THE CHURCH AS EVANGELIST

THE CHURCH
AS
EVANGELIST

George E. Sweazey

1817

Published in San Francisco by

HARPER & ROW, PUBLISHERS

New York, Hagerstown, San Francisco, London

FIRST EDITION

Designed by C. Linda Dingler

Library of Congress Cataloging in Publication Data

Sweazey, George Edgar
  THE CHURCH AS EVANGELIST.

  Bibliography: p. 245
  Includes index.
  1. Mission of the church. 2. Evangelistic work. I. Title.
BV601.8.S86   1978   261.2   77–20452
ISBN 0–06–067776–7

78 79 80 81 82 10 9 8 7 6 5 5 4 3 2 1

To my nephews
Rev. Donald L. Barker   *Rev. Robert S. Barker*
With affectionate admiration

And in memory of their mother
Catherine Sweazey Barker

Contents

Preface   ix
1. The Urgency of Evangelism   1
2. The Objections to Evangelism   27
3. The Church Is the Evangelist   46
4. The Definition of Evangelism   52
5. The Supporting Structures   73
6. Making Contacts   85
7. Cultivating Christian Faith and Knowledge   106
8. Conversion and Decision   113
9. Youth Evangelism   129
10. Using Lay Callers   137
11. Instructions for Evangelistic Callers   159
12. Evangelistic Sermons   184
13. Commencing Church Membership   193
14. The Message of Evangelism   210
15. The Spiritual Qualifications for Evangelism   232
Notes   241
For Further Reading   245
Index   251

Preface

This book is written to help congregations reach outside themselves to bring people to Christian faith and living. A new concern for evangelism is stirring in American church life. Denominations are refurbishing their neglected departments of evangelism. Seminaries are offering new and popular courses on it. Not for decades has it been as easy to get lay members to conferences on evangelism. This is not a nostalgia for old times. Both conservative and liberal churches are looking at evangelism in a new way. God is ready to make this a source of incalculable good. God is always ready, but it is not as certain that we will be. The frightening possibility is that what looks like a new opportunity for evangelism could play out in frustration. There is much help that congregations will be needing. This book is an attempt to give that help.

One barrier to evangelism, with which I try to deal, is the failure of many Christians to recognize what Christ can do for life. They take their faith so much for granted that they are not aware of the difference it makes. Most church members are ethnic Christians. They have never experienced the contrast of the before and after. They feel no great urgency to bring others to their ancestral cult. They need to see clearly the life-transforming effect of faith in Christ and the dreadful loss for those who miss it. They need to be made achingly aware of the many ways in which the world is lost without Christ.

A whole syllabus of errors keeps church people from evangelism. It is widely supposed to be presumptuous, bad-mannered, manipulative, naive, insensitive, and spiritually irresponsible.

Many insist that a church's first task is to evangelize itself. It is said that no evangelism is needed except a good life, or a good church program, or care for human needs. This book deals with such crippling misconceptions.

Many Christians and congregations are kept from evangelism by not having any idea how to go about it. Those who long to help others know what Christ can do cannot think how to start. There is a great deal more clarity about wrong ways than about what could be right. It is often assumed that any sort of evangelism that has been successful in the past must be out of date. This book attempts to show, in down-to-life detail, what church people, singly and together, can do to help others become Christians. This is unabashedly a how-to-do-it approach. Conversion is a miracle, but it is not magic. God in his mercy has given us a part in the most joyful of all accomplishments, the bringing of someone to a saving knowledge of Christ. Our part will be better done if it is done with intelligence and care. We need to consider what we can do, step by step, in the whole process, from making the first contact with those who profess no allegiance to any faith or church, to telling and showing them what Christianity is, to leading them to commit their lives to Christ, to giving them a sound start in the Christian life and in the church.

Evangelism is inhibited by the idea that it requires special gifts. Many fine Christians have sadly concluded, "I am not the type." This book tries to show the normal, natural ways by which believers, of all abilities and temperaments, can help others discover the wonders of the life in Christ. This is essential because ordinary lay members must do most of the evangelizing.

An extended theology of evangelism is not offered here, but I have found it necessary to deal theologically with the timely and timeless purposes of evangelism, with its message, and with what conversion and salvation are. Included is some discussion of what the Church is, where it is, and whether bringing people into it is a necessary evangelistic goal.

I examine the heretical dichotomy between social action and evangelism because if either is neglected the other suffers. Saying that the Church is failing in evangelism because it has gotten too preoccupied with social action is like telling an exhausted person to quit exhaling and just inhale. An evangelism that does not reveal Christ as the Lord of all life defrauds its converts with a fractional Christianity. And Christian social action that neglects evangelism is cut off from its source.

Theoretical problems are looked at realistically here. Queries about whether God has other ways of salvation for people in other lands and eras can be put aside by the recognition that in most of our communities Christ is, in fact, the only way. Only through him are our neighbors likely to come to an adequate knowledge of God, or to worship, or to spiritual fellowship. We cannot answer all the questions about how God is in Christ, but we do know that our best and highest conceptions of God come from seeing him in Christ. In theory it is absurd to think that congregations like ours could bring anyone to Christ, but in reality congregations that are just as inadequate as ours are doing it. We might suppose that people would resent being intruded on religiously, but experience shows that they rarely do; the common problem is not spiritual intrusion but spiritual loneliness.

A chapter on the spiritual qualifications for evangelism is included because these are the most important factors in its success. But I warn against the mistake of thinking that a church should become spiritually qualified before it attempts to evangelize. We do not become spiritually qualified by thinking of ourselves. It is in reaching out to others that church members become more aware of what they believe, more grateful for what God has done for them, more dependent on the Holy Spirit. "First renewal, then evangelism," usually means in fact that there will be little renewal and no evangelism.

Everything in this book rests on the conviction that *the Church is the Evangelist.* Evangelism is not a solo performance, it is a team accomplishment. It is the work, not of an individual, but of a fellowship. Every member of a church, and every organization and activity, should have a part in it. This is the reassurance for those who know that by themselves they could not possibly lead anyone to faith. They say and do all they can, then they trust the church to do the rest that is needed to win those who are brought within its influence. The Church is put on earth to let human beings know of the blessings God offers through his Son. Every member of the Church is given both the obligation and the opportunity to have a part in this.

My earlier book on evangelism (*Effective Evangelism,* New York: Harper & Row, 1953; revised edition, 1976) came out of my experience as a city mission, small town, and urban pastor, and as the director of evangelism for my denomination. This present book comes from my later experiences as a pastor of suburban churches and as a seminary professor of evangelism. This book is not a revision of the other one, which was given the updating I thought it needed in the new edition that was published in 1976. When anything that is written on evangelism is finished, it is soon obvious that a great deal more needs to be said. *The Church as Evangelist* says more about some of the subjects that were treated in *Effective Evangelism,* and it gets into others that were not mentioned there at all.

Attempts to avoid using male terms for both sexes inevitably run into wordings that are either wrong or hopelessly clumsy. I clipped this from a church bulletin:

MINISTER: Hear the good news!
PEOPLE: If a person is in Christ, they become a new person.

It is news that *a person* is *they,* but it is not good news. I had to give up struggling against common English usage. Our language provides no singular personal pronouns without gender, but uses masculine terms for both sexes, possibly because the masculine seems to be less definite. When I sometimes submit to the necessity, it is not because I like it. Surely one of the happiest developments of our time is the growing recognition of how much the Church gains when it literally claims the promise, "Your sons and your daughters shall prophesy." The place of women in every phase of evangelism is of the utmost importance. A church that does not make the most of women's insights and abilities will be sadly handicapped.

I use a capital *C* in referring to the universal Church or a denomination, and a small *c* for a congregation.

Bible quotations are from the Revised Standard Version unless there is such a notation as KJV (King James Version), NEB (New English Bible), or TEV (Today's English Version).

1

The Urgency
of Evangelism

―――――――――――――✧――――――――――――――

THE PERSONAL NEED

Evangelism makes us face the question, "Does everyone need Jesus Christ?" It could seem possible for Christians to be grateful for their faith without thinking that all others should accept it. There is no doubt that the Bible presents the gospel as God's saving truth for all mankind. Christians throughout history have believed that Jesus Christ came to the earth to give what every human being needs most of all. But is it true? Every day we meet admirable, lovable people who never seem to give a passing thought to anything religious. Can we really think of them as lost and needing to be saved?

Let us think of this in terms of real people. A church I know of has a list of those it hopes can be brought to faith and church membership. Here are some of them. There is a young housewife who sings in the choir, but only, she insists, because she likes to sing. She is the sort of person who could make you lose your religion because she is so good and generous and loving without any professed religious faith at all. Her parents were church members, but in school she got so entangled in the concept of a God who is man who is God that she decided that something so irrational could not be taken seriously. Can I believe that she has to profess the Christian faith so that she can be born again? It looks as though she has already been born as the very sort of person God intends.

There is a couple from Iran. The husband came to this country to study engineering and ended up with RCA. He is Moslem and his wife is Jewish. They send their children to the church school, and they sometimes attend the services, but they have inhibitions that have never let them join a Christian church. They are two of the most attractive people one could know—gentle and artistic, with a beautiful home life and a quality of culture that is above the average. It would be hard to insist that they should become Christians so that they might be more like the rest of us.

Another couple were Protestants until they discovered the joys of a liberating faith and became members of the Ethical Culture Society. There is no branch of that Society in their town, so they often attend the church, but their real loyalty is to those spiritual values that are made known through the great souls of all ages. They are an admired couple who have done a great deal of good in the community. It would seem doctrinaire to hold that they have abandoned the way of salvation and are lost in outer darkness.

Are there any reasons for believing that people like these need Jesus Christ? Yes, there are. Here are some of them:

1. The Observable Difference Faith Can Make. This first motive for evangelism is the least theological. It is simply that faith in Christ visibly changes the way people live and what they are. Christians cannot escape this test. They like to point out that a church is not a museum where saints are on display, but a hospital where sinners are having their disorders treated. Our Lord said that the Church would be like a mixed wheat and weed patch, so we cannot expect the members always to look better than the people outside. But if there is truly a new life in Christ, there ought to be some evidence of it—and there is. A friend of mine who has lived in North Africa says you can tell whether an Arab is a Christian by the way he walks down the street. One of Ellen Glasgow's novels describes a lily pond in which sits "Old Mortality, a green bullfrog with a Presbyterian face." There should be such a thing as a Presbyterian face. I have the strong impression that among people who have an ardent faith in Christ you are likely to get the feel of freedom, and a zest for living, and wide-ranging interests. There are so many loving people who are not Christians that it is a little fanciful to sing, "They'll know we are Christians by our love." But if the test groups are large enough, you should know. A scientist is said to have had two of his three children baptized and to have kept the other one for a control. Single examples may be misleading, so such tests have to be made on groups. A scientist I know used exactly that group method. His parents had not had any church interest, but when his children approached school age, he began to wonder whether religion had anything they needed. In the laboratory where he worked he learned who had church connections. Then he studied them to see whether they seemed to have any special qualities that were desirable. His observations convinced him that they did. On as coldly rational a basis as that, he and his wife began to go to church. But it did not stay cold, and for thirty years they have been two of the warmest, most grateful, and most useful Christians I have ever known.

In most communities there is a good deal of evidence that a lively religious faith is likely to be a powerful force for good. When a boy or girl begins to show a religious interest, it is a hopeful sign. Statistics gathered by sociologists show that when a couple participate in some religious group, there is a considerably better chance that their marriage will turn out well. Wherever I have lived, the labor and leadership that church people gave to good causes was far larger than their proportion in the population. In the town where I grew up, it was only in the church that I ever heard racial wrongs condemned.

In the 1950s, a bill was introduced in the legislature of a southern state proposing to end church tax exemption because the churches were the only organizations that were actively opposing segregation. During World War II, it was the churches that criticized our government for such matters as excessive bombings and the mistreatment of prisoners. In St. Louis, where I was living, there was a threat to cut the Church Federation off the air because it spoke so frankly for the Christian conscience in broadcast sermons that commented on war policies. Church women's groups spent hours of study to lay the foundations for the acceptance of what later became the United Nations.

Let us think again of those people about whom I raised the question, "Does everyone need Jesus Christ?" From the list of those whom the church hopes to bring to belief, I selected the ones who seem to be doing best without a Christian faith. But even with them, there is more that needs to be said. The choir member and the couple who left the Christian Church come from strongly religious families. They have Christianity in their bones, if not in the front of their minds. They are still travelling on the religious momentum that their parents imparted, but their children will have less of this. Perhaps not until their grandchildren will the real results of living without faith be evident. The Iranian couple come from Moslem and Jewish families, but when they came to America they broke those ties without forming any other. Their children will be a long way behind where their parents started. There is probably nothing in the immediate environment of any of these persons that regularly reminds them of God or puts spiritual interests among their material preoccupations.

But now, having said all this, let me admit what is obvious. I have failed to show that Christians have desirable qualities that non-Christians cannot have. I might fall back on the French saying, "The good Lord does not settle his accounts at the end of the month, but he settles them at last." But I should be surprised if the non-Christian persons I have described do not remain strong, generous, and upright all their lives. I am convinced that in the mass you can see that Christians have something special. But I cannot offer that personal opinion as a motive for evangelism for anyone else. We can expect Christians to have the Christian virtues; we cannot expect others not to have them.

There is no moralistic motive for evangelism. It cannot be shown that you should win people to faith in Christ so that they can be as good and as happy as Christians are. Here we confront the essential Christian principle that God will not compel belief. Job complained that "the just upright man is laughed to scorn [but] the tabernacles of robbers prosper" (Job 12:4, 6, KJV). God will not buy our love with business success or good health, and he will not bribe us to accept Christ by making this the only way to have the finest personalities or morals. The motive for taking Christ as Lord must be free choice, and not the promise of being rewarded with admirable and lovable qualities. And the motive for wanting to help people come to Christ must also be based on faith.

2. The Unseen Relationship with God. The Christian faith can be derived from the best and shortest of all definitions of God: "God is love" (1 John. 4:16). Love cannot exist in isolation; love has to share good things. Therefore God made human beings. The whole purpose of our existence, the reason we are alive, is to live in love, with God and with each other—and to enjoy God's gifts, the greatest of which is himself, as he comes within our reach in Jesus Christ. To live without the daily sense of God's presence is to be out of touch with reality. Not to be in conscious communication with God is to miss the blessing we were created to enjoy. It is the thought of that dreadful loss that impels Christians to evangelism, though they can never have demonstrable proof that anything is being missed. Some time ago, I heard of the death of the husband of the young housewife who sings in the choir. The news increased the sharp regret I have felt at the failure to bring her to faith. I am sure she has endured her loss bravely and with grace. But I deeply believe that the knowledge of Christ's presence could have been her greatest help.

At the start of the Epistle to the Romans, Paul seems to undercut evangelism. He readily admits that human beings do not need Christ in order to know God and goodness—"for what can be known about God is plain to them, because God has shown it to them" (Rom. 1:19). Here Paul can get loud applause from all the commonsense people who insist that evangelism is presumptuous. Paul seems to be right with them when he continues, "Gentiles who have not the law do by nature what the law requires" (Rom. 2:14). So who needs a church? Why not get rid of the whole clutter of hymns, and sacraments, and mumbled Scriptures, and muttered prayers, and hallelujahs to a risen Lord?

But that conclusion from his words would have been wildly inconceivable to Paul. Of course God in his love gives a knowledge of himself and of his will to every human being. That is what you should expect a God to do. But the marvel that Christ reveals is that God did not stop there. "He humbled himself" (Phil. 2:8). He came to earth in human form to act himself out upon our stage. He shared our lot so that he could teach and demonstrate divine truth in terms that we could understand. He revealed the redeeming love upon the cross, and he rose from death so that we might rise into new life. We would expect a God like ours to give his inner light to everyone, but this far greater marvel of God's love is also meant for everyone. It is the wonder of such mercy that sent Paul out in an abandon of joy, flaming with his eagerness to tell about it. There is our burning motive for evangelism. We must go out to tell all who do not know God that "God was in Christ reconciling the world to himself" (2 Cor. 5:19).

3. What Every Human Being Needs Most. The evangelist's belief that everyone needs Jesus Christ might seem presumptuous, because no one can read the secrets of another's heart. Why should we assume that everybody needs what we do? But there are some important things we can know about every human being.

You know that everyone you meet is going to die. When we are young, threescore years and ten seem like forever, but we soon have to face the maddening inadequacy of our brief time on earth. Unless we can come to terms with the looming threat of death, its gloomy shadow can darken all our days.

Everyone must live under the foreboding that all who are most dearly loved are going to die. Those who cannot find how to deal with this daily dread will never be free from fear and melancholy.

Everyone you know will have to meet disaster. If you have lived in the same town long enough, you will know that behind every front door there is some heartbreak, some dreadful memory.

Sin is each one's grim reality. Not all will know it. Saints know that they are sinners; sinners think they are doing as well as anybody should expect. But all human beings have reasons to dislike themselves: they cringe from recollections that they cannot change, they live behind masks to conceal who they really are, they are torn apart by inner strife, they are poisoned by resentments.

You can know that every person who walks toward you on the street is lost without an answer to such questions as: "Who am I?" "Why am I here?" "Are love and goodness more than phantoms?"

You can be absolutely sure of two things: first, for everyone on

earth the difference between great and hopeless living depends
on being able to cope with death, sorrow, disaster, sin, and meaning; second, Christ came into the world to enable human beings
to deal with these very things triumphantly.

4. Our Own Knowledge. The immediate motive for evangelism must be autobiographical. Has Christ done anything for
you? If so, you know that he can do as much for anyone. In a
strange way this motive may be weak for many in the Church.
Most Church members are ethnic Christians. Just as in northern
India there are goat-herding tribes and brass-working tribes, so
most of us were born into a Christ-worshipping tribe. We are
glad we were, but there may be no great feeling of urgency about
bringing into our ancestral cult those who have their own tribal
practices. We ethnic Christians never get very eager in evangelism until we have looked within ourselves and discovered in the
most personal terms how Christ has changed and blessed our
lives.

To put the matter bluntly, have you been saved? Many modern
Christians do not talk easily about saving souls. For most of us,
baptism and confirmation were expected rites. We do not know
when we were converted. We are aware of no stark contrast
between before and after. Children of the covenant are inclined
to think they did it all themselves. It may be that your parents or
your church, from before your earliest memories, were pointing
you toward Jesus Christ so that your course across the years has
been determined by that slant.

But think back now. There may have been a time when, like
most adolescents, you were trying out various personalities. You
were crude and then polite, selfish and loving, bitter and cheerful, while your parents looked on, nonplussed and aghast. When
you finally settled into the personality that is now most typical of
you, did your religious faith have anything to do with it? There
may have been a later period when you speculated about the
purpose of your life. Should your goal be money or self-fulfill-
ment, pleasure or service to humanity? When you finally came
upon the course you have been travelling, was there another
hand than yours upon the rudder of your life? Every life has times

of critical decision, crossroads where the choice will determine everything that lies ahead. You have probably had many such crises—in your work or in decisions about right and wrong. There may have been a crisis in your marriage, a dreadful time that lasted weeks or months. Then you and your husband or your wife came through it and have meant more to each other since than you ever did before. When you made your critical decisions, did Jesus Christ have anything to do with them? If today you are a different person and at a different place than you ever would have been without him, then you can say in all literalness that you have been saved, converted, transformed, born again.

When we recognize how much we owe to Christ, we know that he can do as much for everyone on earth. He is not the Lord of any special nation, or temperament, or social class. He is Lord of all. Faith in him is the most critical need of the university president and the illiterate ragpicker, of the Eskimo fur trapper and the couple who just moved in across the street. A passion for evangelism would explode in our churches if the members and ministers suddenly woke up to the fact that what they always thought they believed is actually true. The only way theology can come to life for us is to have it come into our lives as we become gratefully aware of what is meant by salvation, reconciliation, repentance, and regeneration. With that, we birthright Christians can have a new convert's eagerness to tell others what Christ can do.

Dr. Gordon Seagrave, the heroic Burma missionary surgeon, said that if it hurt an evangelist half as much to lose a case as it does a surgeon, the church might get somewhere. We can all know what he meant. When a surgeon loses a case, he suffers over the dreadful thing that happened. When we come back from an evangelism call with no sign of anything accomplished, we put the information card into the "little chance" section of the evangelism file and think, "That was a nice young couple, but you can't win them all." And then we go on to something else. If we saw this experience as it really is, we would be saying, "Lord, that must not be, it cannot be! Show me what to do!" Our hearts are not torn by the stark disaster of a life that is lived apart from Jesus Christ. It would transform our churches if we felt in the bottom of our hearts what we affirm in the top of our minds.

THE ONLY WAY TO HAVE THE CHRISTIAN FAITH ON THE EARTH

Well-worn illustrations are likely to be apt conveyors of important truth. One of these tells that Jesus, after his ascension, was asked by the angels how the human race was to find out what he had done for them. He answered that he let eleven people know about it and told them to tell others who would spread the news. "Do you mean," the astonished angels asked, "that if they do not do this, all the benefits of your incarnation, your ministry, your atoning death, and your resurrection will be thrown away?" "Yes," said Jesus, "I have no other plan." This story is told so often because what it says is so startling. An omnipotent God's mighty acts for the world's salvation depend for their effect on what flighty human creatures do.

Within a hundred years, or a little more, Christianity could become as dead as the religion of the Pharaohs. In that time, all the Christians on the earth will have been replaced by those who, without evangelism, will remain non-Christians. One might imagine that Christianity could be transmitted by such means as literature, songs, and Bible study. These can be powerful aids to evangelism, but one rarely hears of anyone coming to faith in Christ without the direct influence of some person or group.

It is significant that the instruction to evangelize is the only commandment that Jesus repeated in all his last appearances to his followers. In Matthew it is: "Go therefore and make disciples of all nations, baptizing them in the name of the Father and of the Son and of the Holy Spirit, teaching them to observe all that I have commanded you" (28:19–20). In Mark the injunction is: "Go into all the world and preach the gospel to the whole creation" (16:15). Luke reports that Jesus said that "repentance and forgiveness of sin should be preached in his name to all nations" (24:47). In his very last appearance, as recorded in the Acts, Jesus said, "You shall be my witnesses in Jerusalem and in all Judea and Samaria and to the end of the earth" (1:8). There was a time when many in the Church opposed missions because, as a Deacon told William Carey, the pioneer missionary, "If God wants the heathen to be converted, he will convert them." This controversy impelled someone to ask the Duke of Wellington why he believed in missions. The old soldier answered with a question: "What were your general's marching orders?" What our Lord has told us to do is very clear.

We may believe that divine providence would not let Christianity disappear from the earth, but we know it can disappear from parts of the earth and grow weak in others. If the Christian faith were as visible as light, watchers on another planet would see a slow flickering, with bright areas turning dark and dim areas blazing into light. The Moslem conquest almost extinguished the knowledge of Christ, which had been becoming brighter, all across North Africa. The Dark Ages, when Christianity in Europe was shadowed by superstition and empty formalism, were succeeded by the light that came from a widespread seeking through the Bible for essential Christianity. Each of us is personally responsible for the brighter shining or the disappearing of the Christian faith where we live and in our lifetimes. Perhaps God will never let faith in Christ die out on the earth, but it can clearly die out in our neighborhoods.

Only God knows who is or is not a Christian, but no one can be a Christian without Christ. We cannot make anyone a Christian—only God does that. But God has left it to us to pass on that knowledge of Christ which makes Christianity possible. A Christian is someone who thinks about Christ, whose daily decisions and attitudes are formed by a conscious reference to Christ, who conceives of God as Christ revealed him, who knows Christ, not just as a dead hero, but as a living Lord. That is why the evangelism which tells who Christ is and what he does is so infinitely important. Without evangelism there could be no Christian faith on earth. Christ has no other plan.

MAKING THE CHURCH A GREATER SOURCE OF GOOD

Without evangelism the Christian Church, like the Christian faith, would vanish from the earth. The Church is always like a boat above Niagara Falls—it is steadily drifting toward extinction. Its members are dying, and they are not being replaced from within the Church. Its birthrate is too low, and too many will be lost. Moreover, church membership is not passed down. The faith of our fathers is not something we inherit; we have to acquire it for ourselves. Begetting puts children into their parents' racial group, but there is no natural process that puts children into their parents' religious group. If the members did not labor unceasingly to reach out to bring others into the Church, it would be done for.

There is danger that the urge for institutional aggrandizement will become the motive for evangelism. This is a sin that none of us can quite escape. It is a satisfaction to add names to a church role. The members like to feel that they belong to a growing concern. The minister wants to have impressive evidence of his accomplishment. When I was pastor of a church and looked over the statistics for the year, I could never keep from thinking thoughts like, "If we could have gotten four more, we would have broken last year's record." We readily bring into the church the world's measurable standards of success. We do not want a rival congregation to grow faster than we do. A church split can produce a burning zeal to add new members, as each side strives to outdo its opponents. But none of the wrong motives for adding members to a church make the right motives any less important.

1. The New Members Need the Church. A first right motive for bringing people into a church is the desire for them to have the benefits it gives. Christians believe that Christ put his Church on earth to provide blessings which every human being needs. You yourself are the test case for that. Have you gotten anything important from the Church? If not, it is strange that you waste your time on it. But if you have, then you must long for others to enjoy the good things you have found.

Sometimes it is hard to identify our ecclesiastical organization with the Church that Christ put on earth. The local clutter of councils and commissions and administrative chores, the denominational assemblies and bureaucratic procedures, do not seem much like the simple Church of the New Testament. But there is no use dreaming of an idyllic state in which Christians can love and serve the Lord without budgets or buildings or committee meetings. A young man helped to organize an *Anti-Church for*

Christian Radicals as a reaction against the religious establishment at his university. It had no stated membership. It was bound only by the sharing of the Eucharist. The protest was needed. But from the beginning the group had a treasury, and a mailing list, and a committee to get out the mailings. It also used a copying machine, which is the engine that keeps church mechanisms going. If this group survives long enough to make an effective protest against religious institutions, it will become one of them.

The scorn of numbers can be unrealistic. If a sermon helped fifty people, it is too bad a hundred did not get to hear it. If it is good to save five marriages, it is twice as good to save ten. When Jesus said, "Feed my sheep," he left us no room to be indifferent either to how many or how well. The New Testament Church was never indifferent to numbers. It counted up how many were converted by Peter's sermon. Paul in jail rejoiced that he was getting the gospel, not just to a few, but to "the *whole* praetorian guard." Quantitative references are frequent. Throughout the Acts, the blessed word *many* echoes the refrain of triumph—*many* were cleansed of evil spirits, *many* believed in the Lord, *many* were baptized, and *many* forsook their trust in magic (8:7, 9:42, 17:12, 18:8, 19:18).

Some churches do not want to grow. They do not want to bring in strangers who might be uncongenial. The coziness they enjoy quenches any flicker of evangelism. A minister told me how his leading officer cut off a proposal to do something about evangelism by saying, "I like our church the way it is; I don't want to see it get big." We might sympathize with a car dealer who told the salesmen, "Let's not try to sell too many cars; I don't like a large agency." A Red Cross worker might say, "Let's try not to make this a big operation." But a church with that attitude ceases to be a church. Its reason for existence is to bring the blessings of the life in Christ to everyone it can reach. When it relinquishes that purpose, it becomes an empty shell. A church dare not let its evangelistic purpose be taken from it by a lack of pews or parking space. There are ways of coping with physical limitations; there is no way to cope with unconcern for human needs.

It is natural for those who love their church to think that it is just the right size, but there is no right size. It would save much rebuilding and inefficiency if an expert could show that a congregation is most effective spiritually when it has fifty, two hundred, one thousand, or three thousand members. No one ever has. Each size has advantages. If your church is growing, it can have more staff and equipment and programs at a lower cost per member, so that more of its income can be used for missions. If your church is in a situation where it has to shrink, it need not be disheartened; the members and the minister can feel closer to each other. It can still do great things. The right size for every church is as large as it can possibly become by doing its utmost to bring everyone in reach to the blessings that Christ put his Church on earth to give.

The idea of improving a church's quality by receiving few new members and giving them meticulous attention is self-defeating. A church that plays down evangelism will not do much good with those it does receive. The exciting purpose that evangelism gives to a congregation, the spiritual intensity, the sense of getting into real life, will be missing. When more are joining, the program to give them a sound start in the Christian life and in the church can be better. There will be the feeling of great things happening. In many ways, in a church *more* makes for *better*. An increase in church attendance is likely to improve the Sunday services. As a Church School grows, its teaching is likely to get better. When fellowship groups become larger, they can offer more interesting programs.

There are countless dispirited little congregations whose great need is numbers. Only stern parental compulsion can make children attend their drab Sunday Schools. Visiting preachers hit and run. Most such congregations are drearily ingrown; not for years have they done much to add new members, but nothing except active recruitment can lift them from their tiresome ruts and give them the numbers they need to become adequate centers for Christian nurture and inspiration. A Nebraska minister wrote about the only church in a little town. It had few members, one officer, and no pastor. "After the evangelism training school," he said "eight ministers in the county decided to do Christ-centered visiting there. Members and friends of the church caught the vision and followed the example. The community was deeply stirred. Twenty-two members were received into the church on Easter, nineteen of them on profession of faith, and ten more soon after. The church has now grown greatly, is well-organized, and is a real power for good in the community."

In the mid-sixties, when many congregations and denominations began to decline in membership, there were heroic attempts to ascribe this to their virtues. A theology of failure became popular. It was held that, since Jesus was rejected, his Church will be rejected if it is faithful. More members, new congregations, popular programs are the world's standards of success—so the Church must expect diminishing numbers, fewer congregations, and declining interest. It became popular to say that what the Church needs most is a time of no growth. After a period of shallow activism, the dropping away of the uncommitted members will give the hard core of sacrificially dedicated followers of Christ a chance to be the Church. If the Church is fearlessly speaking for Christ in an evil world, it can expect to attract few to membership, and to alienate many who are on its rolls.

There is truth here that some of us are too likely to slight. Congregations that are trying to be faithful will come up against practical issues in which a refusal to compromise will estrange some members. Other congregations achieve phenomenal growth by offering only Christ's promises and suppressing his demands. Statistics by themselves tell nothing. There are churches in difficult locations where just slowing down the decrease is a glorious spiritual achievement.

But none of this means that Christians are supposed to fail. Christ was crucified once and for all, and the Messiah's role is not ours. His death made the cross the symbol, not of defeat, but of triumph. That triumph does not guarantee big memberships or new buildings. But it does mean that the Church is not supposed to be feeble or to fail in its task of bringing human beings to faith in Christ. Ours is the post-Pentecost Church that was promised power from on high. If failure had been the Church's intended fate, nothing would have happened outside the upper room. Christ intended for the Church to grow. The account does not say, "The Lord subtracted from their number day by day those who were being saved." Paul does not report, "I planted, Apollos watered, but God gave the decrease." It was the Church's intended success that spread the gospel from Jerusalem to Rome to Gaul to here. If the Church today is shrinking, it is not a sign that something is right, but that something is disastrously wrong.

2. The World Needs the New Members. Evangelism strives to bring people into Church membership, first, because the new members need the Church and, second, because the world needs the new members. The purpose is not to preserve and enlarge an institution but to make the Church a more effective instrument for God to use. The Church was put into the world to be the channel of God's love. The Church reaches the world through its members. It is through them that the Church offers salvation, declares righteousness, denounces evil, ministers to the distressed. Where the members go, the Church goes. The more members there are, the more outlets there are for God's love.

The Reformation creeds speak of the "invisible Church" and the "visible Church." The visible Church is not visible in its buildings or its books. It is visible only in the bodies of its members. It is through their bodies and their voices that the spiritual, invisible Church of God breaks into the realm of sight and sound.

The New Testament has the supremely beautiful picture of Christ's Church as "his body, of which we are living parts" (Eph. 5:30 NEB). Jesus Christ has not been physically absent from the world since he was born in Bethlehem. When that body of flesh and blood that served him in Palestine was no longer present, he moved into the flesh and blood of the members of the Church. "The Church is the present form of the incarnation." The Sacrament by which it lives makes Christ physically take over a communicant's bones and tissues. Paul follows his description of the Communion service by saying, "Now you are Christ's body, and each of you a limb or organ of it" (1 Cor. 12:27 NEB).

Paul used the word *member*, which means a part of a body, to show the connection to Christ of someone who has joined the Church. We therefore want to add "members" to the Church because we want to extend Christ's body. The members are in the world to do what Jesus would be doing if he were present in the flesh where they are, walking where they walk, meeting those they meet. They should comfort where he would comfort, say what he would say, condemn what he would condemn. The Church wants more members because it wants to have Christ present on as many scenes as possible. It wants him to be in more banks and schools and filling stations. It wants more members who look to Christ as Lord to be writing the editorials, turning the levers in the voting booths, taking part in the discussions at the women's clubs. If evangelism is designed to enlarge an institution, a larger institution is all that it will get. But if it is designed to put into the world more committed followers of Christ, it will be doing what the world most desperately needs.

THE SAVING OF SOCIETY

An endurable society depends on human character, and on the very sort of character that Jesus Christ imparts. Corrupted hearts are the sources of the diseases with which the world is sick—the exploitation of the defenseless by the powerful, the established inequity between the rich and those who are condemned to benumbing privation, unequal justice in the courts and penal systems everywhere, murderous hostilities based on differences of race or nation. Any remedy of these sicknesses requires changing human beings. Walter Rauschenbusch was the great prophet of the Social Gospel, but he was also a realist who ceaselessly insisted that the first requirement for a better social order is "a new mind and heart." He declared that the practical reforms for which he labored were impossible without "converted men." He said: "No outward economic readjustment will answer our needs." "The social order cannot be saved without regenerate men." "If the church comes to lean on social preachings and doings as a crutch because its religion has become paralytic, then may the Lord have mercy upon us all."[1]

A humane society requires not only God-given character but also God-given wisdom. The most skillful social engineering cannot put together structures that will work. Understandings are needed which political and social scientists cannot supply. God designed his children to live together in ways that were revealed on earth through Jesus Christ. Other ways will be crossed up with the essentials. When Dr. Sorokin was head of the Department of Sociology at Harvard University, he said, "Given the values of the Kingdom of God, the worldly problems of food and drink can be solved in passing. But without the Kingdom of God we are doomed to a weary and torturing pilgrimage from calamity to calamity."[2] It is easy to pile up quotations from distinguished statesmen and historians who declare that the escape from our morass is to be found in the teachings of Jesus Christ. But the only way to increase the practice of Christ's teachings is to put into the world more people who look to him as Lord.

There is much to make us wonder whether there is enough goodness and wisdom in human beings to enable them to operate our increasingly complex society. As the world's soaring population speeds us toward the horror of millions starving, there does not seem to be enough brains or discipline to avoid it. When the nations send their experts and managers to a conference on food problems, there is plenty of evidence of sin, but not enough evidence of the readiness for exertion and sacrifice that a solution will require. The only serious product which the clashing selfishness and hostility in one such conference permitted was a discussion of triage, a system of rational decisions about who dies first. We are facing the prospect that terrorist gangs and tawdry dictators may soon have the use of weapons that can murder millions and make large areas of the earth's surface uninhabitable.

We tolerate the bumbling and inefficiency of democracy because there is no other form of government that we prefer. But as social tensions or the economy become increasingly hard to manage, we may wonder how much longer we can have our first choice. A democracy cannot exist if its citizens are incorrigibly selfish or corrupt, but it can be successful if there is in most of its citizens enough discipline, decency, honesty, and compassion. Every big city is an island whose inhabitants depend for their survival upon such workers as truckers, electricians, doctors, and policemen. If some strikes could not be settled, many would die. With such a possibility impending, the Governor of New York threatened to use the National Guard to get the garbage hauled.

The garbagemen said that if he did, they would fight. What would have happened then? Our hold on orderly existence is precarious. The shocks of recent years have made Americans uneasy about dependabilities that we used to take for granted. We were brought up to believe that our country always won its wars because it was always in the right. We used to tell ourselves that, though city machines or courthouse gangs might be corrupt, it was at the top political level that the real soundness of the American character is revealed. We used to dismiss as fantastic fabrications any charges of criminal acts committed by our armed forces or security agencies. There is now the uneasy feeling that we may be acting out the American drama on a platform whose moral underpinnings have decayed.

The assumption that our country and our world urgently need more people who believe in Christ runs into the evidence that many Christians do not have the qualities that a good society requires. Sociological studies discover, for example, a shocking degree of prejudice among church members. Professor Gordon W. Allport summarizes his studies of the social attitudes of church members by saying: "Belonging to a church because it is a safe, powerful, superior in-group is likely to be the mark of an authoritarian character and to be linked with prejudice. Belonging to a church because its basic creed of brotherhood expresses the ideals one sincerely believes in is associated with tolerance."[3] A study by E. L. Streuning of nine hundred faculty members at a midwestern university graded their ethnic and racial hostility. Those who attended church irregularly showed the most hostility, with a grade of 25; next came those who never attended church at all—14.7; while the lowest score was made by those who went to church most often (at least eleven times a month) —11.7. The nominal and devoted members are poles apart.

All of this emphasizes the need for an adequate evangelism. Many in the Church have never been brought to understand the full meaning of the Christian faith. People may come into membership with their selfishness unchanged. But no one can come to a true faith in Christ without becoming a saving factor in society.

There were famous American churchmen in the last century

who were widely admired as Bible-believing, born-again, Spirit-filled Christians and yet were completely heathen in their business and political relationships. They were like Hosea's unturned pancake, done on only one side. They were the products of churches that conceded half the field to Satan. He was to be relentlessly resisted in the private area, but in the public sector he was allowed to ravage undisturbed. Individual sin was to be condemned, but cooperative sin was not the church's business. The church was supposed to implant the Christian virtues but never to point out their application to the larger problems of mankind. The converts of an evangelism that is so constricted will in truth have only a limited value for society.

Some church people are confined in their social outlook because their religious development stopped too soon. Children learn first about Christianity in the most personal terms. They know that those who love Jesus will be kind and truthful, and will mind their parents and say their prayers. They never hear that Jesus cares about welfare policies or legal aid. If their religious understanding does not develop beyond this stage, they may later think that if a church gets into social matters, it has forsaken its religious function. Adult converts also are likely to experience the wonders of the life in Christ in the ways that are most intimate. Without help, they may never discover more than that. So if a church sees its evangelistic purpose as accomplished when new members, perhaps with deep feeling, profess faith in Christ as their Savior, those members may never rightly understand that their faith also can heal a sick society.

The church is the evangelist. The sort of congregation that is deep in its ministry to a troubled world is the sort whose evangelism will put into the world new members who are applying Christ's teachings to the whole wide range of human needs.

Since the first century, the Church's application of Christ's love and righteousness to the world's problems has been handicapped by those who insist that the last days are at hand. Because the present social order will soon be gone, they say, Christians should not waste their time trying to improve it. And since the corruption of the social order is the sign of the Lord's return, Christians should devote their efforts to preparing believers to receive him. Noah did not make futile attempts at flood control; he gathered those who were to be saved into the ark. For nineteen centuries, some Christians have been allowing enmities to grow into wars, famines to build up, and the unjustly imprisoned to languish in their cells because the end of the world was at hand. When Francis of Assisi was working in his garden, someone asked him what he would do if he knew the world were going to end that day. He said, "I'd hoe my garden." When the Lord does return, we will want him to find us, like the servant in the parable, doing what we were told to do (Matt. 24:45–46). We hope he will find us ministering to the earth's defrauded and distressed, and preparing all those we can reach to receive him as their Lord.

The healing of the world by the love of Christ will always be a matter of degree. With every child that is fed, with every wrong that is righted, the Lordship of Christ is extended by that much. His rule does not have to wait until a majority become his followers. Christians are called to be the saving leaven in the lump. By their urging and example they can influence many who give little thought to Jesus Christ. God has put into all human hearts the ability to respond to what Christ taught. The Christian ideals of love and peace can awaken those same ideals in others anywhere on earth. The policies of any free country can be powerfully influenced by a devoted Christian minority. The leaven does not have to be the whole lump, but the more leaven there is, the more powerful its working will be. When a church brings one more person to look to Christ as Lord, it has advanced his Kingdom by that much.

Through most of this century, American Christians have suffered a sinful and unbiblical distortion of the faith. When I enrolled at my theological seminary, I discovered that the students were recognizably divided between the evangelizers and the social gospellers. That polarity has distinguished denominations from each other, and has identified parties within denominations. It is as though Christians had to choose between the Christ of the Great Commission and the Christ of the Great Assize.

Actually, there were two Great Commissions. The one we usually call that was the commandment to evangelize. It was of such supreme importance that it is recorded in every account of Jesus' last words to his disciples. In Matthew it is: "Go therefore and make disciples of all nations" (28:19); in Mark: "Go into all the world and preach the gospel to the whole creation" (16:15); in Luke, Jesus says that "repentance and forgiveness of sins should be preached in his name to all nations" (24:47); and in the Acts he says, "You shall be my witnesses" (1:8). Obedience to that commandment is the supreme test of loyalty to him.

But Jesus also gave a supreme test just before the crucifixion. He pictured the last judgement and told how his true disciples would be separated from the unfaithful. There is just one distinction—the true disciples will be the ones who have carried out his Great Commission to care for the distressed (Matt. 25:31–46). So his final commandment to evangelize never mentioned ministering to the hungry, the sick, or the imprisoned; but his test of true discipleship never referred to evangelizing. Did Jesus not know his own mind? But there is no contradiction here. There is just one commandment by which all will be tested—the commandment to care for those in need. Looking out over the city in all its misery, it was physical suffering that Jesus mentioned. At his departure into the heavenly glory, it was spiritual needs of which he spoke. Each implies the other. Those are the twin aspects of the gospel. That is why so much of the talk about the polarization of the Church is absurd. The Church was born polarized. You are not allowed to choose whether to be an evangelistic or a social-gospel Christian. The world can never have enough of either. Our Lord has made both his absolutes.

We need to hear Paul's exasperated question, "Is Christ divided?" (1 Cor. 1:13). Most of us are inclined by temperament to lean, at least slightly, toward one side or the other. But we have to carry our duties on both shoulders if we are going to be upright followers of Christ.

The situation is confused by those whose motives are negative. There are congregations that talk endlessly of soul-winning, but most of those they win are disgruntled members of other churches. Their supposed zeal for evangelism is really an escape from Christ's social righteousness. On the other hand, those whose faith and religious feelings are unsatisfying may throw themselves into social action as the only religious expression they can have. This may be revealed by an unstable passion for a succession of social causes.

Right now there are highly welcome indications that the schizoid condition is being healed. The new generation of seminary students is increasingly impatient with the senseless old division. There is a new style of church life that springs from a lively awareness of the need to follow Christ in every part of life. From this comes an eagerness to tell others about Christ or to send a committee to talk with the mayor about bad housing.

Heartening evidence of the coming together of what has been heretically put asunder can be seen in the increasing social concern of evangelicals. (A label never rightly designates a many-faceted religious outlook. Perhaps I may slip past this difficulty by defining an evangelical as someone who calls himself an evangelical.) This development was seen in a 1965 meeting of evangelical leaders who decided that a study of the evangelical position on social matters was overdue. From this came the very significant book by Sherwood E. Wirt, *The Social Conscience of an Evangelical,* which reports what is happening: "The typical Gospel church of our day is not the fundamentalist enclave it was at the turn of the century. Its congregation still wants its minister to be fervent, dedicated, evangelistic, and Biblically oriented, but a new element has entered the picture. Today's evangelical congregation wishes its pastor also to be imaginatively and effectively cognizant of the social ferment going on about him. . . . Some evangelical seminaries have forged ahead of the congregations in the matter."[4] Wirt shows that the slighting of social concerns by American evangelicals since 1900 was a denial of both their history and their dependence on Scripture.

At the World Evangelism Conference in Berlin in 1966, eleven hundred evangelical delegates showed a new turning to social concern. A conference in Minneapolis in 1969, with its expression of repentance for past neglect and its call for attention to social issues, received a good deal of attention in the press because it so astonished many who had not known of this growing emphasis. There was more surprise when an organization of evangelicals was formed in 1972 to support Senator McGovern, the socially liberal candidate for the presidency. The social emphasis was documented in an impressive Declaration of Evangelical Social Concern that was drafted by fifty prominent leaders in Chicago in 1973. There was a confession of sinful silence when God required condemnation and healing action. The list of social evils was long and specific. There was an acceptance of Christ's "claim on our total discipleship till He comes." After the massive International Congress on World Evangelization in Lausanne, Switzerland, in 1974, a majority of the twenty-four hundred delegates signed a statement which said, "We express penitence both for our neglect and for having sometimes regarded evangelism and social concern as mutually exclusive. . . . We affirm that evangelism and socio-political involvement are both part of our Christian duty. . . . [But] we reject as a proud, self-confident dream the notion that man can ever build a utopia on earth."

At the second annual Calvin College Conference on Christianity and Politics, held in 1974, it was emphasized that, "In our quest for new forms of social/political engagement today, we must not be thought of as siding with Protestant liberalism, but rather as expanding the evangelicalism that nurtured us and brought us to a saving knowledge of the Lordship of Jesus Christ." Evangelicals believe that it is their traditional insistence on Christ's Lordship and their loyalty to the Scriptures that inspire their new concern for economic and racial justice and for world peace. They insist that evangelicals have historically been in the front of the struggle for social righteousness; it is only the long period of acceptance of the status quo that makes the present concern for social reform seem new.

History supports this. During the Reformation in Europe, it was the most evangelically minded Christians who were most insistent on social reform. In England, it was the evangelicals, with their emphasis on the relevance of religion to daily life, who did most to tame the barbarities of the early industrial revolution. English historians—Green, Lecky, and Trevelyan—believe that England escaped a revolution like that in France only because of the Wesleyan combination of evangelism and social action. John Wesley said, "The Gospel of Christ knows of no religion but social; no holiness but social holiness." The English trade-union movement started in Methodist meeting houses. The Wesleyan revival roused concern for public health, hospital care, prison reform, and public education. Lord Shaftesbury, an evangelical who remained in the established Church, expressed his faith through sixty years of public life that were dedicated to social reform. No other leader of Parliament ever did as much to secure legislation which improved the condition of industrial workers. His real constituents were the laborers in mines, farms, and factories, the insane, chimney sweeps, women, children, and slum dwellers.

American revivalism, in the first two-thirds of the nineteenth century, was deeply concerned with social reform. It transformed the ruthless individualism of the frontier. Slavery was the most agonizing social issue, and many of the leading abolitionists were fervent evangelicals. Early Holiness leaders insisted on equal rights for black people and for women. The first Free Methodists intended the "free" in their name to have both a political and a religious meaning.

The social concern of evangelicals seems likely to continue. Professor Richard Lovelace, of Gordon-Conwell Seminary, says: "I find that practically none of the young evangelicals I teach will accept a gospel which lacks the dimension of social healing. To them injustice and oppression are sins just as serious as heresy and adultery. . . . Many of the young I know are aflame with an unnatural—or supernatural—urgency to get into the inner city, and they are determined not to carry on in work which does not include both social and evangelistic components."[5]

Among non-evangelicals there is less evidence of a healing of the division into rival gospels. Their leaders are still inclined to discount evangelism by seeing it only in terms of its least creditable distortions. The best evidence of a new emphasis on evangelism by those who have been committed to social action is found in local congregations.

THE THEOLOGICAL MOTIVES FOR EVANGELISM

Anyone who compiles a bibliography for evangelism will be impressed with how much of the literature comes from warmhearted Christians who believe that Satan is a present enemy, that a hell of endless torment awaits those who have not explicitly accepted salvation through Christ, that the Bible is in every word infallibly inspired, and that Christ is coming soon. Such beliefs are so prevalent in much that is written and said about evangelism that those who do not share the beliefs may think that evangelism is not for them.

When those with a more liberal theology think through the implications of what they believe, they can have overpowering motives for evangelism. But this is an extra step which the literal minded do not have to take. Abstractions lack the immediate force of graphic and definite conceptions. Compassion is more readily aroused by the thought of agony in eternal fire than by the thought that rejecting Christ may have extended handicaps. Dread of a sinister Devil who is always on the prowl has an urgency that is not found in the belief that sin may turn out to be unwholesome. One who is convinced that salvation can be found only through his own Church will, if he has any heart at all, throw himself into evangelism with more fervor than will someone who thinks that God can be found in any Church, or in none at all. We may praise broadmindedness, but in the hydraulics of the spirit it is narrowness that builds up pressure. A preacher who can lift up the Old Book with the assurance that every line is the word of God will find more proof texts for evangelism than will a preacher who leafs through the ancient writings with the hope that somewhere in them there may be a more than human truth. Those who dismiss the old-time motives for evangelism as simplistic need to ask themselves whether they have a more rigorous approach. The rejection of evangelism, by those who want to be intellectual, can be just as emotional as the most fervent revivalism. So they shirk the mental exertions which a serious consideration of evangelism should require.

Evangelism is not tied to any specialized theology. It is simply a way of communicating whatever conception of Christianity one may have. A Christian church has to have something to say. A church that has nothing to offer has no reason to exist. Those who do not think that truth is important are intellectually bankrupt. If you think that God offers human beings anything at all in Jesus Christ, you cannot fail to be eager to let them know about it. If you believe there is a cataract of lost souls plunging into hell, then to save any one of them is as urgent as snatching a baby from a burning building. But if your conception of the future state is not nearly that distinct, or if that view raises moral questions for you, you may still have powerful motives for evangelism. Perhaps all you can say is that life goes on in some form after death in the direction that it was pointed before death. So those who in this world were inclined toward Jesus and what he represents will move on closer to him—which is a beautiful way to think of heaven. Those who were inclined away from the God we know in Christ will be moving farther from him—and that is a dreadful enough conception of hell without adding demons and pitch-forks, as the Bible never does.

Or perhaps all you are really sure of is the tragic loss of those who live out their time on earth without knowing what Christ could do for them. Bruce Larson says the immediate question for all of us is not life after death but life after birth. When Robert Louis Stevenson lay ill in Samoa, he received a note from a clergyman who asked if he would like a minister to talk to him "as to one in danger of dying." Stevenson declined, but he said he would be very glad to have the clergyman talk to him "as to one in danger of living." It is dreadful to think of anyone missing for even a single day the wonders of the life in Christ. The purpose of evangelism is not just to save people from dying without Christ, but to save them from living without him.

The first way to come to a theology of evangelism is not to look through the library, but to look through your own life. Identify what Christ has done for you. Recognize your blessings. Think of the great certainties that keep you on your course. When you have done that, you can go out with all of a new convert's eager-ness to help others have what you have found.

2

The Objections
to Evangelism

1. Evasions. One of my students, as research for a term paper, visited pastors in his area to ask what they were doing in evangelism. Most of them told him that nothing special was needed because normal church work is the best evangelism. This is the old fallacy that if you make a good product, you do not need to tell about it. The whole advertising industry demonstrates that this is not so. It is even less true of churches than of mousetraps. A church is thought of by outsiders as a private club. Its good work will not attract outsiders to it. Few who are not members will ever notice it.

One minister expressed several common illusions when he told the student that the mission of the church is "to be a Christian presence, and to serve without thought of growth or proselytizing." Semantics could find this a striking example of how "slur" and "purr" words obscure reality. "Presence" is a code word for failure. A church institution that pays no attention to religion assures its supporters that it is offering a Christian presence, though no one has any idea what a "presence" is.

"To serve without thought of growth" sounds beautifully Christian, but the desire to grow is the real expression of unselfishness. The church thus described is, in fact, spending almost all its efforts and money on itself, and becoming smaller every year. The members serve with no concern for how few they are serving so long as they themselves are served.

To "proselytize" is to take adherents from other religions by unworthy means. This church has probably never had a chance to take anyone from another religion. What the minister really renounces is a concern for the spiritual needs of those who are adrift.

The eagerness to think of evangelism only through its caricatures often reveals a guilty conscience. To think of it only as "proselytizing," or as "this 'come to Jesus' stuff," or as a membership drive may offer an escape. An article in one of my denomination's magazines demonstrated great acuteness in showing why seizing strangers and demanding, "Friend, are you saved?", is not spiritually valid. That is not a practice that we staid people need to be warned against.

2. Personal Insecurities. Our personal insecurities may make us intent on finding reasons to avoid evangelism. We may be uneasy about our own uncertain faith. We may know we are inadequate examples of what a Christian should be. Our lack of self-confidence may make us shrink from appearing doltish or undignified. A sort of xenophobia may turn us rigid at the thought of talking about religion with people outside the church. We may shrink from giving the time and energy that evangelism takes.

3. Manners. An able young instructor at my seminary told me, "I just have a gut feeling that evangelism is bad taste." Reluctance to intrude into other people's religious feelings, or to reveal our own, inhibits evangelism. It might seem that a decent reserve would keep well-mannered people from infringing on the sacred privacy of another person's relationship with God.

Brash, insensitive approaches are, of course, to be avoided. But too great an awe for religion's sacred intimacies may be more sentimental than real. There are spiritual depths which no one else can share. But there are also spiritual realities which we can never discover by ourselves. A God of love made us with a need for fellowship. We were not created for isolation, and there are experiences with God which we can have only in company.

For the heathen, God is arcane, unmentionable, occult. Jesus came into the world to reveal the everydayness of the holy. He put God within reach. He made the realm of the spirit something that Christians can talk about and share. It is not inviolably private and sacrosanct.

The great problem for many people outside the church is spiritual loneliness. They do not suffer from being intruded on, they suffer from being let alone. They need to be set free from sterile isolation. There are things they want to talk about that they have never had a chance to discuss with anyone. There are thoughts they ache to share. They welcome someone who will be open with them and give them a chance to open up. Church workers who fear to broach the deepest subjects are often astonished at how ready people are to talk about God and the meaning of life. Not all conversations make great progress, but one almost never hears of a rebuff. Our usual mistake is not being overly intrusive but overly reserved. I have never had anyone show any irritation at my prying when I managed to get to the question of where he or she stood religiously. But there must have been countless times when I was too hesitant to get on such subjects with those who would have welcomed them. The fear of being offensive was the real offense.

Leonard England, Director of *Mass Observation,* a British public opinion poll, said: "There is little difficulty in talking to people about religion. . . . People like talking about religion—many of the investigators in my organization regard a religious questionnaire as something of a rest cure after some commercial subjects."[1]

Some have felt that a personal religious discussion might be possible with intimate friends but insufferable with strangers. Friends do have a special access, but the truth is that many people would rather open up their hearts to those whom they do not often see. That is why travellers are often astonishingly ready to tell each other about all sorts of personal matters. They will not meet again, so there is no reason to be guarded. Even Jesus found that those in his hometown were not as open to him as strangers were.

It is sometimes said that before we impose our witness on people, we must show that we care about them. That is true, but we can overestimate how long it takes to show we care. People will know immediately whether we really care about them or are just performing a duty. Some of the most caring relationships are formed almost at once.

There are good reasons for feeling tension in talking about spiritual matters. Such talk cannot be offhanded. It imposes the effort of hard thinking and of finding words for what is not often expressed. It may be this, more than any sense of impropriety, that makes us hang back. A silence that we try to excuse as good manners may really be bad manners—an unwillingness to put ourselves out for someone else.

One day on a plane my seatmate, to whom I had been talking for a while, suddenly asked, "Are you going to heaven?" He was a sophisticated looking man, and I assumed he was joking, so I answered, "Not this trip, I hope." But he was not joking; he was asking whether I was saved. I could not possibly have resented that sort of warmhearted concern about my welfare. The encounter made me wonder about myself. I had the same reasons for getting to that subject that my seatmate had—but he did it first. And I would have used a more circuitous approach—he came straight out. By any right definition of good manners ("the loving way of doing things"), his manners were much better than mine.

4. Manipulation. The dreadful word *manipulation* has been used to discredit evangelism. Applying skilled psychology to get people to join a church so that they may be trophies for the minister and sources of income for the congregation would be bad. But that still leaves unselfish, spiritually sensitive evangelism as something very good. Sometimes it is assumed that any attempt to influence another person religiously is an infringement on that person's freedom and therefore "manipulative." But any contact between human beings is manipulative. If you speak to me, or just wave to me, you have done something to me and shrunk my independence. In any encounter, I am being shaped by you. That is why Sartre said, "Hell is other people." But so is heaven. Any good effects that we have on other people are the result of good manipulations. Since we cannot help affecting other people, even by avoiding them, we are obliged as Christians to make the sort of contacts that will do the most good to others. It is hard to see how a preacher, who every Sunday uses his training in persuasion to do something to a room full of people, can decry evangelism as manipulative.

5. Presuming to Do God's Work. It has been objected that bringing souls to Christ is God's doing, and not a matter for evangelistic techniques. The work of the Holy Spirit cannot be programmed. The dealings between a human being and God are not a proper area for the practice of evangelism's vaunted skills.

But God works through human beings. He uses doctors to do his healing, friends to bring his comfort, parents to teach his truth to his children. We are the channels through which the Holy Spirit works. It is Christ who saves, but his salvation is made available to the world through Christians. There is an inevitable Semi-Pelagianism in all church work. The things a church tries to do are impossible without God's miracles, but the miracles will not be granted if the church members do not do their part. "The wind blows where it wills," but unless someone hoists the sails, it will bring no ships to port.

One of Rabindranath Tagore's poems says: "No: it is not yours to open buds into blossoms." That is beautiful—but there is more to be said. The gardener cannot pry open the buds, but he can put them where they will be opened by the sun. It is the old story of "You should have seen this garden when no one but God was working here." God in his love has given us incomparable dignity and importance by moving over to make room for us in his occupation. As parents, farmers, teachers, and evangelists, we are "workers together with him." Jesus described the evangelist as reaping a harvest that he had nothing to do with making ready, but the reaper's role is important (John. 4:35–38). All workers in evangelism feel ridiculous. They know that what they are trying to do is absurdly beyond their ability. But they have the trust that if they do their little parts, God will do his big one.

Our big danger is lack of faith that God will do his part. We are tempted to discount what our churches do in evangelism—tiresome committee meetings, labored sermons, embarrassed callers, distracted classes, exuberant youth conferences, sentimental retreats—as having nothing that will deeply change human lives. But we are seeing only the human part of it. How often Jesus must feel with us the exasperation he expressed when his disciples could not heal the epileptic boy because they did not have faith that God would do his part (Matt. 17:14–21). We are right when we think that we and our congregations, with all the carefully worked out evangelistic procedures, cannot be expected to have much effect on anyone. We are wrong if we do not recognize that through such unimpressive means lives have been transformed by finding their new center in Jesus Christ. The only possible reason for believing that our kind of evangelism can do that is our observation that it does.

6. Our Lives Are Our Evangelism. There are some who believe that no other evangelism is needed because our real witness to Christ is the way we live. They insist that the gospel is not in captivity to words. We evanglize, not by talking, but by revealing what Christ has done for us. As Henry Drummond said, "The best argument for Christianity is a Christian."

There is a truth here that must never be forgotten. Jesus said, "Let your light so shine before men, that they may see your good works and give glory to your Father who is in heaven" (Matt. 5:16). In First Peter it is said that the good deeds of Christians will incline the Gentiles toward the Christians' God (2:12). It is Christian lives that attract people to Christianity. Augustine told how the saintly Ambrose made him receptive to the truth: "I began to love him, not at first as a teacher of the truth, which I despaired of finding in thy Church, but as a fellow creature who was kind to me."

Colonel Raymond Robins as a young man joined the gold rush to Alaska. As his party struggled over the mountains, through glaciers and deep snow, he noticed that there was one man who always helped the others, cheering them up, getting them to their feet when they fell under their heavy packs. One evening Robins found this man reading the New Testament, and he asked, "Why don't you ever lose your temper, as we all do?" "I suppose it's because I'm a Christian," the man answered. "Oh, hell, that doesn't mean anything. What's the real reason?" "It means something if you're a real Christian," the other man replied. For eighteen years Robins had had no religious interests, but now he got a New Testament and began reading it. That was the start of his career as a great preacher and social reformer.

It can also work the other way around. Paul concludes a passage on hypocrisy by warning, "The name of God is blasphemed among the Gentiles because of you" (Rom. 2:21–24). Nietzsche was not unfair when he said, "You will have to look more redeemed if I am to believe in your Redeemer."

Our lives are our credentials as evangelists. Our influence on others depends most on what we are. Laurence Housman said, "A saint is one who makes goodness attractive." If we do that, if people sense in us a genuine kindness and devotion to Christ, then they will be receptive to what we have to say about the Christian faith.

All of this is just as true of congregations. A church whose worship is halfhearted, whose resources are devoted to its own benefit, and which is stratified into social cliques can do little in evangelism. But a loving, praying, praising church, whose members care about each other, and whose strength is being poured out for the good of its community and world, can have a valid and powerful evangelism.

Christian lives are both a preparation for evangelism and a result of it. They are pre-evangelism and post-evangelism, but they are not evangelism. The most beautiful Christian life in a community will not bring another human being to the daily thought of God, or to prayer, or to a knowledge of the saving truth until those are made explicit. The most faithful congregation, that is giving itself unsparingly to human needs, will make admiring outsiders who remain outsiders to the Christian faith until the possibility of accepting it is made personal.

Augustine's affection for Ambrose made him open to Christianity, but it did not make him a Christian. Ambrose had to put in many hours of instructing and motivating before Augustine was converted. Colonel Robins's friend turned him toward Christ, but a good deal more had to happen before Robins was ready to confess his faith.

A friend of mine, who was a conscientious objector during World War II, was assigned by the government to alternative service in an impoverished area of Puerto Rico. After the war he persuaded his denomination to take over support of the work he had been doing. His motives were deeply religious, but he explained that he was not going to try to force religion on people or to risk making rice Christians. He and his wife and their associates would do all they could to love and help the people. Then when someone asked, "Why are you doing this?", they would explain, "There was a Man named Jesus. . . ." But after two years the policy had to be changed because no one ever asked the question. The people used the clinic, the nursery, the fertilizer, and the improved breeding stock without ever wondering why it was given. So the workers started a Sunday School and prayer meetings. These were so successful that a church was founded.

The knowledge of who Christ is and what he did and does is conveyed by words. The fad for dismissing language as inauthentic slights intelligence. Linguistic studies can demonstrate that language is inadequate for containing all of any basic truth—but there is no other form of communication that serves as well to transmit thoughts. The One who conveys conceptions from the mind of God to human minds is called, "the Word." The Creator who gave human beings the gift of speech enabled them to tell about him: "O Lord, open thou my lips, and my mouth shall show forth thy praise"(Ps. 51:15).

Keith Miller said, "I had for years decided I would *live* my faith instead of *talk* about it."[2] Then it came to him that this was like being cured of a dread disease by a specially skilled physician and then trying to help others by displaying one's own sound condition. Such a man would walk through a hospital trying to radiate health when what the poor sufferers needed was to know about the doctor and the treatment.

It is not entirely modest to say, "I don't need to talk about Christ; when you look at me you'll see all of him you need to know." No one lives out an adequate witness to the Christian faith. You cannot, just by being good, reveal that Jesus Christ is the divine Savior who died for your sins and now lives as your Lord and ever-present helper. No congregation is so radiant an embodiment of Christ that people can be transformed just by observing it.

If Christians who long to share their faith could do it only by the way they live, they would feel obliged to sound a trumpet to announce how good they are. There would be reason to insist that all a congregation's good works should be done under church auspices so that Christ may have the glory.

Evangelism does not have to be indirect or disguised. The demonstration of love that is most likely to bring lives to Christ is the act of going out to people, letting them know what Christ can do for them, and asking them to take him as their Lord.

7. Not Individuals but Structures. Some ecumenical and denominational leaders insist that the transformation of the major structures of society has always been the Church's major task, from which it has been distracted by evangelistic enthusiasms. A former top official of the World Council of Churches told a worldwide Christian Assembly: "When you begin to see again that the Church is not in this world in order to save individual human souls but in order to be the herald of the Kingdom of God, then you put the Church again in a cosmic framework. . . . When we get out of that narrow pietistic view of evangelism which has characterized most of our Churches far too long, then you become aware of the full challenge of the vast masses in all countries that are outside the life of the Church."

A story in the *New York Times* reported that there is "a new wave of missionaries now coming to Africa in increasing numbers. These missionaries are now concentrating almost entirely on helping the Africans build better countries. 'Proselytizing is a dead dodo today,' " one of them declared.

The language of evangelism has been misapplied to make this sound acceptable. Evangelism has been defined as the "redeeming" of social structures. Individual sin is regarded as a by-product of social sin. But this confuses figures of speech with realities. You can no more redeem a social structure than you can kill an engine. A stock market cannot be wild, though stockbrokers can be. A corporation cannot sin, though it can be administered by sinners. A government agency cannot have a change of heart, but its officials can. All devices, including social structures, can be "converted" to good uses only when the users are. To talk of Christianizing society makes it seem too easy. It is like "christening" (making a Christian of) a battleship. Social orders will be brought under the control of Christ when those who compose them are.

The Church does not have to choose between transforming individuals and transforming social structures. Each will be incomplete without the other. The bringing of God's Kingdom requires both.

8. The Time Is Not Right. It is sometimes assumed that church life moves in cycles, like business depressions or sunspots, so there is no use trying to force evangelism when the time is not right. We will have to wait until some mysterious urge starts the lemmings migrating into the churches again.

A lessened emphasis on evangelism might be ascribed to the times in which we live. Confronted by the emergencies of international tensions, racism, the population outgrowing the food supply, Third World unrest, exploited masses, and depletion of the earth's resources, the Church has no leisure to spend on making converts. The demand now is for social reform.

Or it might be said that not much can be done in evangelism when the Church is at a spiritual ebb tide. Many of the major denominations are suffering from a depleted vitality, as is shown by their decreased attendance, loss of mission giving, and shrinking Sunday Schools. We can hope that this is one of those low seasons of the soul that will pass; but until it does there is a poor prospect for evangelism.

But this is like saying that now is a poor time for breathing. The Church cannot exist without evangelism, because the act of evangelism is a vital function. When it ceases, the Church is cut off from its source of life. It is no accident that the recent loss of vigor in American Churches coincided with a period of inattention to evangelism. There is a vicious downward spiral. Less evangelism in the Church makes for less spiritual vitality, which makes for less evangelism. . . . For the Christian life the words, "I have it because I share it because I have it because I share it . . . ," can be written in a circle, and so can the reverse, "I don't have it because I don't share it because I don't have it because I don't share it. . . ."

There are no special seasons for evangelism, and no special decades. The obligation to make disciples is not periodic, and the power to do it which the Holy Spirit gives is not turned off and on. "Behold, now is the acceptable time; behold, now is the day of salvation" (2 Cor. 6:2). Jesus knew the disciples would find many reasons to postpone evangelizing the despised Samaritans, and that waiting for a better time would always be a temptation; so he told them, "Do you not say, 'There are yet four months, then comes the harvest'? I tell you, lift up your eyes, and see how the fields are already white for harvest" (John. 4:35).

We remain on *hold* when all systems are *go*. No person and no congregation need be a victim of the Zeitgeist. What others are not doing does not limit either our obligation or our opportunity. We do not have to wait until a rising religious interest among Americans makes evangelism easy. People who need Christ now should not have to live out their lives while a church is waiting for some conjectural better time to tell of him.

What really rises and falls is the concern for evangelism in the Church. The fault "is not in our stars but in ourselves." The Holy Spirit is always ready. When any group or person shows concern, that can be the signal that an up-cycle is commencing. The cycle is not a cultural or historical phenomenon—it is in us. What we do can mark the start of a new springtime of the spirit. In evangelism, the right time is always now.

9. God Never Intended Everyone to Be a Christian. The belief that God in his mercy sent his Son to be the Savior of every human being runs into a difficult reality. Most of those who have lived on earth have never had a chance to hear of Jesus. Would a loving heavenly Father make salvation through Christ necessary but impossible? The burning urge to share Christianity made it the world's most widely known religion. (The Encyclopedia Britannica's count of adherents, which is very inexact but significant, is: Christian—944,065,450; Muslim—529,108,700; Hindu—514,432,400; Buddhist—248,516,800; Confucian—205,976,-700.) But after almost two thousand years, Christianity is still a minority faith, and with the far more rapid population growth among non-Christians, Christianity is becoming a smaller minority every year. The world can never be brought to Christ, because it is constantly filling up with little unbelievers. If the Student Volunteers had ever been successful in bringing "the world to

Christ in this generation," they would immediately have had to start again.

It is embarrassing for the evangelist to have to declare that the minority faith into which he luckily was born is the one that God intends for all mankind. That claim does not seem to be confirmed by history.

In the early years, that problem did not appear. Peter's declaration that the time was at hand when God would pour out his Spirit upon all flesh and the old order on earth would be ended was taken literally, so that the Christians' advantages were only temporary. But as the years rolled by, the Church had to explain why God offers all men a salvation which most of them have had no chance to take. There are various ways of getting at this problem:

(a) *God's inscrutability.* Old Testament Jewish thought would have forbidden puzzling over this. Two things were certain: God is righteous, and his ways are beyond our understanding. Orthodox Christian theology took its cue from this. God's offer of salvation to only a minority is not for us to criticize. All are under the curse of sin and fully deserve damnation. It is only God's incomprehensible mercy that offers a chance for real life, here and hereafter, to the elect whom he has enabled to hear the gospel and accept it. To one who believes in a sovereign God, that logic is inescapable. There are many who profess to accept it, though they labor at evangelism and plead for conversions as though human agency had something to do with what happens. Predestination is a doctrine you can neither live by nor deny.

(b) *Uncertainty about Jesus' words.* Modern Christians strain for more credible solutions. Some Bible scholars believe that the oral recollection available to the gospel writers included additions to what Jesus really said. They suspect that the earliest tradition shows that he intended the gospel only for the Jews. The later Pauline extension of the Christian mission to include the Gentiles may have caused the broadening of the scope that was ascribed to Jesus at the ends of the Gospels and in the Acts. So the unaltered account would have shown that the truth Christ brought was to be offered to all the world through the Jews, though it was never intended that all human beings should take the Jewish Messiah as their own or should become members of his Church. Form criticism does not offer this as a firm solution, but as a possibility.

(c) All can know Christ. An always available approach to the problem is suggested by the prologue to John's Gospel: "He was in the beginning with God. . . . The true light that enlightens every man was coming into the world" (John 1:2,9). So all human beings, including those who never heard of the Man of Galilee, have known the Son of God in their hearts. The Holy Spirit has offered to their consciences the love and goodness which Jesus Christ revealed. Since *name* in Bible usage refers to the essential character, many have known the "name" of Christ without ever hearing the vocal sounds by which he has been called. The divine truth that has been given to enlightened spirits is stored up and passed on through the traditions of religious groups, so that non-Christians can have it, not only by direct illumination, but through their institutions. Thus all humanity has been offered a chance to accept Christ or to reject him, even though so far most have missed the special benefits that are now offered through his incarnation.

Justin Martyr, one of the ablest second-century defenders of the Christian faith, said that Christ "is the reason [Word] of whom the whole human race partake, and those who live according to reason are Christians, even though they are accounted atheists. Such were Socrates and Heraclitus among the Greeks, and those like them." The more rigid Church fathers dismissed the high moral teachings of the Greek philosophers as having been given to them by Satan as a seductive front for heathenism. St. Francis Xavier, who labored to take Christianity to the Orient, believed that the Hindus and Buddhists worshipped demons who devilishly introduced some truths that agreed with Christ's as sugarcoating for their poisons. Christians today are more likely to agree with another Jesuit, the modern scholar Karl Rahner, who says that the world is full of "anonymous Christians" who formally disbelieve in Christ or the Church, but who have nevertheless made a personal and total surrender to the truth of an "unknown God." A revered Protestant, Archbishop William

Temple, said: "An atheist who lives by love is saved by his faith in the God whose existence (under that name) he denies."

Then what reason was there for the Incarnation, and why should evangelists bother to tell people what they already know? Christians answer that there are degrees in revelation. God reveals himself through nature: "The heavens declare the glory of God." God and his will are revealed through history, in what happens to persons and to groups. Far more than this, he puts the knowledge of himself in every human heart. Then there is the special revelation in the Old Testament. But beyond that, "when the time had fully come, God sent forth his Son" (Gal. 4:4). This is the fullest truth, expressed in the most complete way that human beings could ever comprehend. In comparison to the knowledge of God that everyone can have, it was like the difference between the astronomy of the great observatories and the astronomy that everyone can have by gazing at the sky. We can glimpse the difference by thinking of what we would have known of God or goodness by ourselves, and what we know through Jesus Christ. It is this special wonder of God's love, revealed in Jesus Christ, that evangelists long for all to know.

This still leaves the inequity between those who have been granted the fullest revelation in Jesus and those who have missed it. But at least this moves the problem from the realm of awful ultimates to that of the earth's puzzling injustices. We do not know why God permits disparity in health, happiness, and religious knowledge. We do know that he intends the inequality to give occasion for mercy and the righting of wrongs. Christ's supreme commandments require his followers to help those who are less fortunate—*physically* ("as you did it to one of the least of these my brethren . . .") and *spiritually* ("go therefore and make disciples . . .").

(d) Saving truth in all religions. Some people try to solve the problem of a merciful way of salvation to which most human beings have no access by believing that there are many ways to saving truth through the religions of mankind. Though these differ widely at the lower levels, they get together at the top. While God was revealing himself in one form to the Hebrews, he

was giving himself in other forms to his well-loved children in India, Polynesia, and South America. Each path can be the right one.

The trouble with this solution is that its necessary assumption is untrue. The religions do not get together at the top. The Scythians thought of their highest God as infinite ferocity. They sought his favor by heaping up pyramids of human skulls and packing their temples with the living bodies of captives with their hands and feet cut off and their eyes gouged out. Various religions have found their highest virtues embodied in gods who were deceitful, licentious, monstrous, depraved. The central symbol may be a bolt of lightning or a lamb, a lotus blossom or a cross. The contrasting styles of living in India and Pakistan come from essentially different religious views. Both sides of a contradiction cannot be true. If the Viking conception of God is right, the Christian conception must be wrong. Opposite qualities are inculcated by different religions—meekness or vengefulness, action or passivity, hopefulness or resignation. A traveller said, "When you see a troop of priests beating drums to frighten demons out of a sick child, you have to recognize that theology does make a difference."

Christians have sometimes distinguished the noble and ignoble religions: the noble ones are those that offer valid ways to God. This still leaves great masses of mankind in the darkness of ignoble faiths. The noble religions are judged to be higher because in them can be found teachings that are similar to those of Christianity—though these may not be the ones the adherents regard as most important. So Christianity is set apart by Christians as the truth by which all other religions are evaluated. The Jesuit scholar Avery Dulles says: "Many theologians today hold that the great religions of the world contain authentic elements of divine revelation and should therefore be treated with great reverence, even though on some points they stand in need of correction."[3] Professor Ronan Hoffman, of the Catholic University of America, allows that Christians may want others "to practise more faithfully that religion which they in good conscience believe to be the right religion for them, at least in those matters which we also consider to be true and good."[4] If the Christian faith is regarded as the normative truth which other religions may more or less approach, then the conception of many parallel paths to the same goal is gone, and the longing to bring people to the Christian faith remains.

(e) Syncretism. It might seem reasonable to think that each religion has a fragment of the truth and each has errors. Thus the best religion for mankind can be found by combining the truths each has to offer, and by subjecting each religion to the criticism of the others. A *World Bible* could bring together the greatest treasures from all the sacred writings. A *Congress of Religions* could identify the weaknesses of each religion as it is viewed through God-enlightened eyes that have not been blinded by prejudice and familiarity.

A major problem with syncretism is its long history of failure. The idea is as old as enlightened human thought, but nothing like a world religion has ever been built out of a collection of parts. To abandon the hope of doing that may seem like a surrender to human weakness. But only a few free spirits ever show much interest. It may be that this is not the way to come to truth. A religion can be understood only from the inside. Commitment has to precede perception. "The unspiritual man does not receive the gifts of the Spirit of God, for they are folly to him, and he is not able to understand them" (1 Cor. 2:14). A Moslem could not see why most Christians find the Koran unendurably boring. Beautiful passages in the Oriental Scriptures will seem to nonbelievers to be great literature, but more like *Aesop's Fables* than a message from beyond all human thought. Much of the Bible is of little interest to those who do not regard it as God's word.

Christians should welcome every chance to gain insights from those of other faiths. We American Christians can be sure that Buddhists or Hindus could point out distortions in our faith and practice which we do not see. We need to find more ways to have religious discussion with non-Christians. But to replace evangelism with efforts to put together a universal religion would be self-defeating. The participants would have to be ready to give up their most cherished beliefs if differing ones seemed more appealing. An exchange of loosely held beliefs does not seem likely to produce a sublime religion.

(f) *Witness, not conversion.* Some insist that Jesus' commandment to witness to all nations never meant that every person was to be made a Christian, but that there should be a Christian witness everywhere on earth. It is to be that of a faithful minority, the leaven in the lump. Some European theologians use the Latin phrase *pars pro toto* to describe Jesus' intention. He does not call everyone; he means for the *pars,* the part, to represent all humanity.

Giving up the belief that the gospel is intended for every human being raises hard questions. The Biblical problems involved are not just a matter of proof texts, though there are many of them. The belief that "at the name of Jesus every knee should bow . . . and every tongue confess that Jesus Christ is Lord" is woven too fully into the fabric of the New Testament to be separated from it. Should the witnessing minority be a tenth, or would a millionth be enough? If some do not need Christ, does anyone? If he is Lord, is he not Lord of all?

The missionaries who took the Christian faith from Palestine across oceans and mountains and centuries were not sociologists. It was not the desire to implant a Christian witness in diverse societies but the yearning to save lost souls that impelled them. Without that urgency, few of us would now be Christians. It is our concern for individual human beings, in our communities and everywhere, that will make us long to pass on the Christian faith.

(g) *The "Cosmic Christ."* Some recent theologians have tried to get at the dilemma of God's sending a Savior of the world without letting most of the world know of him, by the conception of the "Cosmic Christ." Just as the New Testament Christ was a radical reinterpretation of the Old Testament Messiah, which was hard for the Jews to accept, so the universal Cosmic Christ is a reinterpretation of the New Testament Messiah, which will be hard for conventional Christians to accept. It will require them to progress beyond the Christ whom they look on as their tribal Lord. The Christ beyond the Jesus of the Gospels, like Tillich's "God beyond God," will be the one toward whom the whole creation has been straining.

The concept is sometimes associated with Teilhard de Chardin's Omega Point. The progression from Jewish Messiah to

Christian Messiah to Cosmic Christ is like the progression from Teilhard's Biosphere to Noosphere to Omega Point. The Lord of the Future is the one toward whom all faiths have been pressing; in him the differences that separate them will be done away. He is the creative Word that is latent in all religions and in humanism. He is the reconciling Word that modern communication technologies have made urgently necessary in our new "global village." There can be a heady excitement in this conception —partly, perhaps, because no one knows just what it means. It can set off some soaring speculations, but these do not seem to have much bearing on my neighbor's needs or on my groping for some way to help him.

(h) *Nonessentials.* As we worry about the great masses who seem to be largely outside the plan of salvation, the hard issues may appear to be nonessentials: Baptism—a sign; the Church—an association; conversion—a possible form of psychological reorientation. If we could regard these as dispensable, could we not share the good news of Christ with more freedom, and would not non-Christians receive our advances with less wariness? The great need is to let human beings know who Christ is, and what he did and taught. Whether or not they ever go through the external forms may not matter much to their souls or to God.

But it cannot be quite that casual. God did not send his Son into the world to be one of the good influences, but to be the Savior. Faith in him is more than admiration of his character or approval of his teachings. Accepting him as Lord and Master is always marked by something definite. A secret and unacknowledged faith would be precariously unspecific. It would be hard to find a life that has been transformed by Christ apart from any observances or expected fellowship with other Christians. We can hope that now, for the first time in history, communication satellites, radio, television, and the growth of literacy may make it possible for everyone on earth to hear the essentials of the Christian faith. But it will take more than this to bring the full blessings of the life in Christ.

(i) *Where we live.* We may speculate about God's provision for people in remote ages and distant lands, but we know what Christ has done for us, and we know that he can do the same for those we bring to him. We may wonder about other religions, but we know that where most of us live the only likely choice for those who are not Jews is Christianity or no recognized religion. In the Missouri town where I grew up, it was simple fact that "there is salvation in no one else, for there is no other name under heaven given among men by which we must be saved" (Acts 4:12). Without Christ, I would have had no worship, no definite religious teachings, no church. If someone says, "We have no right to urge people to join our church; God can be found through many faiths," we have to wonder what mosque or temple he has in mind. We do not hold back from sharing our bread with someone who is starving because there might be other bakeries. We may be uncertain about the human race, but if we know one person who greatly needs what Christ can do for life, our motive for evangelism is overwhelming.

Evangelism is self-validating. Christ makes his followers care deeply about the physical and spiritual well-being of people who are next door or on the other side of the world. This caring is the evidence that Christ truly is the Savior that the whole world needs, because only that sort of caring can save a world that seems to be rushing to destroy itself by its selfishness and enmities. Clyde Beatty said that the moment in his act that he dreaded most was the one when the big cats that are natural enemies— lions, tigers, and leopards—discovered that they were close together in the same small cage. That is the moment to which our swiftly shrinking world has brought us. Peoples whose differences make for hostility, and who have been separated, are now thrust sharp against each other—politically, militarily, economically, culturally. And they now can swiftly annihilate each other. Democratic societies seem to be becoming ungovernable because of the clash of selfish power groups. Only a religion that makes people more lovingly concerned about other people than they are about themselves offers any hope. The religion of the Good Samaritan, of the Savior who gave his life for sinners, of the martyred missionaries can supply what our fractured world most desperately needs. It is the longing to evangelize that makes it valid.

3

The Church Is the Evangelist

The most pressing practical question in evangelism is "What do you do?" The more important something is, the more necessary it is to learn how to do it well. Jesus made it clear that right methods are important. To help his disciples get more from praying, he told them: (1) "Go into your room," (2) "shut the door," (3) "pray to your Father who is in secret," and (4) "do not heap up empty phrases" (Matt. 6:5–13). Then he gave them a model prayer. Jesus laid down detailed instructions for evangelism. When he sent out the twelve (Matt. 10:5–20) and the seventy (Luke 10:1–11), he told them whom to approach, what to say, where to go, where to lodge, what to do about expenses, how to deal with opposition. He told the seventy to go in pairs. The New Testament is full of instructions for evangelists: "Be wise in your behavior toward non-Christians, and make the best possible use of your time. Speak pleasantly to them, but never sentimentally, and learn how to give a proper answer to every questioner" (Col. 4:5–6, PHILLIPS). "Maintain good conduct among the Gentiles, so that . . . they may see your good deeds and glorify God" (1 Pet. 2:12). "Always be prepared to make a defense to any one who calls you to account for the hope that is in you, yet do it with gentleness and reverence" (1 Pet. 3:15).

The love of Christ and the love of people are the sources of evangelism, but there must also be some knowledge of how to go about it. Many Christians who would cut off their right arms to help some friend come to faith in Christ do nothing because they do not know what to do. Church people lie awake wondering how to help their troubled neighbors know what Christ could do for them; but nothing happens, because they have no idea how to start. Ministers and lay officers, who feel a responsibility for evangelism and discuss it at their planning meetings, may never actually do anything about it, because nothing they can think of seems right.

Part of the problem comes from supposing that any method which has been successful in the past must be out-of-date. There has been a demand for new methods for our new age, and none have been discovered. They never will be. No really new method of evangelism has been discovered for almost two thousand years. I can think of only about ten ways to evangelize: by means of sermons, classes, friendship, partnership in humane tasks, home contacts, conversations, church fellowship, intimate groups, the arts, and the communications media. There may be others, but they are not likely to be new. Whatever is just right for our jet age will be an updating of what has long been used. It will have to be more contemporary than the morning paper in its vocabulary and its adaptation to modern ways of thought and living—but it will not be new.

One result of the discounting of the old ways of evangelism has been a preoccupation with the marginal and fanciful. At a national Church assembly some years ago, the Workshop on Youth Evangelism was led by a campus pastor. He dealt only with how to work with hippies, who, he said, were about 5 percent of the students on his campus. So all the time of the pastors and lay delegates, who wanted to know how their churches might reach youth, was devoted to this colorful, but very small, minority. Experimental and innovative evangelism should be encouraged, but it should not displace the less exotic but more needed ways. It is fascinating to try to get to artists through arts festivals, or to scientists through church-and-science seminars, but most of the artists or scientists who become Christians will be reached through the normal life of congregations.

There is just one basic method of evangelism. It is the one to which all the others have to be related. It can be described in just five words: THE CHURCH IS THE EVANGELIST. The evangelist is not a person at all, but a fellowship. God put his Church on earth as his intended instrument for evangelism. Evangelism is a team accomplishment. The evangelists are not the revival preachers or the zealous "personal workers"—they are the whole congregation. As the preparatory papers for the 1954 Assembly of the World Council of Churches put it: "Our need is not so much for more evangelists, but for an evangelizing Church. . . . The Church itself must be the true means of evangelism."

This does not minimize the classical conception of the evangelist as the warmhearted Christian who lays a loving hand on someone's shoulder and asks, "Isn't it time you gave your life to Christ?" That is important. But that is not how most people become Christians. With most it is the church—working through pastors, teachers, friends, youth leaders, and their parents—that opens up the gospel to them and calls for their commitment. The normal way for adults to be brought to faith is across the growing edge of some congregation. The basic method of evangelism is to draw people into a fellowship of Christians and through that fellowship to bring them to a knowledge of Christ and a desire to give their lives to him.

Right here there is a question that towers up a mile high: "Can those who are brought into the life of your congregation come to know Christ there?" If not, then all you are really running is a religious racket, and the sooner you close it up and sell the building the better it will be for everyone. But if there is no real Christian life, and no presence of Christ in your church, then why are you there? There is probably much about your church that you need to criticize. No doubt it could be much more clearly Christian. The longing to evangelize makes members more aware of their church's weaknesses and more eager to make it what it ought to be. But God throughout the years has used ordinary ministers and members and church life to work his extraordinary miracles in human lives.

To see the whole church as the evangelist can correct the ruinous old misconception of evangelism as a *special activity,* for *special people,* at *special times,* and make us recognize that it is a *normal activity,* for *all the church people, all the time.*

1. Not a Special Activity. Evangelism has been damaged by the tendency to regard it as a peculiar enterprise. So the emotional crusade and the occasional campaign were brief interruptions in a church's normal life. It is the assumption that evangelism has to be unusual that makes it impossible for many churches to think of any method that could be right for them. Evangelism does sometimes need special events—the Church School Enlargement Program, the Enquirers' Class—but these are useful only as a part of the evangelism that is going on all the time. Every organization and activity in the church should be serving evangelism through their regular operations.

This must not encourage the old evasion, "Everything we do is evangelism." Everything is nothing. The self-centered church that makes no attempt to evangelize tries to hide its failure by claiming that its Christmas cantata, or every-member-canvass, or officers' retreat are "real evangelism." An ecumenical Department of Evangelism made its major project the turning of unused bits of real estate in cities around the country into "Miniparks." That was a good thing for someone to do, but as the chief accomplishment of the agency that was supposed to help churches bring people to faith in Christ, it did seem somewhat indirect. I heard an enthusiast in a church meeting declare, "If fixing up our kiddie's playground isn't evangelism, I don't know what evangelism is!" Truer words were never spoken. To "evangelize," in the Bible and in church usage through the years, has meant to make Christ known so that people might take him as their Savior. To seize that word for other meanings leaves this as a duty with no name, and a duty with no name will be ignored.

But everything that a church does can be used for evangelism. It can attract outsiders, or reveal Christianity, or help new members start the Christian life. This gives every church activity an inspiring and exciting purpose.

2. Not for a Special Sort of People. Evangelism has been crippled by the assumption that only those with unusual gifts or a special temperament can evangelize. Many who long to help others know Christ have sadly concluded, "I don't have what it takes." No one has all that it takes, but anyone who says to a friend, "How about coming to church with me next Sunday?", can be an evangelist. Anyone who helps plan a program that will give Christian insights to nonmembers is evangelizing. This is not the only sort of witness that Christians should give. We should all be trying to become more capable of sharing our faith. But even the most inarticulate can be evangelists.

Lay Christians need to know that Christ's commandment to bring others to him was addressed to all disciples. A layman cannot hire a minister to keep the commandments for him, whether the commandment be "You shall not steal," or "Love your neighbor," or "Be my witnesses." The gospel was not spread by specialists. Edward Gibbon, the historian, said that the most important reason for the rapid spread of Christianity was that "it became the most sacred duty of a new convert to diffuse among his friends and relations the inestimable blessings which he had received."[1]

Two corruptions tended to rob ordinary Christians of this function. One was clericalism. During the Dark Ages it was assumed that only priests were used by God to make Christians. The second corruption was territorialism, by which all who were born within a Christian realm were seen as Christians and members of the Church, whether or not they recognized it. Most of the major Churches that came out of the Reformation denounced clericalism but retained territorialism. Thus they did not evangelize but tried only to rouse the latent faith of inactive Christians. Calvinism's doctrine of election, and its teaching that children of Christian parents were born into the covenant, inhibited evangelism. During and after the Reformation, the Churches of the "called out," like the Anabaptists, did most of the evangelizing. They insisted on a personal response to Christ's invitation. In America the major Protestant denominations, including those that sprang from territorial European Churches, forswore both clericalism and territorialism. This returned them to the early Church belief that evangelism is every Christian's responsibility. Most American Calvinist Churches, after a struggle with the logic of predestination, officially accepted responsibility for missions and evangelism. It is the Churches which lay most stress on lay evangelism that are growing.

There is no such crime as practicing Christianity without a license. Churches have to show *all* their members how they can be faithful to Christ's commandment to evangelize. The members need the reassurance that their church is backing them up. When they have done their best to bring people to faith and to the church, then it can take over and do what a member alone could never do.

Evangelism detached from the Christian fellowship must be incomplete. Private conversations, tract racks in bus stations, street-corner preaching, broadcasts, beach ministries all offer opportunities to get the saving word to those who need it. But the weakness of all such methods is that they exist in midair. If they do not lead to some continuing association with Christians, their value is likely to be temporary.

3. Not at Special Times. Seasonal flurries tend to make evangelism a hit-and-miss affair, so that most of its force is lost. Bringing people to faith in Christ usually takes more time than a week of meetings or a Lenten time of doorbell-ringing offers. There are no closed seasons for the fishers of men. The evangelistic church has to be working all through the year to get outsiders to participate, to introduce them to the Christian faith, and to lead them to commit their lives to Christ.

4

The Definition of Evangelism

Understanding what the word *evangelism* means is extraordinarily critical. People can be repelled if the definition is too narrow or misled if it is too broad. It is a Biblical word, and what the Bible means by it puts some limits on capricious definitions. It comes from the Greek *eu* ("good") and *aggelia* ("message"). The exact equivalent in Anglo-Saxon is *god* ("good") and *spell* ("spiel" or "speech"), which combine to make *gospel.* The New Testament uses the word exclusively for proclaiming the good news of Christ. Everyone is entitled to his own definitions, but a meaning for *evangelism* that has no connection with Biblical sources is not Christian terminology.

Uncertainties about what evangelism is have been a chief barrier to doing anything about it. A Committee on Evangelism can waste many meetings, and leave some members angry and frustrated, by disagreement over what their assignment is. Exactly the same problem scatters the effectiveness of a denominational Department of Evangelism. A conference on evangelism can have most of the attenders grumbling, "This isn't what I came for!" Efforts to avoid this paralyzing disagreement have produced an impressive anthology of definitions that have been officially accepted by Church bodies, from the World Council of Churches to local congregations. These do not end the arguments. I have wondered whether a way out might be found by giving all the popular views equal standing. Making church members better Christians might then be called "Evangelism A." The witness to Christ by good deeds could be "Evangelism B." Bringing people to an acknowledged faith and Church membership could be

"Evangelism C," and so on. Thus a State Association could vote on a motion to have a workshop on Evangelism C without a long wrangle about what evangelism is.

As this book gets into methods, the sort of evangelism that is intended needs to be defined. The definition given here is practical, not theological. It has a congregation in view. It intends to show, step by step, how a congregation brings people to Christian faith and living. Its order is the order in which the methods of evangelism will be taken up.

DEFINITION OF EVANGELISM

Evangelism is *every possible* way of reaching *outside* the church:

To make *contacts* with definite persons,

To *cultivate* their knowledge of Christian faith and living,

To lead them to *confess* Christ as their Lord and Savior,

To bring them into *Church* membership, and

To help them *commence* Christian habits and church
    participation.

This definition identifies progressive stages, each of which is incomplete without the others. Its model is not an assembly line but the one Jesus used: "first the blade, then the ear, then the full grain in the ear" (Mark 4:28). The sad mishaps in evangelism come from slighting any one of these essential stages. It may help us to remember these five steps if we think of them as: Contact, Cultivation, Confession, Church membership, and Commencing. Let us consider what this definition says.

Evangelism is every possible way . . . Whenever someone says, "The sort of evangelism I believe in is . . . ," beware! That is a sure sign of distortion. Evangelism cannot be of only one sort. The specialists in pulpit evangelism, personal evangelism, or educational evangelism offer only a fragment of what a congregation's evangelistic program ought to be.

A church must have many ways to evangelize in order to reach those of various ages and personalities. There may be no door into a church for young people past school age, single adults, those with little education, or the highly educated. A church needs ways to appeal to people of all tastes and temperaments.

Churches often wonder about cooperating with special evangelistic programs with such names as *College Christian Fellowship, Business Women's Gospel League,* or *Senior Citizens' Crusade.* If such an organization has a message and methods that are soundly Christian, and if it does not try to be a substitute for the Church, and if it is doing good in an impressive way, then it may be a useful partner in evangelism. But it can be only one of the many ways of evangelism that a congregation needs.

Reaching outside the church . . . Conscientious people may be troubled by this emphasis on reaching *outside.* They may wonder, first, whether we have any moral right to specialize on the outsiders when we have so many merely nominal members right in the church. This looks suspiciously like concentrating on the outsider's needs as an escape from our own failure to be what Christians ought to be. Second, thoughtful church members may wonder whether we do not need to get spiritually ready before we undertake something as demanding as bringing people to faith in Christ. Can they learn what Christianity is by what we are able to tell them, and by what we are? Do we have the sort of church that will show those who are brought to it the wonders of the life in Christ?

These are basic questions. The spiritual qualities of the church members are the most important human factor in evangelism. But bringing people to an acknowledged Christian faith has to be sharply distinguished from improving those who have already been brought in. The psychology and methods must be wholly different. It is judgemental to identify fellow members as unconverted. Nonmembers know they are not professing Christians, but church members think they are converted and that they are in the church by as good a right as anyone's. All sorts of practical difficulties come from the failure to distinguish evangelism from the spiritual nurturing of church members, or from the restoring of the inactive.

It is wrong to delay evangelism until something is done to make church members better Christians, because that is what is going on all the time. It is the purpose of every program and worship service. It is the outsiders who have to be brought to the church's influence. The insiders are already there.

The plan of first reviving the church and then starting to evangelize is a mistake because it does not work. Churches do not become more spiritual by being turned in upon themselves. Christians do not thrive from an intense preoccupation with their spiritual state. Church members who ignore those outside while they are seeking their own spiritual benefit are not likely to have any benefit. A candle under a bushel soon goes out.

In the New Testament, the receiving of spiritual gifts is always coupled with the use of them: "The measure you give will be the measure you get" (Mark 4:24). The Holy Spirit's power is given to us to use: "You shall receive power when the Holy Spirit has come upon you; and you shall be my witnesses" (Acts 1:8). Archbishop Temple said, "The primary purpose for which the Spirit is given is that we may bear witness to Christ. We must not expect the gift while we ignore the purpose. A Church which ceases to be missionary will not be, and cannot rightly expect to be, spiritual."[1]

It is doing evangelism, not thinking about it, that revives a church. A blocked tongue makes for a stale spirit. A Christian who is trying to explain the Christian faith is being freshly reminded of its wonder and beauty. Evangelism brings a new dependence upon prayer and a rediscovery of its power. When a preacher is laying the gospel before those who have not accepted it, he is reminding the church members of great truths they may have forgotten, and calling them to renewed dedication.

By its evangelizing, a congregation is treating in itself the very diseases with which a modern church is plagued: self-centeredness, materialism, unclear faith, spiritual insensitivity, exclusiveness, formalism, and being walled off from the world. Evangelizing is literally a congregation's redeeming feature.

If a tainted church could not make Christians, evangelism would have ended before it started. Think of the harsh charges that the New Testament makes against some churches—legalism, sexual scandal, quarrelling, class distinctions—the list is long and appalling. But those same congregations were winning multitudes to a transforming faith in Christ. We have the treasure in earthen vessels, but the vessels are not what we are offering.

Unworthy though we are, the good things we have to say about Jesus are completely true.

If we were to delay evangelism until the church was spiritually ready, we would wait forever. Every congregation will remain only fractionally Christian. All Christians have unconverted areas in their lives. That is why the effort to get spiritually ready for evangelism so often leads to nothing. No one ever becomes qualified. Many a congregation or denomination has laid out an evangelism program that makes the first year a time of preparation, and the second year the time to start winning lives for Christ. It is a matter of record that in a large proportion of these programs the second year never comes.

1. To Make CONTACTS with Definite Persons. Evangelism most often breaks up for the lack of anyone to be evangelized. A congregation may be inspired to set up a strong Evangelism Committee. Its members read books and go to conferences and lay out a fine program. Then they look around and cannot find anyone to approach. In some stable communities it is assumed that all but the hard-core resisters are in some church. That assumption comes from looking over people's heads. When the belief that there was no need for evangelism was questioned in a town that I know of, there were some surprises. No one had thought of the manager of a chain store, who had come with his wife from Chicago some years before. They turned out to be quite interested in having a church home. There were two brothers and their families who ran a confectionery. People had supposed that they belonged to some exotic Balkan communion which put them out of reach. They had been in town for twenty years before someone invited Alexis to the Men's Brotherhood at the Disciples' Church, where they have ever since been lively and grateful members. We still greatly need Jesus' instruction for evangelism, "Lift up your eyes, and see . . ." (Jn. 4:35).

At the other extreme are the big-city churches, with countless numbers of those who need a faith packed close around them. But the physical proximity means nothing until there is some sort of social proximity. Until a church has contact with real persons, with names and faces, there is no way for evangelism to get started.

2. To CULTIVATE Their Knowledge of Christian Faith and Living. If by some super-salesmanship a church could bring those with whom it makes contact immediately into its membership, it would be the worst thing that could happen to them and to the church. Those who come in at a low level of understanding and commitment are likely to remain there, and the church would be filling its membership with those who have little idea of what a church should be or do. Those who come directly from active membership in another church may not need much preparation, but all others will need some time to learn about the Christian faith and life before they can rightly profess their faith and make their vows. When church joining is too easy, people will think that it is not supposed to make much difference in what they are or how they live.

Dr. Philip Schaff, in his *History of the Christian Church,* says that, back almost to apostolic times, a period of preparation for full church membership "was, on the one hand, a bulwark of the church against unworthy members; on the other, a bridge from the world to the church, a Christian novitiate, to lead beginners forward to maturity. The catechumens or hearers were regarded not as unbelievers, but as half-Christians, and were accordingly allowed to attend all the exercises of worship, except the celebration of the sacraments. They embraced people of all ranks, ages, and grades of culture, even philosophers, statesmen, and rhetoricians. . . . The duration of this catechetical instruction was fixed sometimes at two years, sometimes at three."[2]

Of course, the converts to the early Church came from a heathen world. Not only did they have no background of Christian understanding, but they came from religions which were in some ways the reverse of Christianity. That is true in parts of the world today. But in countries where there have been strong Churches, almost everyone has some Christian knowledge. Those who have never seen inside a church know whose birthday Christmas is and what Easter celebrates. Everyone knows some scraps of Scripture, and the stock of songs that all Americans can sing includes a few that are strong statements of Christian belief. Those who think they have no Christian faith are likely to make assumptions about honor, sportsmanship, and decency that are influenced by Christian teachings. A person who says, "I am not a Christian, but I believe in God," is likely to mean, without recognizing it, ". . . in the sort of God that Jesus revealed." So it might be felt that in our culture even non-Christians do not need the prolonged instruction and reshaping that is required for those who have had no exposure to any Christian thinking.

But with most of our churches the question is not whether we will have a two- or three-year period of preparation, but whether we will immediately snatch into Church membership anyone who can be persuaded to say yes. At least some brief time of preparation is clearly needed. In a country like ours, there is the double task of imparting information and correcting misinformation. The passed-on ideas from Christian sources that finally come through the world to outsiders pick up some contamination on the way. Even mature Christians keep discovering that the Jesus they would like to have is not the one God gave them. Those who have largely made up their own conception of him may have a good deal of unmaking to do. The Christmas baby and the apparition who accompanies the Easter bunny leave a good deal of latitude for invention. The world can capture the Church through the preformed assumptions about Christianity that new members bring in with them.

The period between the first contact and the confession of faith has to provide for:

(a) Instruction. Those who are growing into Christian faith need to learn who Jesus is, what he promises, and what he demands. They need to learn how Christians live so as to get the most for themselves and to do the most for others. They need to learn what the Church is and what Church members ought to do. The evangelism program can try to provide for this growth by getting newcomers to attend church services, classes, and meetings of organizations. It also looks at all this to see whether it is supplying the sort of knowledge that seekers need. It offers books, pamphlets, and conversations.

How much do Christians need to learn? Some of the religions are available only to sages, and to them only after years of grinding study. But Christianity is within the reach of children, though it is inexhaustible for scholars. A slow-witted illiterate may be a better Christian than is the most erudite theologian. Brilliant minds and long study can be powerfully used in the service of Christianity, but they are not what it takes to be a Christian. People are not educated into the Christian life; they come by a miracle of God's grace.

The marvellous democracy of Christianity is possible because religion for the Christian is a person. It is not ritual, law, philosophy, esoteric lore—it is a life-dominating love for Jesus Christ. Children and the unintelligent can be powerfully aware of persons, and they can be deeply devoted to Christ. But this does require a certain sort of learning. You cannot love someone you do not know. Those who are able to confess their faith in Christ have to have some knowledge of who he is.

It is possible to be moved by religious-sounding words with no sense of what they mean. Someone can say with deep emotion, "I take Jesus Christ as my Lord and Savior," with no conception of what is meant by "take," or "Jesus," or "Christ," or "Lord," or "Savior." It is then less a statement of faith than an incantation, and closer to the *Arabian Nights* than to the gospel. Conversion is a miracle, but it is not magic.

A preparatory period should not be slighted, because people are teachable then as they may never be again. Before they have joined, they are curious about the Church. They want to know more about the faith they will be asked to profess. They are wondering what will be expected of them. But the reason they have then for wanting to come to classes and to read will be gone once they have accepted themselves as established members of the Church.

(b) The feel of faith. Christianity brings about a special state of the heart, an emotional makeup, a way of responding to life. This is a direct result of faith in Christ, but it is also caught from Christians. A church tries to bring outsiders into its fellowship until they begin to feel as Christians do.

A young British army officer, who had no Christian background, told of his experience of this: "It all began when an army friend persuaded me to spend a weekend at Lee Abbey. There, under the inspiration of the Holy Spirit, I saw something which

I had never seen before: a large gathering of Christian people of all ages enjoying themselves on holiday together. I found this as enlightening as it was refreshing. Here were people who had so obviously found what I had been seeking zealously elsewhere and in various ways with so little success. It was in the train going back to Catterick that I put my life into God's hands and knew that He had received it."

A good evangelism program tries to help newcomers get the feel of faith by getting them to participate in the church's fellowship organizations, devotional groups, worship services, and social action. It tries to establish personal friendships by arranging for visits in their homes and for invitations into the homes of members.

(c) Testing. Those who would immediately join the church and immediately disappear may not persist if the joining is delayed. Those who have enough interest to come to one meeting to be received but not enough to come to five preparatory classes are not enough in earnest. Father John A. O'Brien, the noted Catholic evangelism leader, says, "Be quick to instruct and slow to baptize."

It might be supposed that some of the weakly interested, who might eventually become good Christians, could be kept from drifting off by quickly making them church members. But experience shows that raising the requirements does not reduce the number who join. People value what is made to seem important. What is easy to get may not be considered worth having. It is the denominations that make high demands of their members that are growing the most rapidly.

There can be no fixed estimate of how long this second stage of evangelism requires. Those who transfer from active membership in another congregation may be ready as soon as they have had a chance to learn about their new church home. The time for the preparation of youth communicants may depend on the traditions of the denomination. Adults may become ready to be new church members in two months or two years. They should be received as soon as it can be rightly done. Delay with not much happening would indicate that the church was unconcerned.

Someone should be keeping a watch on prospective members to be sure that everything possible is being done to draw them toward the church and to build up their understanding. As soon as they are mentally and spiritually able to profess their faith and become church members, an opportunity to make the decision should be offered.

3. To Lead Them to CONFESS Christ as Their Lord and Savior. When people have been attracted to the church and have learned there about Christian faith and living, the great hope is that this faith will come to dominate their lives. The church needs to make them know that Christ cares about them personally and is asking for their love. The great goal is the time when they will be ready to give their lives to him and to take him as their Lord.

This is too critical and personal for the church ever to be satisfied with just having a good influence or with creating a favorable attitude to Christ. The idea that Christ wants each person's devotion is not poetic imagery, it is literal fact. It is so actual that until we have consciously accepted Christ's love and given our love to him, we have rejected someone who is reaching toward us. We are inclined, in our ordinary thinking, to regard the Christian faith as a set of statements about truth which we may believe or doubt. It *is* that—but one of those statements of truth says that there is a God who knows and loves and cares about every single one of us. Jesus expressed this by saying that the heavenly Father knows how many hairs are on your head. Jesus came to the earth to express the divine love for each of us, and through him we love God. If this is so, then Christian faith is not just the acceptance of a set of truths. It is an intensely personal relationship. It is a love for Jesus Christ that responds to his love for us. The evangelism program tries to bring people past the state of interest in religion and to the state of an actual relationship with Jesus Christ as a living and a present Lord.

This personal relationship with Jesus will not have its full power unless we are conscious of it. There might conceivably be unconscious Christians, but our being with Jesus will mean far more to us if we are aware of it. And our awareness will not be definite until it is expressed. We exist in a physical world, and nothing ever seems quite actual unless there is some tangible evidence of it. Thoughts without acts are insubstantial. That is why evangelism tries to bring people to a declaration of what Jesus means to them. The decision to follow Christ is made in the secrecy of one's own heart, but something must be done about it. The Bible emphasizes both the tangible expression of our faith and its secret part: "If you confess with your lips that Jesus is Lord and believe in your heart that God raised him from the dead, you will be saved" (Rom. 10:9).

Professor William James told how to anchor good intentions: "Seize the first possible opportunity to act on every resolution you make. It is not in the moment of their forming, but in the moment of their producing motor effects that resolutions communicate the new 'set' to the brain. . . . No matter how good one's sentiments may be, if one has not taken advantage of every concrete opportunity to act, one's character may remain entirely unaffected for the better. . . . When a resolve or a fine glow of feeling is allowed to evaporate without bearing practical fruit, it is worse than a chance lost; it works so as positively to hinder the discharge of future resolutions and emotions. . . . If we let our emotions evaporate, they get into a way of evaporating."[3]

Letting one or two intimates know of our faith would have some of the benefits of expressing it. But there are reasons why it has to be openly declared. It is not wholly a private matter. It is impossible to be a complete Christian apart from others who believe in Christ. Anyone who makes a public profession of faith is taking his place within the fellowship of believers. We are both private and social beings. A faith that you have not made known can have a meaning for your private self, but it will be unrelated to the social part of you.

A decision to follow Christ that few others know about will be precarious. It gains substantiality by existing in the world where other people are. We are less likely to waver and be unfaithful when our associates know what our commitment is.

Dietrich Bonhoeffer said, "The road to faith passes through obedience to the call of Jesus. Unless a definite step is demanded, the call vanishes into thin air, and if men imagine that they can follow Jesus without taking this step, they are deluding themselves like fanatics."[4] The first act of obedience to the call of Jesus is to let it be known that we have heard his call and accepted it. "Whosoever therefore shall confess me before men, him will I confess also before my Father which is in heaven" (Matt. 10:32, KJV).

4. To Bring Them into CHURCH Membership. Right here we might hesitate. We can see well enough why it is important to bring people to faith in Christ, but why must this lofty purpose descend from the spiritual to the organizational? We should certainly remind converts that a church can be of immeasurable value, but do we not have to recognize that a sincere faith in Christ does not always have to be expressed through church activities? Christians may not like organ music, or liturgy, or sermons, or group activities. It seems likely that some people join the Church because it is the only way they have to be recognized as Christians. They want to take their stand for Christ and be counted among his followers, but they never intend to be active members. So they come to the church to be identified as Christians just as they might come to be certified as married, and they are happy in the knowledge that they do not have to come back. It might seem better to offer a certificate which would say that a person, having upon examination been found to have a valid belief in Christ and an intention to be his faithful follower, is therefore to be known as a Christian. Then enrollment in a congregation, with promises to attend services and to contribute time and money, could be optional.

The great purpose of evangelism is to bring people to faith in Jesus Christ and to a desire to live a Christian life. But does living a full Christian life require becoming a member of the Church? If it does, then this is a secondary purpose, and evangelism is incomplete until those who have come to faith have also become Church members.

The New Testament leaves no doubt that Christ established a Church that was to be made up of his followers. Throughout Christian history it has generally been assumed that a Christian would be in the Christian Church. Martin Luther said, "Any one who is to find Christ must first find the Church. For how can one know where Christ is, and where faith in Him is, unless he knew where His followers are? Whoever wishes to know something about Christ must not trust to himself, nor by the help of his own reason build a bridge of his own to heaven, but must go to the Church, must visit it, and make inquiry. Now the Church is not wood and stone, but the company of people who believe in Christ; He must keep in company with them, and see how they believe, and teach, and live."[5]

The historic faith has been that the Church is not a human institution at all. As Paul told the Philippians, "We are a colony of heaven" (Phil. 3:20, MOFFATT). God set his church on earth as an outpost of heaven to give blessings that every human being needs. I once said in print, "There need be no embarrassment about making evangelism a 'join-the-Church' program. It was that in the New Testament." A professor of church history commented on that in a religious journal, "Here we leap lightly over the centuries, and make the assumption that our particular institutional form of the church is the New Testament Church!" I needed that correction of my too offhand treatment of a serious matter, but I do not think the centuries are as far apart as the professor does. Christians need to be in a recognized fellowship of believers today for the same reasons that they needed to be in Paul's Corinth or Polycarp's Smyrna, and they can usually find that fellowship in their hometown congregations. The colony of heaven is still here.

The failure to understand the Church is a chief barrier to evangelism. Church members will have no great zeal to win their neighbors to a dispensable religious club. But the Church is much more than that. In the visible Church, spiritual realities that are always and everywhere become now and here. In this material world, a disembodied religion is impossible. In the Church, the divine perfection is made manifest through what is imperfect. The visible Church is where the invisible breaks into the world where we live. Such realities as the Body of Christ and the Kingdom of God cannot be identified with any earthly organization. But they become manifest and locatable through the Church that we know.

(a) The Church is the Body of Christ. Through the Church, Christ's spiritual presence is tangibly made known. Jesus was born on earth to put the ineffable and the wholly other onto our scene and within our reach. The visible Church continues this incarnation. Christ comes to us through his Church. We know him there as we could never know him by ourselves—We know him through the worship, the Sacraments, the teachings, and the sense of his presence that we have where those who love him are gathered in his name. We find him in the Church in what he is doing in us, and through us, and in the lives of others. He is in the Church in such a special way that the Bible says that the members of the Church are members of his body. It is an aspect of the Christian's union with Christ.

The Church is on the earth to make Christ known, and to keep those who know him growing in their knowledge of him. Amid all the soul-stifling pressure of material cares, participating church members are reminded of the spiritual. The Bible's revelation of God and of his will is kept in the consciousness of those who are often in a church, and there they are helped to understand the Bible. Year by year the Church gives a supportive framework for Christian living, with its regular promptings to worship, with its calls to service and self-sacrifice. Those who are getting what a church has for them may not always be the best Christians, but they do have the best chance to be.

(b) The Church is the Communion of Saints. The New Testament knows nothing about a Christianity for isolated individuals. Those who share the same great faith in Jesus Christ are inevitably bound together in a loving and supporting fellowship. Many of the greatest blessings that Christ has for us, he gives us through each other. A solitary Christian must be disabled and deprived. There are Christian insights we never get except through other people; there are spiritual experiences we cannot have alone.

J. Milton Yinger, in *The Scientific Study of Religion,* says: "Can there be an 'individual' religion? There can be religious *aspects* of private systems of belief and action. A complete religion, however, is a social phenomenon: it is shared, and it takes on many of its most significant aspects only in the interaction of the group."[6]

We experience the Communion of Saints when we are with Christian friends whose hearts kindle ours. We experience it in the life of our congregations. We experience it in large assemblies when we feel a surprising intimacy with people we have never seen before. We experience it in our sense of being one with Church members "from every tribe and tongue and people and nation" throughout the earth. We experience it in our knowledge that we are close to people who have left this world but are still near us in that fellowship which even death can never break.

When people join the little church down the street, they are not just getting a line in its membership list and the right to vote in its meetings. They are taking their places in an awesome company that includes their ancestors and the great Christian heroes. They have come into a heart-to-heart relationship with their new friends in the church, and with those who wrote the hymns they sing, and with the Apostles, and with the Lord who makes them all a loving family.

(c) The Church is the Holy Catholic Church. When you join the little church down the street, you go at the same time through the doors of every other church in town. When you move from outside to inside the church family, you are becoming at the same time a Catholic, Methodist, Episcopalian. In any city in the world, when you walk into a Christian church building, you can know you are right back home again. Becoming a member of one denomination does not cut you off from the others, it puts you with them. You may not like some of their hymns or agree with all of their views, but you worship the same Christ, who is made known to you in the same Bible, and offers you the same salvation, and has taught you the same Lord's Prayer.

David M. Stowe says in *Ecumenicity and Evangelism* that history reveals "the necessity for a message to have a social bearer, some sociological apparatus to carry it in mission. This must also be a permanent embodiment, one that bridges the generations and builds up a cumulative effect in society at large." The Church is such a social organization. It is a visible structure that joins present, past, and future—Occident and Orient. Christianity is not a twentieth-century American phenomenon, and evangelism has not achieved its goal when it has attached the believer to a neighborhood Bible-study group or a businessmen's prayer breakfast. Those are useful activities, but Christians need the sense of belonging to a company of faith that joins us with the followers of Christ in all nations and all centuries. There is no sanctity in mustiness, and forms of music and prayer that were just right for medieval German peasants may be quite wrong for us. But we sometimes need to know that we are sharing in the worship that was used by Christ's followers in the centuries past and will be used in the centuries to come. We need an established Christian community that can sustain us for a lifetime, where deep and lasting friendships are maintained, where grandchildren and grandparents share a spiritual home.

Callow flings at the "institutional Church" leave us to wonder what other recognizable Church there could be. The institutional Church is a Church that is definite, that is there. It is because we have a real Church that we have real Sacraments. The divine Being was incarnated in weak human flesh. Because of that, the Church has the related mystery of divine grace conveyed through physical and commonplace materials. The Sacraments belong to the Church; they have been transmitted through the Church; they would be unknown without the Church. There is no reason for people who set no store by the Church to want to receive from the Church the Sacraments of Communion for themselves or Baptism for their families. Anyone who believes in the Sacraments will not be satisfied with an evangelism that leaves people cut off from the Church through which the Sacraments are given.

The Church is not a tool for the gospel, it is a part of the gospel. The great benefits that the Church has for Christ's followers are among the gospel's promises.

(d) *The Church is the Kingdom of God.* References to the Kingdom in the New Testament are not simple, but some of them clearly mean the visible company of the followers of Christ. To join the Church is to become a citizen of a country in which Christ is King. This Kingdom has its own laws and its special way of life. The early Christians, who might have worshipped secretly, openly admitted that they were members of the Church, though they knew it might mean their martyrdom. By this they made it known that Christ, not Caesar, was their king. That is still a reason for becoming a member of his Church, and that is still a reason why the Church has martyrs. Joining an evangelistic movement or a campus fellowship does not bear that sort of witness.

Christ's Kingdom is set over against the kingdoms of this world. An institution has to be confronted by an institution. The united expression of Christian conviction can be much more effective than the separate efforts of individuals. The gospel would have far less influence upon society today without the organized Churches and the pressures they can generate. Christians join Churches so that they can combine with those who share their faith in combatting the evils of the world. If evangelism does not bring those it leads to Christ into the Church, it keeps his gospel from having its full power.

Now comes the hard question: *Where is the Church?* If we believe that God put the Church on earth to give men and women what they need above all, and if evangelism is incomplete until it has brought people into Church membership, then we have to know where that divine institution can be found. We speak of "the Church" as though we know what we mean, but what we see when we look around us is a bewildering profusion of obviously too human institutions. There are stately cathedrals and storefront meeting places; there are ancient hierarchies and wild sects. Where, on the unbroken continuum, does "the Church" begin?

What certification does a religious group require to qualify as a Church? Lodges use Bibles in their rituals—are they therefore Churches? Is a house-church a Church? Can a dormitory prayer group perform a valid baptism? Can earnest friends at a restaurant order some grape soda and potato chips and celebrate the Eucharist?

Because it is so important to know where the Church is, and so difficult, Christians across the years have tried to find some definite marks of the "true Church." Some have tried to define the Church through its ministry: where there is a valid ministry, there is a valid Church; and there is a valid ministry only where there is an unbroken succession of ordinations back through the centuries to the Apostles and, finally, to Christ himself. The chain of palms on scalps gives a physical continuity. It has recently been proposed that, since the work of the Apostles is assigned by the Bible to all the members of the Church, and not just to the clergy, the Apostolic succession should be traced through the laity. Where people are actually doing what Christ charged the Apostles to do, you have a true Church.

The Orthodox Churches, as their name implies, find the true Church where Christ's teachings have been passed down unchanged through the Apostles and Patriarchs to the Church today. Therefore nothing can be dropped from what the Church has taught, and nothing added to it.

Some Churches have defined themselves through the right observance of the Sacraments, to which the Calvinist Churches have added the right preaching of God's word. State Churches are politically defined. The Churches of the Called-Out are identified by lives that show the marks of the response to God's call. With others the evidence is the possessing of the gifts of the Holy Spirit, which were promised to the Church.

The difference between the "We-Only" Churches and the less exclusive ones is important. There are many Christian bodies which insist that only in them can be found what God has promised through the Church. As a song from the American frontier expressed it:

> And if you will not join us,
> we bid you now farewell;
> For we are bound for heaven,
> and you are bound for hell.

That does have a certain satisfying urgency, but in actual life there never seems to be evidence of that sort of monopoly on grace.

Fortunately, the Bible is not that clear. Unlike traditional theology, the Bible deals in fractions. Jesus said that the Church is like a field in which the wheat and the weeds grow together. The Seven Churches in the Revelation are graded on a sliding scale, from Smyrna, which is rich in good works, at the top, to Sardis, which is dead, at the bottom, with Laodicea, which is lukewarm, in between. That is what we see when we look at the congregations we know best. There are none that seem to be all that the true Church ought to be, and there are none without convincing signs of the Holy Spirit's power. The Church on earth is always fractional, but that fraction is the true Church.

If the radio beams that keep airplanes on their courses also supplied the power for their motors, we might think of the true Church as being on the beam, and the false Church as off. Most of our churches are partly on and partly off this beam of guidance and power that streams out from God across the centuries. Right traditions and the members' devotion to Christ help keep a church on the beam. Even when a congregation is badly slipping from it, we cannot doubt that the beam is there.

For the evangelist, the question of where the true Church is must be of the utmost importance. He will not get his answer from the historians or the theologians. They can tell him what to look for, but they cannot tell him where it is. That answer must finally be personal. You must start with your own congregation. Is there any evidence that the power of God is granted to your church? Do you sense God's presence in the worship? Has your church helped you to be a better Christian? Do you find in the other members traits of love and goodness that seem to be from clear out of this world? Are you in your church aware of a continuity with the Church of the past and with the Church that is still to come? There is no doubt that you will also find in your church and its members many things that you do not like. That is what you would expect from any earthly fellowship. It is the something extra that is not of the earth which indicates that the true Church is there.

If there is nothing extra, if you are convinced that you would be as well off today if you had never been in your church, then you have a pressing problem. For your own soul's good, you must immediately leave your church and find a real one. As a Christian you cannot doubt that Christ's Church exists on earth or that it can enrich your life.

Because there is a true Church of Christ on earth, getting those who believe in him into it is of the utmost importance for evangelism. About A.D. 250, St. Cyprian said, *"Extra Ecclesiam nulla salus,"* which is usually translated, "Outside the Church there is no salvation." That is, no doubt, what Cyprian believed and what many since him have taught. But the Latin word *salus* can also mean "health." Evangelists do not have to believe that only Church members get to heaven. But they may believe that a Christian cannot be fully healthy outside the Church. They may know that God grants through the continuing company of believers a sustaining experience of his presence, and of loving fellowship, and of power for great living that could never be had apart from it.

Church members often fear that trying to get others to join their church will seem like building up the institution or like implying, "What you need is to be more like us." That might indeed be true if the first emphasis were on joining the church. But if the appeal has to do with coming to faith in Jesus Christ, then joining the church is usually expected. Without faith in Christ, there is no good enough reason for joining a church; but with faith in him, there is no good enough reason for staying outside. A new awareness of Christ is likely to bring a desire for a church and for the company of other Christians. When two callers had invited an older woman to join a church in an Illinois town, she answered, half-humorously, "I have lived without the church for eighty years, and I can die without it." They recognized that they had been on the wrong subject, and one of them said, "You can say that about the church, but can you say that about Jesus Christ?" When they had talked about that for a time, she decided that she wanted to confess her faith. They never had to speak about the church again, because she took it for granted that she would become a member.

5. to help them COMMENCE Christian habits and Church Participation. The most critical stage of evangelism comes after people have made the great decision to give their lives to Christ and join the Church. In the weeks that follow, tremendous issues are in the balance. The grip of old habits of thinking and living will be strong. The natural inclination is to continue as usual, with such minor alterations as a new club membership requires.

But the Church is unlike any other organization. To join it requires moving into a new world, with a completely distinctive sort of acts and attitudes. *Church membership is not a connection, it is a way of life.*

For the convert who has decided to take Christ as Lord, it means becoming a new sort of human being. For those who have thought of themselves as Christians, and have decided to make it explicit, a great deal has to be different. If their open acknowledgement and Church membership are real, then their use of time and money, their bearing, and their relationships must change. Those who have transferred from another church may be in a precarious state. The new church will not seem like the dear one they have left. Everything that is different about it will seem wrong. They will be confronting a crowd of strangers. Unless their new church tries hard to help them through this difficult time, they may never be quite happy or feel at home in it.

The great sin of incomplete evangelism is that it abandons new church members to sink or swim, which is why so many of them sink. There is a great deal a church should do to give them a sound start in the Christian life and in the church. It has to put arms around those who have just stepped inside the door and go with them for a while until they have learned to walk in the new way. This is the subject of Chapter 13.

5

The Supporting Structures

There is a strange paradox in evangelism—*it is a church's most urgent and least pressing duty.* Of all a church's tasks, evangelism is the one that can most readily be neglected.

A minister can be ordained and go through years of his ministry without ever talking about religion with anyone who is not already a member of a church. If he submits to the natural pressures of his work, that is exactly what will happen. Almost all his dealings are with church people. He is walled off from the world in a religious ghetto.

In my seminary class in evangelism, I asked the students to report on conversations about religion that they had had with persons who were not members of a church. Some very interesting conversations were described, but it was startling to find that all these second- and third-year students reported on conversations that they had had before they came to the seminary. In college they had been associated with people of all sorts. As students for the ministry, on the campus, and in their weekend fieldwork, they associated only with church people. Unless something happens to change the way things naturally work out, the law might be: *The first stage in giving up evangelism is to go to a theological seminary; the final stage is to become the pastor of a church.*

A minister never has time to make his sermons as good as he knows they ought to be. He never does all he should be doing for the members of the church. He may know it is his duty to be reaching also to those outside, but if they are neglected their feelings will not be hurt. There is nothing that requires him to pay attention to strangers. But if he does not, he will be haunted by the knowledge of a broken obligation. He cannot keep from remembering the Lord's words, "I have other sheep, that are not of this fold; I must bring them also." There is a deep inner conflict in a ministry that is preoccupied with the voting, dues-paying members of a church. The lay workers have exactly the same problem. They never catch up with what needs to be done within the church.

A church that yields to this natural tendency cannot escape the penalty. The old rule still holds: "Evangelize or fossilize." Karl Barth put it more precisely: "One thing must prevail: 'Proclaim the Gospel to every creature!' . . . Where the Church is living, it must ask itself whether it is serving this commission or whether it is a purpose in itself? If the second is the case, then as a rule it begins to smack of the 'sacred,' to affect piety, to play the priest and to mumble. Anyone with a keen nose will smell it and find it dreadful! Christianity is not 'sacred.' . . . It is an out and out 'worldy' thing, open to all humanity: 'Go into all the world and proclaim the Gospel to every creature.' "[1] Around the unevangelizing church, there will inevitably be the stale odor that Barth found so repellent.

1. The Congregation. A congregation must take arms against its tendency to neglect evangelism by giving it a strong place in the church government. It is dismaying to see that many congregations are far better organized for everything else—for education, music, meals, recreation—than they are for their most important task. Consider, for example, how much more planning most churches devote to bringing in money than to bringing in human beings. This does not show that they are materialistic; it shows that there is more incentive to work for visible than for invisible results. The Stewardship Chairman can say, "We got a twenty percent increase in giving." The Evangelism Chairman cannot say, "We got a twenty percent increase in Christian faith." Moreover, short-range needs are more pressing than the long-range ones. If a church gets no money, it dies fast; if it gets no members, it dies slowly. Most churches are better organized to raise money for evangelism overseas than they are for their own evangelizing.

In most denominations, giving evangelism a strong place in the church government will require assigning it to an important committee of the Official Board (the Diaconate, Vestry, Session, or whatever else it may be called). It is a mistake to assign evangelism to a committee that has some other major responsibility. There might be some logic in combining it with Membership or Spiritual Life. But if the Committee on Evangelism has to care for something else that is immediately pressing, such as Christian education or worship, then the evangelism duty is likely to be the one that is postponed.

It is important for the Evangelism Committee to be expected to report at each regular meeting of the Board. Here again, the reason is that evangelism is a church's most urgent and least pressing duty. There are no external pressures that force an Evangelism Committee to do its work. But after several meetings of the Board in which the Evangelism Chairman has responded, "No Report," he or she is likely to begin studying and planning. The Committee reports to the Board what is happening in evangelism and brings in any proposals that require Board approval.

Enthusiasm for evangelism builds up. A new Chairman or committee member is likely to start out both unconcerned and uninformed. Church committees do not meet because they have business; they have business because they meet. It is after they have overcome their inertia and gotten into the work that they get excited about it. If committee members rotate out of office, there must be ways of rapidly educating and kindling a new group every year.

The minister usually has the best chance to stir a lively interest in evangelism in the congregation and Committee, though there are churches where enthusiastic lay leaders are the chief source of the fervor. The minister can be the inspirer and guide, as well as one of the evangelism workers. It is better for evangelism to be regarded as a lay enterprise than as a ministerial task with which lay members are giving a helping hand.

The Evangelism Chairman should be one of the ablest and most respected lay officers. The qualities of this Chairman can be crucial for a church's success in bringing people to faith in Christ. He or she can help the minister overcome the inevitable tendency to postpone evangelism. I can recall meetings when I tried hard to avoid the Chairman's eye. Then on the telephone the next day, he would say, "I was wondering last night whether you were going to bring up the calling program. Don't you think we ought to set the dates?" Such a Chairman is one of the greatest blessings a congregation and its minister can have.

Evangelism is the work of the whole church. It is therefore wise to expand the Committee by adding to it representatives of all the organizations and activities that are important for evangelism. In a large church these could be from the Church School and from the groups for women, men, singles, couples, youth, older people, and stewardship. When the Committee meets with these added members, it may be called the Evangelism Commission (or Council). In a large church the Commission may have forty or more members. In a small church it might have just the minister and two lay members. The Committee attaches the program to the Official Board, but the whole Commission develops and operates it. Overorganizing is a menace, but the Commission is not a fifth wheel, it is a steering wheel. It offers an easier way for doing what would otherwise have to be done with more strain and distraction.

The Commission needs a special annual meeting at which it takes a searching look at the church's whole evangelistic work and lays out plans for the year ahead. This meeting can come just after new members have come onto the Commission, and can provide for their orientation.

The Evangelism Commission has to start by identifying its task. The word *evangelism* has been so abused that the Committee members may have no idea, or very wrong ideas, of what they are to do. A new Commission will have to make a basic study of its purposes and methods. A definition of evangelism can clarify the purpose, and deciding on the definition can be educational.

The Commission needs inspiration. There should be hard thinking about the motives for evangelism—in the Bible, in each one's religious experience, and in the needs of persons and of the world. There needs to be assurance that God changes human lives so that the results of the Commission's work can be clear beyond what anyone could do. Reliance upon prayer and the use of prayer are critically important for the Commission.

The Commission needs to be very clear about just what it wants the church to do. It needs to see the whole picture of evangelism as a linked series of steps, not just as scattered activities. This book's description of the five C's—(1) Contact, (2) Cultivation, (3) Confession, (4) Church membership, and (5) Commencing—is intended to make the process plain (see p. 53). The results of evangelism are spiritual and invisible, so it tends to become vaporous. Its methods therefore must be specific, with a clear understanding of who does what and how. Who seeks new pupils for the Church School, and when is it done? What is the process for getting a new member's first financial pledge?

The Commission's purpose is to bring the whole church into evangelism. It therefore needs to see what part every organization, activity, and member can have. It needs to describe in detail what each can do to draw people toward the church, to prepare them to be confessing Christians and church members, and to establish them in the Christian life and in the church.

It can be useful to outline all this in writing and have it duplicated. This can keep before the Commission what is to be done and serve as a checklist for the performance. Such a description might start with the definition of evangelism. Next could come the ways by which the church members can be made eager for evangelism—by sermons, prayers, programs, publications, etc. Then could come a listing of what each part of the church should do to make contacts, reveal the Christian faith, bring newcomers into the church family, and give new members a sound start.

A Commission needs all the knowledge it can get. The minister, members who know what has been done in other churches, and leaders from outside can all supply ideas. Members can be sent to evangelism training conferences. Books and pamphlets can be circulated.

A Commission meeting has three sorts of business:

(1). It checks on how well the plans it has made are being carried out. Are the teachers using the slips on which they are supposed to report new families? Have the names of new couples been sent to the Couples' Club?

(2.) It considers what else should be done and how to get it started.

Should there be a club for employed young adults who have rooms near the church?

(3.) It pools information on what is happening to people. What did the visitors learn about the new family? Has the man who joined the church two months ago been attending? What happened to the girl who for a while seemed so happy in the choir? A representative group will have the needed information that no one person could supply. Collective wisdom can be the best guide to what should be done next for people.

Evangelism can be anchored against a congregation's tendency to let it drift, not only by lodging it firmly in the church government, but also by lodging it firmly in the church calendar. If, before the church year starts, the dates have been set for what is to be done—the calling, the sermon series, the enquirers' classes —then the plans will be made and these things will be done. But if the intention is to wait until the right time comes, it never will. Needed workers, who cannot break engagements three weeks in advance, might have readily promised to serve if they had been asked earlier.

2. The Denomination. What congregations do in evangelism depends critically on the help they are given through their denominations. A local church can be very successful by itself, but what most churches do, and how well they do it, can be greatly increased by strong denominational leadership.

This can be given at various levels. Denominations differ in their structure, but most of them are organized at the national, regional, and district levels—like the nation, the state, and the county. There may be employed evangelism leaders at all these levels, or the professional staff may be concentrated at the national level, with volunteer committees of pastors and lay members giving leadership in the regions and districts.

There are essentials that a denomination can supply:

(a) Prompting. Because of every congregation's tendency to drift away from evangelism, outside reminders are perpetually needed. The leaders, through meetings, denominational publications, mailings, and travelling speakers, can keep incentives for evangelism before pastors and congregations. The national evangelism staff can work with the staffs of other agencies—such as

those for Christian Education, women, men, and youth—to help them keep an emphasis on evangelism in their programs.

The principle that agencies should offer help to local churches only when they ask for it may be right for some sorts of church work, but it cannot be right for evangelism. The churches that are giving no thought to evangelism will not ask for help, but they are the very ones that most need stimulation. The churches need regular prompting because nothing is fixed. A strong work in evangelism can dwindle away, and churches that for years have shown no interest can become enthusiastic.

(b) Methods. Churches that want to reach out may not know what to do or how to start. Full-time evangelism leaders can acquire the knowledge that pastors do not have time to get. They can travel, observe, study, and discuss. The right methods in evangelism are not devised by technicians; they are found out by success and failure in thousands of churches. The best ideas come to those who are on the job. Denominational leaders have the wide contacts that enable them to learn where good things are happening, and they can pass the methods and the inspirations on to other congregations.

The denominations can learn from each other. There have been times when the evangelism leaders of the ecumenical denominations, and of some that are not ecumenical, have met twice a year to share their thinking and their methods. They have used each other's literature and leaders. These denominations have had at times what was, in many ways, one common evangelism program to which all were contributing. This has been of immeasurable benefit to the local churches.

(c) Materials. Many of the most needed printed and audiovisual tools for evangelism have to be produced in quantity. These can give motivation and instruction in evangelism, courses of study for youth and adult new-member classes, appealing presentations of the Christian faith, aids to devotion and Bible study, and information about the denomination. Cards for the file, for calling assignments, for decisions, and for church attendance registration can be supplied.

(d) Updating. Local churches get out-of-date and out-of-touch in their conception of evangelism. Pastors become attached to what they learned early in their ministries. Denominational leaders can help them understand how the Christian faith can best be presented in terms of contemporary thinking and new situations.

(e) Conferences. Pastors, Evangelism Commission members, and lay workers need help. They need the inspiration and knowledge that a training conference can supply. A denomination can put such conferences within reach of most churches. It can supply able leaders for them. A conference may offer the attenders a chance to observe or to get experience in evangelistic work. The give-and-take among the delegates can be stimulating. Conferences can start lively evangelism programs in churches that could have been persuaded in no other way.

(f) A denominational program. A national program with a special name is simply a way of getting major attention for something that is of major importance. It gives the whole denomination the sense of doing something great together. A series of conferences that would otherwise be held in five cities with five hundred attending can, as a national program, be held in twenty-five cities with five thousand present. A national program can get congregations to undertake work that their minister might have urged in vain.

3. The Theological Seminary. It has long been recognized that the success or failure of evangelism depends very much on the institutions in which ministers are trained. As Father John A. O'Brien, of the faculty of Notre Dame University, has said: "Our seminaries hold the key to the solution of the convert problem in America. In their hallowed halls our future priests are trained. It is evident that the training in the technique of recruiting prospects and instructing them must be given in the seminary. In addition, there must be imparted to them that quenchless thirst for souls which will drive them in all their priestly years to search, in season and out of season, for the sheep that are lost, strayed or stolen."[2] In a sense, a class in evangelism should be a seminary's basic course because the benefit of all the other classes depends on having people in the churches. It is frustrating to be giving better and better training to ministers who will be dealing with fewer and fewer people.

Year after year, the national assembly of my denomination passes solemn resolutions that request its seminaries to give more attention to preparing their students for evangelism. I have never heard of any of these directives being mentioned in a meeting of a seminary's faculty or trustees. But they do reveal the Church's recognition that what the seminaries do is critically important for evangelism. I suspect that the ministers at the assemblies vote so massively for these resolutions because they blame their seminaries for not giving them the training in evangelism that they have found they badly needed.

For most of Protestant history, ministerial training gave no time to the practical matters which we attempt to dignify by calling them "practical theology." There were abstract courses in classical rhetoric, but it was not until homiletics was admitted that any teaching of methods was countenanced. In the first quarter of this century, standard seminaries began with some embarrassment to offer instruction in Christian Education. Then Pastoral Care became generally accepted. Evangelism is still lagging. Many seminaries seem to assume that a minister is supposed to pay attention only to those who are already members of the church.

There could be several reasons for the dearth of instruction in evangelism. One of these might be uncertainty about whether there is enough solid material on evangelism to provide for an intellectually respectable course. This uncertainty can be ended by examining the content and bibliographies of any of the many impressive courses. Or it might be thought that this is one of the needed disciplines that ministers can master after they leave school. But the whole pressure of parish life keeps this from happening. Observation shows that if a minister is not started into evangelism before graduation, he is headed toward a lifetime of neglect. Or it may be felt that a minister's effectiveness in evangelism does not depend on what he knows but on what he is. If he loves people and loves the Lord, then he is sure to have an evangelistic ministry. But that sentiment has little connection

with reality. Of course an evangelist has to be a good Christian.
But Christianity is not radiated. It is shared by getting in touch
with definite people and opening up the Christian life to them in
definite ways. Unless ministers learn about those ways, they will
be ineffectual in evangelism.

That was exactly my experience. I have never known more
lovable Christians than the members of the first church where I
was a pastor. Their background had been Christian for generations. I was their private family chaplain, employed to be the
cleric for a self-contained group. I could not help knowing that
a minister should be more than that, and every year I discussed
with the church officers what we might be doing in evangelism.
They were very much in favor of it, so the next year we would
discuss it again. We could never think of any method of evangelism that seemed right for us. So when I left after seven years, the
church people were about the same ones who had been there
when I came. I had done what I had been trained to do, and that
was all.

My next pastorate was in a city where the district denominational body, in all ignorance, put me on its evangelism committee. Its chairman was having a notable evangelistic ministry in his
own church, and he was devoted to helping other churches do the
same. He was a strong character who had no patience when we
skipped meetings or slighted assignments. The result was that I
learned from him the things I should have learned about evangelism from my seminary. But it cannot be counted on to happen
that way. Except for my good fortune in having been put on that
committee with that chairman, I might have gone through all my
pastorates as incompetent in evangelism as I was in my first one.
If a minister's schooling does not propel him into evangelism, his
churches never will.

It might be hoped that students would get what they need for
evangelism from their classes in theology, Bible, administration,
preaching, and pastoral care. These should all be helpful, but
solid training for an evangelistic ministry cannot be picked up
from odds and ends. It takes a substantial course to teach a
minister how to use his public and private opportunities for evangelism, and how the whole church can be used to attract people

from outside and to lead them into Christian faith and living.

Seminary courses can be classified as library-centered or congregation-centered. This is not a distinction between the academic and the practical. A course in theology may be congregation-centered, while one in worship may be library-centered, with impressive scholarship and little awareness of what goes on in real churches. A library-centered course in evangelism may be valuable, but it cannot be the basic course. The only evangelism course one seminary offered was described as "based on a study of Luke and the Acts, examining especially the verbs and adverbs for evangelistic content." The essential course has to prepare ministers to lead their congregations in evangelism. It may be uncertainty about that subject that prompts seminaries to list as "Evangelism" some courses that properly belong in the History or Biblical departments. A course on American frontier revivalism or on the doctrine of the atonement cannot properly be listed as "evangelism."

Students can have wildly impractical views about evangelism because they approach it as the scholastics approached nature—with deductive reasoning unchecked by any observation. What is taught will be far better remembered if there has been some laboratory experience. Only by trying can some students lay to rest their anxieties about evangelistic conversations or preaching. To teach with the hope that two or three years later students may try out what was said is poor pedagogy.

Some seminaries arrange with nearby churches to use their students for evangelistic calling. Each student goes out as the teammate of a layman from a church to call on that church's evangelistic prospects. The seminary teacher may instruct the callers, or the church's minister may do it. All reassemble after the calling for a report of the experiences. If the class is large, several churches may be needed to supply the calls and the teammates, and the callers may all be instructed together.

Fieldwork programs may be expected to offer opportunities for evangelism to seminary students through calling, preaching, and work with youth. If there is an unspecific understanding that such things may develop as the year goes along, they usually do not. But if they are specified as a part of the arrangement, there can be some valuable experiences for the students and for the churches.

Some seminaries make available to churches in their area teams of two to eight students who offer several sorts of help—calling in homes, training callers, preaching, conducting youth meetings, and inspiring couples' clubs.

Some seminaries put evangelism among the required courses. Their position is that evangelism cannot be elective for a minister and should not be elective in his education. When it is not required, it may be chosen only by the minority of students who already have some background in evangelism. Those who need it most are not likely to elect a course which deals with something they have never thought about. Most of the students are young lay men and women, fresh from college, who have not had a normal church connection since they finished high school. With all the exciting elective courses that a seminary offers, they will not prefer one called "evangelism." So it can be expected that most students in this situation will go into their ministries with the immense handicap of not knowing what evangelism is or caring much about it. There is therefore the great problem of how to build up the enrollment in evangelism courses.

The atmosphere of the institution can be of great help in this. It can give evangelism academic standing if it is made the subject of lectureships, visiting speakers, and publications. The members of the faculty can speak of evangelism in their classes in terms that make it seem important. Student organizations can be encouraged to undertake various ways of drawing people in the communities around the seminary toward the Christian faith—as through beach ministries, fellowship centers, retreats, and gospel teams.

6

Making Contacts

As we think of where the contacts for evangelism come from, we have to face the fact that most of them come from within the Christian sector. That is where most Americans are. The total membership reported by the Christian Churches is well over half the population of the country. It is estimated that more than 90 percent of the people in the United States "have at least some church background and claim religious antecedents they have not repudiated."[1] Churches that baptize babies rarely have to baptize an adult who is received on confession of faith; most of their "converts" have been pledged to Christ in infancy. Almost all the "adult baptisms" that such churches report are of boys and girls from the communicants' class. We probably rarely receive into the Church anyone who has not had at least one grandparent who was an active member of a Church.

This may seem shocking to those who dream of evangelism as taking the good news of Christ to those who have not heard it, but most of those we approach already know the main Christian beliefs. Evangelism in the United States is very different from what it was in the New Testament, or what it is in non-Christian lands today. It is easier in that we do not have to start with complete ignorance of the gospel, we do not have to loosen the hold of non-Christian religions, and we do not have to work against a hostile culture or the threat of ostracism from friends and families. But our evangelism is harder in that those who have rejected Christianity or become indifferent to it may be more difficult to sway than are those to whom it comes as a soulshaking new revelation. Even people who rarely think of Christ, read the

Bible, or pray may not be interested in any change, because they regard themselves as Christians who do not happen to be enrolled in a religious group. The fact that most of our evangelism is a reclaiming of those who have a Christian background does not mean that it is not infinitely important. The result can be a real conversion and the transforming of a life.

But we cannot be indifferent to those who come from outside the Christian segment of our society. We believe that Christ is the Savior for every human being. We believe that Christians have been told to bring the knowledge of Christ's love to everyone. We believe that the wonders of the life in Christ are not intended for just a special sort of people. Our desire to share what we have found has no ethnic limitations. We send missionaries to those who are not Christians in other countries. But in our own country, with people who are explicitly not Christian all around our churches, we tend to overlook them. The habit of passing up in our evangelism those who are not "our sort of people" is a denial of the gospel. Approaching such people requires no special knowledge or techniques. Drawing them into the life of the congregation is the basic method. Knowing how to offer friendship is the necessary skill. Often non-Christians in America have dropped away from their ancestral faiths. They are drifting, with no religious moorings.

Evangelism can be an attempt to save the safe, to keep nice people nice, to assemble the respectable. I have caught myself, after a contact with a repairman or a store clerk whom I found specially likeable, thinking, "Here is someone who ought to be in our church; I'm going to find out if there is a church connection." If I were behaving as a Christian, I would feel that urge most strongly with those who do not seem to be of the church type. Karl Barth wrote in his last major work, "On the basis of the eternal will of God we have to think of every human being, even the oddest, most villainous or miserable, as one to whom Jesus Christ is a brother and God is Father. . . . If he does not know it or no longer knows it, our business is to transmit this knowledge to him."[2]

Our contacts for evangelism may be too confined, not only religiously, but also socially. We tend to look for those who are most like ourselves in education, income, and culture. By this we miss the meaning of Christian love and corrupt the church with divisions and exclusion. Many a personal evangelist has gotten into trouble for trying to introduce into a snobbish church converts whom the members regarded with distaste.

Cultural differences among congregations are not always the result of sin. People who know they will be welcome in any congregation may still choose a church where they will feel most at home. A preacher who gives the most help to the highly educated may not be the best one for those whose favorite reading is the comics. The devotees of country music may be driven out of church by music that best lifts the souls of those who love the classics.

There may be good reasons for trying to evangelize people within their social groups. Donald A. McGavran, on the basis of his extensive knowledge of missions, shows that coming into the Christian faith is much more likely if it does not require abandoning one's own social group and joining a strange one: "Human beings like to become Christians without crossing linguistic, class, or racial barriers." When illiterates were required to join congregations of educated Christians, years of missionary labor resulted in only tiny churches. When they were introduced to Christianity and organized into churches in their own groups, there were mass movements into Christianity. Moreover, "men understand the Gospel better when expounded by their own kind of people."[3]

Dr. McGavran points out that the command which is translated, "Make disciples of all nations," says in the Greek, "of all *ethne*," which means, not "nation," in our sense, but any ethnic sector—tribe, class, language, race, or inhabitants of an area. This can be a command to make Christians of ethnic groups— workers, students, castes. So Paul's strategy of "to the Jew first," and Peter's willingness to let the Jewish Christians in Galatia keep their Hebrew customs, and Jesus' telling the Syrophoenician woman, "Let the children first be fed," were all examples of dealing evangelistically with separate groups.

Letting new Christians be excluded from each other would have to be a temporary expedient, as it turned out to be in

Galatia. But it might permit taking the Christian faith to tribes or castes or social groups that at the start could not be merged with others. The eventual fruit of the spirit may not have to be a requisite for baptism.

American churches have been reproached for having their own cultural constituencies, but this has made it possible for people of every sort of culture to have a church that is right for them. Americans also have the advantage of having no official church from which the masses could feel alienated. In 1843, a Vicar at Leeds, in England, wrote Bishop Wilberforce of the estrangement of working men from the Church of England: "They consider the Church to belong to the party of their oppressors; hence they hate it, and consider a man of the working class who is a Churchman to be a traitor to his Party or Order—he is outlawed in the society in which he moves." More recently, a French evangelist said, "The proletariat have deserted the churches, or else by staying in the churches they have deserted their class." Tom Allen said of his parish in a working-class area of Glasgow, "They reject the Church because it represents another type of secular culture diametrically opposed to their own. . . . The Church is separated from the working-classes by its subservience to a *bourgeois* culture."

Thoughtful persons have found warnings for Americans in the estrangement of European working classes from the Churches, but the wide variety of major Churches in America makes the situation different. Laboring people in this country belong to churches whose worship and ministers have what they need. Their denominations on the national scene are as imposing and influential as their employers' denominations. Professor H. Richard Niebuhr, after a detailed study, concluded, "It appears that the percentage of church members who are also members of trade unions corresponds by and large with the percentage of the population in general that is in these unions."[4]

A Christian church must welcome people of every race and class and culture. Every sort of exclusion is sin. But Christians may freely choose to gather in churches with those who are like themselves. As soon as that is said, however, we have to recognize that it has grave dangers for evangelism. The pastor of a small and dormant church in a midwestern town explained that the evangelistic denominations got "the sunbonnets and overalls," while the special field of his denomination was "the substantial people." Churches which see their ministry as restricted to some social class divide the body of Christ. They are likely to be indifferent to the religious needs of those outside this group.

It has been supposed, though there are many obvious exceptions, that religious people are likely to rise in the world. John Wesley said, "Religion must necessarily produce both industry and frugality and these cannot but produce riches." So families, at least in succeeding generations, tend to move from the churches of the poor to the churches of the prosperous. As they become better educated, they become dissatisfied with the intellectual level of the churches of their origins. Sometimes they take their denominations with them. The evangelism secretary of a denomination which started among the less well educated said, "Our churches are beginning to move across the tracks. Someone else is going to have to go in where we are moving out."

Thus we have the picture, partly apocryphal, of the churches of the poor converting people from the world to Christianity, and the upper-class churches staying alive by taking members from the humbler churches. I once heard a minister say, "They go to the revivalistic churches to get salvation; then they come to us to find out what salvation is." Fortunately, there is little evidence that this happens. A church that is not interested in bringing people to salvation can have no idea what salvation is. But this distorted picture of the flow from the bottom to the top can keep consciences in upper-level churches from feeling guilty about their small efforts in evangelism. They like to believe that, in the Lord's economy, evangelism was not assigned to them. One problem is that when families have advanced to religion at that level, they keep on advancing right out of any church.

Our letting churches be socially segregated also produces a reverse snobbery. A factory worker and his wife, whom I knew, were invited to join one of the more prosperous churches when they moved from a farm to a city. They became popular and influential leaders and very happy in their friendships there. But the young man's fellow workers at the factory made jibes at him for being a social climber. And their parents sorrowed because their children had left what the parents thought was the only denomination that truly believes the Bible. Those with fewer worldly honors may be quite insistent on their spiritual superiority.

Cultural differences create the unsolved problem of how to relate churches in changing neighborhoods to their new neighbors. The dwindling congregations that now come from a distance do not want the kind of church life that would attract the sort of people who have moved in near the church. Some endowed churches can maintain their beautiful buildings and expensive music without any participating members, which is almost what some of them are doing. When staid churches try to reach those of a different social level, they may not have the touch. Their denomination on principle cannot permit the Gospel Tabernacle sort of program that might be popular. Any solutions to this problem will be a great gain for evangelism.

The gospel is the glad news that what Christians have in Christ draws them together. The love they share annihilates the worldly divisions that set human beings against each other. Jesus prayed "for those who believe in me . . . that they may all be one" (John 17:20–21). The Church is to display to our sadly fractured world a model of what the human family should be. But from the very beginning, the sins that fragment society made divisions in the Church. Paul writes sadly to the Corinthians, "I hear that there are divisions among you" (1 Cor. 11:18). He tells the Ephesians that Christ "has broken down the dividing wall of hostility . . . that he might create in himself one new man in place of the two" (Eph. 2:14, 15). He reminds the Colossians that, in the Church, national, racial, and class distinctions are abolished, "but Christ is all, and in all" (Col. 3:11). James is indignant at a church that makes distinctions between "a man with gold rings and in fine clothing . . . and a poor man in shabby clothing" (James 2:2–4). It is contrary to all that Christians believe in for a church to try to keep its membership homogeneous by looking for evangelistic contacts only within one social group.

We can recognize that people become Christians more readily if conversion does not require them to move to a different social level. We may admit that people of different cultures prefer different sorts of worship. But we can take care of this, not by having socially specialized churches, but by having socially inclusive churches. We all know congregations that happily include members of a wide variety of sorts. An ardent Christian faith is itself a cultural factor that has a tendency to produce similarity of tastes. The same church can try to please its different members by occasional excursions into both classical and country-style music, and still have a middle level where all can unite. The same preacher can reach at different times toward people with different sorts of *minds,* but most of the time be reaching the *hearts* of all.

The great blessing of an inclusive church is the enrichment the members get as they come to appreciate those who in worldly ways are quite different from themselves. It is true that a church for the highly educated will not be right for the uneducated; and a rich people's church will not be the best one for the poor. But what evangelism tries to build, as it looks for possible new members, is a church that will not be specialized for any group or class. The congregation that will be right for all Christians will give them a chance for close and loving fellowship with those who are of different classes, races, cultures, and interests, but "all one in Christ Jesus." It is at the point of entry that such a church is built.

THE FILE

The holiest object in my church was a battered wooden box. It was a thing of no beauty. The congregation would not have been pleased to have it on the Communion table. It was not displayed among the symbols of our faith, but nothing in the church was more symbolic, for in that box was our file of prospective members. This exaltation of a prospect list does not confuse the church with a sales agency. That list was our mission field. There were many around us who needed to be told about the wonders of God's love, but the only ones who were going to be told by our church first had to be listed in that four-inch space. Almost never did our church bring an adult whose card had not been in that box to a profession of faith in Christ. Each card represented a person or a family whom God loves.

On each card was recorded helpful information, the result of every approach, and recommendations for next steps. The cards were moved among the sections of the file, which were labelled: TO SEE — SEEM INTERESTED — FOR CULTIVATION — FOR COMMITMENT — WILL JOIN — NOT MUCH CHANCE. Moving cards around in the file in this way was not a card game, it was a drama—a drama with vaulting hopes and crushing disappointments.

The whole evangelistic opportunity of a congregation depends on the quality of such a file. When it keeps filling up with likely possibilities, there is a great deal to be done and the hope of great rewards. When the file begins to dwindle, evangelism has to slow down or cease.

A card should never be taken from the file. A copy of the card should always be made for a caller or for any other use. If the original card were mislaid, a person might be lost. Cards that are removed from the file, because there does not seem to be much reason to keep them, should be saved; the record will be needed if the same people are proposed again.

SOURCES OF CONTACTS

1. Friendship. The friendships of church members with non-members are a major source of contacts. It is not surprising that friendship is the greatest drawing power of a religion that is based on love. One hundred and twenty Pittsburgh churches sent enquiries to a sample group of over a thousand adults who had joined them during one year to find out what had brought them. They learned that it was friendship with a church member that had most frequently started a new member toward the church. The report concluded, "The majority underlying factor in the success of evangelism is the friendly layman." A similar and more recent survey in a Houston suburban area found that 37 percent first came because friends took an interest in them and invited them, and 21 percent because there were people in the church whom they respected. All other reasons were far less important.

In most churches the power of friendship is used more or less by accident. A good deal more good would be done if it were used purposely and by plan. Church members need to be frequently urged to try to help their friends have the blessings of a church and of its faith. They can do this by telling them of the great good the church does, by inviting them to the church, and by introducing them to church people.

Members should be regularly reminded to give the church the names of their friends who might be contacts for evangelism, together with all other useful information. This must include information about the friends' church background or religious interest. Without this information the church will find itself trying to entice members of other congregations. The person who sends the information is the best one to give the friend the first invitation to the church. Cards for reporting such names can be in the pews, or sent to the church members by mail, or given out in connection with a sermon on evangelism.

Church members can be encouraged to form friendships with people they know only casually with the hope of helping them find their way into the church. The fellowship of Christians is so close that it tends to make them a walled-off enclave, separated socially from people in the world outside. There are Church members who rarely, except for business reasons, have guests in their homes or friends that they visit who are not also members of some church. The Church cannot be in the world as it should be unless its members show that they care personally about people who are not in a church. An extremely bright young woman came from the Orient to an American church college. She was not a Christian, and converting her became a project for the brilliant campus intellects, who impressed her not at all. She did become a Christian, however, through the influence of an inconspicuous girl student. The new convert's explanation was, "She did not use arguments. She built a bridge from her heart to mine, and Christ walked over it."

2. Daily Contacts. Members can be inspired to form the habit of using their daily contacts to turn people toward the church. Sidney Powell tells of a haberdasher in Illinois who never missed an opportunity to get to this subject. Being a good salesman, he could make his approach friendly and informal. When he sold a man a tie, he would say, "That tie's going to look good on you in church next Sunday. What church do you go to?" A university professor who moved to Knoxville said he was sure he would like the city because so many people he met were interested in helping him find a church home. The man who came to connect the gas, and the librarian and others all said something like, "Have you folks found a church yet? I think you would like ours." But, he added sadly, not one of these was from his own denomination. Only churches which urge their members to do this will get it done.

Those who make such contacts should report them to their church but, again, always with information about the church background, and only after they themselves have made the first approach for the church. Someone who reports about a fellow employee, "I don't know what church he belongs to, but you can find out," is not being very helpful.

3. Church Families. Enquiries about each church household may discover a good many relatives who are not members of any local church. Religion is often a forbidden topic among members of a family. Someone else may be able to talk about faith better than a relative can.

A religiously divided marriage presents a special need. If a husband and wife are members of different churches, there is a great deal of reason for wanting them to be together. A church should always be happy to lose a member to a similar congregation if that will get a couple into the same church. The old feelings of denominational superiority are, happily, disappearing. It is often loyalty to their parents' prejudices that keeps husbands and wives in different churches. They may need to be reminded that Jesus said that those who marry leave their fathers and mothers and belong to each other. Efforts to get couples into the same church can be a very important part of a minister's counsel with those he marries.

When a husband or wife is not a professing Christian, or comes from a non-Christian religion, the problem is harder and the need is greater. Often, surprisingly, they may never have talked in any depth about religion. From the time they met and fell in love, a sense of sportsmanship, tact, or danger may have kept them off the subject. When someone from a church comes to talk with them, they may learn things about each other's views and feelings that they never knew before. They need to recognize that a marriage is enriched and strengthened by religious sharing, and that religious faith will mean more to each of them if they have it together. When a family is religiously divided, it is hard for a husband and wife or for their children to maintain strong religious moorings.

A congregation should do all it can to help non-church husbands or wives of church members to participate in as much of the church life as their consciences will allow, even if it is only the social part. The more a couple have the same friends and experiences, the less they have to live in different worlds.

It would have been impossible for the New Testament Church to have baptized Cornelius or the Philippian jailor without paying attention to their families. Faith was seen as a family matter, and evangelism was directed, as far as possible, not just to individuals, but to households. When a church makes a new contact, it should find out who else in the household might be approached, and list them for its attention. Children in the church school or nonmembers who attend church groups may have relatives who should also be coming.

4. Attendance at Worship Services. Getting nonmembers to attend church services is of great importance. This can best be done by church members in their daily contacts. Their invitations can be specially effective at the seasons that rouse religious sentiments in people outside the Church—at Thanksgiving, Advent, Lent, Holy Week. All through the year, church people should keep trying to bring others—and they need to be reminded to do it. No other form of church advertising can compare with this. This was convincingly demonstrated by what happened at a famous old church in an eastern city. One of the businessmen invited twenty-five of his friends to his office. He talked with them about how much more good their church could be doing if more people could get the benefit of the church services. He asked them to agree to speak about the church to at least six people every week, and to invite them to come. Most of the group promised. As a result of their telling of their enthusiasm for their church, people who had never thought of it came to visit. They were so pleased with the welcome and the service that many of them kept coming. The church became so widely talked about that the whole city was affected, and the church was transformed by the new life it was receiving. Nothing at the church had been strikingly improved. All that was necessary was to let people know what had been there all the time.

People may come the first time because of something special —a musical event or a noted guest speaker. Special Sundays— Scout Sunday, Youth Sunday, anniversaries—can bring visitors. One of the great benefits of children's and youth choirs is their power to bring relatives and friends who have not come before.

Of course, the other necessary part of this is to make those who have come once want to come again. The minister's warm welcome from the pulpit and his handshake at the door are valuable, but it is the friendliness of the members that is most important. People who are naturally friendly and easy to talk to should be stationed near the doors. If this task is assigned without regard to talent, it will get to some who obviously find it painful. The greeters must avoid getting entangled with friends who will keep them from giving their attention to visitors. Official smiles and handshakes are good, but what is really needed is brief conversations that will seem like the start of new friendships. The minister, who is trying to greet everyone, cannot be much help with that. In small churches, visitors are so conspicuous that two or three couples can readily locate and meet them. Larger churches will need multiple greeters at each door. Ushers need training in how to meet people and help them find a pew; the manners of the ushers have much to do with the impression a church makes. But ushers are too busy to get acquainted with visitors.

Greeters need not be intimidated by the hoary story of the glaring dowager who said, "Young woman, I was a member of this church before you were born!" It would be better to have that happen a dozen times than for one visitor to be neglected. Besides, no old-time member whose opinion is worth anything can be other than delighted at friendliness. But it is not necessary to say, "Are you a stranger? Can I have your name and address?" Questions do not have to sound inquisitive. The greeter might say, "I don't know all the people in this church; have I met you before?" Names and addresses can be learned by mentioning something the church can mail: "We are going to be sending out the Christmas season programs. Could we mail one to you?" "Would you like some information about our Sunday School?" The greeter might end the conversation by saying, "They are serving coffee in the meeting room. Could I ask my friend here (any member in reach) to take you over there?" All the information the greeters get is given in writing to the minister or the Evangelism Chairman. It is important to remember faces, and even names, if possible. If visitors are recognized when they return, they feel connected.

Guest Books are useless dust catchers. By the time visitors have been propelled to the book and induced to sign, the same information could have been gotten in an easier way. The only way a church that has many visitors can get their names is by a registration of the attendance of everyone. If visitors are asked to sign attendance cards, few will. If everyone signs, the visitors will too. This is reason enough for the church members to be willing to sign, but their registration has other uses. A church needs to know how well its members are attending Sunday worship, and general impressions cannot be trusted. When a minister looks through the attendance cards on Monday, he will be pleased to find the names of members he thought had not been attending. A group of volunteers, every fourth Sunday, or every Sunday for a month, may mark the attendance in the church-member card file. This sampling can indicate who is drifting off and needing special care. The attendance record is useful when members are being considered for important responsibilities. Attendance cards can also get personal information from the members that would be missed if they did not sign them. There may be spaces on the back of the card for: New Address, Illness, Wish Appointment with the Minister, Prospect for Membership, Suggestion.

The names of nonmembers are copied from the cards. Those who are not known are telephoned: "We were so glad to see you in church on Sunday. I hope you will be back." There will be no need for a house call on most of the visitors. The phone call will find out those with whom there might possibly be a continuing connection. These are recorded and someone is assigned to get acquainted with them and to report.

The time for signing the cards can be made to seem a proper part of worship. It can be called "The Ritual of Friendship," or "The Record of Worship." Separate cards for each worshipper can be sorted alphabetically, with visitors' and members' cards put in different stacks. But a larger card can have spaces for each one in a pew to sign as it is passed along. If they all read the names as the card is passed back, this can be counted as an introduction and an invitation for each one to speak to the others at the close of the service. It simplifies the members' signing if the part of the card that has the spaces for *address* and *church membership* is designated *For Visitors*. Some churches use pads, with a slip for each Sunday, instead of cards.

Having a time in a church service when people are asked to speak to those near them helps visitors feel a church's friendliness. Ministers and members often assume that a church is very friendly because *they* find it so. But the members may be so absorbed in being friendly with each other that they never see outsiders. In our pew racks we had red ribbons that visitors were asked to pin on so the members could greet them. The father of one of our members, who was visiting her from out of town, was so impressed with this that he pinned on the ribbon and, after the benediction, stood at the head of the main aisle, waiting to be greeted. Our members went by, so happy in seeing each other that no one saw him. So he went to the reception room and stood beside the coffee urn. In all the excitement of reunions there, he was not noticed. He said, "I don't think our church will try the ribbons." Even the most friendly church members must be constantly reminded to pay attention to people in the church whom they do not know.

5. The Church School. Many parents who have little religious knowledge or interest want their children to learn about Jesus and the Ten Commandments. Children are ideal links between the church and the world outside. Bringing children from non-church homes into the church school is evangelism in two ways: It brings children who would otherwise not know the gospel to where they may come to know Christ as their Lord. And it gives a tie to families that may be drawn through the children to the church and its faith.

The most rapidly growing denominations recognize how important children are for evangelism. They send out their pickup buses and work constantly at campaigns to bring in more pupils. The shrinking denominations do little of this. Their church schools are more like private schools for the benefit of the children of church members. This was not at all the original purpose of the Sunday School.

Churches that are eager to bring people to faith in Christ should give a great deal of attention to attracting children. There are many ways of doing this. Church members can be urged to look for, and offer transportation to, children in their neighborhoods whose parents will be glad to have them in a church school. Pupils can be stirred to bring their friends. These things are more likely to be done if there are concerted efforts—a *Church School Enlargement Month* or a *Bring A Pal* program. If, because of cultural or racial differences, it is hard to get children to come straight into the Sunday church school, they may first be brought into weekday clubs for games and Bible stories, and then into the Sunday School.

Parents have to be shown that the church needs their cooperation in what it is trying to do for their children. The teachers want to know their pupils' parents. There can be parents' meetings at the church. Parents who know that the school depends on volunteers may be glad to come to the church to help at tasks that do not require religious knowledge. Then, if they do become interested in the church and make friends there, they may step by step find their way into the Christian life.

A church where I once was minister had this statement in its church paper:

Recently I began to wonder what in the world I am doing as chairman of the 1976 canvass committee. There is nothing I find harder to do than talk to this congregation about our pledging commitments.

To answer this I really had to ask myself, "What am I doing in this church at all?" That took me back about twenty-six years when I used to sit in my car on the parking lot, unshaven, reading the Sunday sports page, waiting for our daughter to come from Sunday School.

Some good person changed that by inviting me in. In the years that followed, I met and became involved with some fine Christian people. They, along with a lot of you, introduced me to Christ.

I guess this is the reason I'm chairman of the canvass committee. It has to be done. I have to say to all of us: *Let's step up our pledging commitments so that we may continue to bring the unshaven in from the parking lots of the world and introduce them to Christ!*[5]

6. Church Organizations. Many people make their first step into church life through one of the organizations. They do not at the outset have much understanding of worship or much interest in sermons, but they do enjoy the fine fellowship, the attractive programs, and a chance to discuss important subjects. Drawing people into that first step is one of the most important purposes of every class, club, and group. A great deal more of this will be done if the groups have it before them as a major purpose, and if they are organized to do it. An officer of each group should be responsible for efforts to enlarge the membership. The members should be constantly reminded to try to bring their friends. Unusually attractive meetings can give special occasions for this. The organizations need a clear method for getting information about their contacts into the evangelism file of the church. Having members on the Evangelism Commission keeps the organizations working at this part of their evangelistic task.

In my experience, the organizations that have made the most and the best evangelistic contacts for the church are, in this order: the church school, the women's association, and the young couples' club. Young married people are in a time that makes them specially open to approaches from a church. They are entering into an entirely new sort of living, and they want it to be right. They need to make new friends, and they hope to find the sort that will mean the most to them. Marriage is a new kind of religious experience. When a couple comes to a church to be married, if they know what they are doing, they are recognizing that it is God who gives them to each other, and that they are entering into a three-way contract, with God as the third party to their convenant. There is a mysticism in their love. Babies are miracles—and awesome responsibilities. Many young people who in their school days paid little attention to religion, begin to think about it when they get married. So they may welcome an invitation from another young married couple to join their club at the church. And this may be the start that takes them into a lasting relationship with Christ.

7. Service from the Church. Many people whose motives are not very spiritual may turn to the church for help. They may seek the minister for counsel about a problem—marriage, children, alcohol. People with little religious interest feel forced to have a minister for funerals. Sympathetic persons who want to help others may join a church group that makes surgical dressings, or does parole work, or takes meals to invalids. People may come to a church for good friends or for good times with the campers, square dancers, softball team, or drama guild. The great danger is that those who come for these marginal reasons will be given no glimpse of what the church really is. Ministers and lay members must be continually alert for opportunities to take these contacts deeper than they began.

8. New Residents. When people move to a new community, they are in a state of transition in many ways. They have to make new friends and set up new patterns for living. Those who have not had a church connection may consider making one. They may come to the church just as a place to make friends, and then discover how much more a church can mean to them. They may be wanting a place where their uprooted children can make connections.

On the other hand, people who have been church members in the communities they left may be lost in transit. In the busy time of getting settled, they may postpone looking for a church until churchless habits have become established. A little shopping around among churches where the people are strange and the ways are different may convince them that there is no church available that they really like. They may decide that they will not

find a church that will take the place of the congregation they
have left. "How shall we sing the Lord's song in a strange land?"
may end the matter for them.

The Church must minister to Christians on the move. Some
occupations require frequent changes to new communities. The
larger part of the membership of most congregations has come
by transfer. If they do not have good methods for passing their
members from one to the next, churches will largely disappear.

A great deal of the success in this matter depends on the
churches that are left behind. What needs to be done can start
when people join a church. The membership vows can include
some such promise as: ". . . and if I move away, I intend to find
soon a new church home." When a minister in a church service
welcomes visitors and invites those whose membership is out of
town to join that church, he can add an explanation of why it is
necessary for Christians who move to become quickly at home in
a new church family. By this he will be also telling the members
of his own church what they should do when they move. When
a minister knows that members are leaving, he can bid them
farewell and at the same time give them advice on finding a new
congregation. He can write to a church or a denominational
office in the new community, asking for attention to a member
who has moved there and giving his or her address. When members are slow in finding a new church home, their minister can
write to them. A first letter can have good counsel and a form to
be returned, asking for a transfer of membership. A year later
there may be a stronger and sadder letter, explaining why those
who remain too long without an active church connection must
be suspended from church membership.

Much of the success in getting memberships transferred depends on churches in the new communities. They must be alert
at discovering new residents who are church members and getting invitations to them. When a minister receives word that such
a person has moved in, an immediate contact is urgent. A letter
from another church telling of a moved member must by all
means be acknowledged. Ministers are chronically indignant
about how few such letters receive replies. Church members from
out of town often have a strange wariness when they try out new

churches. They want to feel welcome, but they are uncomfortable about introducing themselves. This gives special importance to the methods for greeting visitors, getting their names, and commencing friendships.

It is necessary for a church to learn soon of both church members and nonmembers who have moved to its community. Most ministers find that their surest source of information is the members of the church. They can be frequently urged to report to the church the names and addresses of new neighbors, or club members, or fellow employees, and to make the first contact themselves. Members of the church who work with public schools, Welcome Wagons, utilities, or real estate can report new arrivals.

Dr. Andrew Blackwood wrote of a helper in his church: "She kept her eyes open for the moving van. The same afternoon she would send one of the children across with a pie warm from the oven. Before Sunday she would call and invite the friends to come with her and her husband to church, as well as Bible school. . . . Kindness on the part of a woman with tact and charm unlocks many a heart. When the mother across the way is pining for friends whom she will seldom see any more, a cheery call by a winsome neighbor is a boon from heaven."[6]

9. Independent Christian Groups. A good many people are brought to a lively Christian interest by independent evangelistic movements such as those on campuses, in the armed services, or among business people. Many who are reached in this way come into churches. Sometimes there is a tendency in the other direction: "I have been a church member for years, and now at last I am a Christian." Even when there are clear differences in style and theology, churches should stay as close as they can to the devoted and conscientious people in these groups.

10. Evangelism Crusades. The best of the mass evangelism preachers try very hard to work with the local churches and to connect those who make decisions in their meetings with congregations. The success in this depends significantly on how well the churches do their part, both in preparing for the meetings and in conserving the results. Many churches find that a large proportion of the names that are sent to them from the crusade are of people they already know about—some of them faithful members of the church. These often mean that church people have been reminded of Christian truths and have been rededicated to them —which is important. But churches cannot count on a crusade by itself to give them a great many new evangelistic contacts.

11. A Census. When a church begins to think about evangelism, someone is likely to propose a neighborhood religious census. That is usually a mistake. The logic is irrefutable. The church needs to know who, within its reach, are not in churches, and this method of finding out is rapid and systematic. It requires no special skill, and it can be fun. So there is a two-week flurry of doorbell ringing, and the church settles back with a feeling of evangelistic achievement—and all there ever is to show for it is a stack of cards.

The problem is usually that the church jumped into the census too soon. It should first have planned in detail what it was going to do with those whom the census discovered. Most of them will be very cold prospects. A church whose evangelism has been directed to those with whom it already has a connection will have had heartwarming experiences and satisfying results. Then, when it turns to those whom a census has discovered, it is in for a bad time. Rudeness is rare, but complete indifference is common. Disheartened workers are likely to give up in discouragement. People who have paid no attention to a church do not intend to. If they have marked a preference for your denomination, it probably means that they think it would be a good one to be buried by. This is not a reason for the church to have no interest in such people. Christ's Church should want them as much as he does. But it must also know that easy methods of evangelism will not work with them.

A census can be of great benefit if a church is prepared to follow it with patient efforts through the church school and church organizations, through much attention from neighbors, through many friendly contacts by the minister, and through callers who may expect to see no results from their good work for many months. This is the "prayer and fasting" sort of labor that is so difficult because its purpose is so great.

A census is also likely to discover a few people who will not be difficult at all. They can make it worth while. But it is astonishing to find how many churches simply collapse when the census has been finished and do not even approach those who seem most ready. That, again, is the result of backwards planning. The follow-up plans have to be made first.

Two situations make a census clearly necessary—a new church and a new housing development. With both of these, the people who are discovered will not necessarily be indifferent. Many may be eager for a church, or at least grateful for an invitation. A census is the best way to let a church and the people near it know about each other.

An ecumenical census is better than one by a single congregation. It gives a good impression of church cooperation; it saves homes from having repeated church callers; and it is a rewarding experience of fellowship for workers from different churches. The filled-out cards are divided among the churches by denominational preference and vicinity. City hall maps show the number of residences in each block. Counting these will show how many workers are needed and where they are to be assigned. Cards have spaces for the names at each address, family relationship, church membership or preference, and age if under twenty-one. Workers need instructions in how to make the call. A page of written instructions and a thirty-minute training meeting are enough. Most calls can be completed at the door, though there will be occasions when a longer conversation is needed.

Instructions and materials for a neighborhood religious census can be had from the evangelism offices of some of the denominations.

7

Cultivating Christian Faith and Knowledge

A church starts its evangelism by making contacts with people outside its membership. Then comes a period of cultivation when the church prepares those people to confess their faith and join the Church.

1. Church Services. One of the most important ways of preparing people for faith and membership is to get them to attend the Sunday services. That is an important purpose of church services. If only well-established church members attend, the services are partly being wasted. Such a closed-in service has the musty aroma of an unaired vestry.

When a worship service is being designed, one of the questions must be: "What will this mean to seekers?" The Scripture-saturated may get a lift from declaring (responsively) that the kings of Tarshish, Sheba, and Seba will bring gifts, but to the uninitiated that has only the charm of nonsense syllables. I recently attended a church service where we were kept scrambling for the prayers and responses through the regular prayer book, a loose-leaf experimental book, and the Sunday bulletin. The church members seemed to know what they were doing, but I could rarely find the place. My conclusion had to be that my sort of people were not supposed to be there. The chief enemy of church worship is boredom, even for church members; those who have built up no emotional attachment to the forms may find them unendurably barren. Every church service should have something that newcomers will find inspiring.

A preacher has to ask himself, "How long would a seeker have to listen to my sermons in order to learn much about the Christian faith?" Some Christian groups insist that every sermon must answer the question, "What must I do to be saved?" This has made for repetitious preaching. It is like requiring every session of Congress to be opened with an announcement that the Constitution has been ratified. There are many other matters with which sermons have to deal. But unless sermons on these matters are clearly connected with the heart of all preaching, which is God's revelation of himself in Jesus Christ, they will be like severed limbs lying around loose. Both mature Christians and seekers need sermons that will connect the solutions to practical daily problems with the basic Christian truths. If a minister recognizes that it would take a long time for the uninformed to learn elemental Christianity from his sermons, then he has to know that the church members also are poorly fed.

Christian worship is a miracle. Its results cannot be understood from its parts. The worshippers can have better music from their record players and better sermons from their books. But they come to the church to worship God because something strange and wonderful can happen there. We try to bring seekers with the hope that they will have an experience with God. James Stewart said to ministers: "Every Sunday morning when it comes ought to find you awed and thrilled by the reflection—'God is to be in action today, through me, for these people: this day may be crucial, this service decisive, for someone now ripe for the vision of Jesus.' "[1]

The ways of bringing those who have a new contact with the church into the church services are much the same as the ways that have been described for bringing those who have not yet had a contact: the invitations of church members, special events or speakers, youth choirs, the pull of special seasons of the year. New friends in the church can add their urging. The minister can tell those who are looking toward the church that he hopes to see them at the worship services. They can be put on the mailing list for the church newsletter or for anything that calls attention to the services (see pp. 95–98).

The use of a social time for making contacts after a church service has been mentioned. It is also valuable at this second stage. It gives those who already have a contact with a church a chance to increase their acquaintance and to see what church life is like. There must be church members in the reception room with the special purpose of seeing that those who are new to the church are not neglected.

If there is a Talk-It-Over or Feed-Back meeting to discuss the sermon, it can be a revelation for newcomers. They may discover for the first time that a preacher is not an oracle who hands down pronouncements, and that preaching is a cooperative enterprise.

2. Classes. A church's regular classes offer an ideal situation for preparing people for faith and membership if they provide, as they usually do, close fellowship with a small group, instruction in Christian truth, and a chance to participate in discussion. A class, like a church service, can be evaluated by asking, "How long would a seeker have to come in order to learn the essentials of Christianity?" If it would take a long while, the class is also failing its members. A church can locate gaps in its program by asking whether there are some people for whom no adequate class is available. Is there a class to which you could with confidence invite a bright young college student, a farm laborer, or a young couple? If not, the church is not fully ready for evangelism.

There are many sorts of classes that serve well: the adult classes in the church school (for the old saints or the young Turks), a women's weekday morning Bible study group, a business people's downtown luncheon meeting, a religious book club, a parents' class, or a midweek service.

A class is its own best recruiting agency. Printed information and mailed invitations prepare the way, but by themselves they will bring few. Enthusiastic descriptions of the class from the pulpit are useful, especially if the class follows the church service. Members of the class can do the most to locate and bring in new attenders. The name of each person with whom the church has made a contact can be sent to whichever class seems most appropriate. Then an officer of the class must be responsible for getting someone to try hard to bring that person to the class.

3. Groups. The church organizations are of great use in this second stage of evangelism. They can offer growth in knowledge, friendships, and a feel for what the church is. Groups for couples, singles, women, men, youth, music, drama, or social action can turn strangers into people who feel at home in the church and understand why it is important. Some groups are like the supper club whose president said, "Most of us take part in serious church activities, but this club is our fun part of the church, so don't ask us to hear a speech on missions." But that club did reveal to newcomers how much church people enjoy each other. The groups should receive the names of those the evangelism leaders hope can be brought into the group life. They need well-designed procedures for bringing them.

A convention, a family camp, or a retreat can be a mountaintop experience for someone who is new to church life.

4. Reading. Much that those who are turning to the church need to know can be given them in writing. Pamphlets and books tell about the Christian faith and appeal for acceptance of it. There can be information about the local church, and the denomination, and church history. Help for devotions and for Bible reading can be given. Both simple and intellectually demanding material will be needed. A mass of reading is an unwelcome sight, so what it is hoped will be read should be given out a little bit at a time. With each piece that is given there should be an enthusiastic commendation. This can turn forbidding print into an object of curiosity. What is given away is likely to be thrown away, so there are more than budgetary reasons for hoping that some of the material will be paid for.

Seekers can be directed to the church library for much that they need. A rolling library shelf can put the books where they will be picked up. A pamphlet rack is handy. A church bookstore will increase the reading.

Written information about the local church is important for evangelism. Attractive advertising can rouse interest. Larger pieces can tell more about the church and what it offers. The importance of this justifies artwork and expense, but some of the most appealing examples are produced in a church office, with clean copying, a beautiful layout, and engaging writing. Some of these will be needed: (1) A description of all that goes on at the church, with times and places of meetings. (2) A street map which shows how to find the church and where to park. (3) A floor plan of the church building. (4) An invitation to become a member, which has in writing a statement of the faith that new members profess and the promises they make. (5) An explanation of how to join the church. (6) An application for membership, with blanks for personal information and, possibly, a list for checking services that are offered to the church. (7) An explanation of church finance, with a description of local and distant mission projects.

A packet is a useful form. A booklet soon goes out of date, but separate sheets or folders can be readily replaced.

5. Enquirers' Groups. There is great value in getting non-church people together to discuss the Christian faith. A minister may organize such a group from those on the list of contacts. It has psychological advantages if a lay person gets the group together and the minister is asked to meet with them. Nonmembers are likely to get more from a group if they are not outnumbered by the church members. The following groups were very successful:

There is a St. Louis church in an area where a good many employed, unmarried young adults from out of town are living. The minister invited a group of them to his home for "Fireside Meetings" on Sunday evenings through the winter. Church memberships and three marriages resulted.

In New Rochelle, New York, where boat owners get together at the town dock, a church couple kept finding themselves in religious discussions. So they suggested to the others that their minister be invited to come to answer their questions. Through a number of weeks they had some very profitable evenings.

A bridge club, about half of whose members had church connections, decided to give up bridge for Lent and to use the evenings for religious study. They worked out their own study materials and made it a wholly lay project.

Three of the paid soloists in a church near New York are in show business. They got some of their musical and theatrical friends together for a series of religious discussions. The minister met with them.

In an industrial community, a minister got some of his church members to invite him to meet with them and their fellow workers during the lunch hour at the factory.

Such groups usually decide in advance how many meetings they will have. People hesitate to get into something that might just go on and on.

There is a danger that these discussions will become just a mental parlor game. People enjoy exercising their acuteness on subtle questions that do not hit them very hard. A sequence I have used seems to help avoid a playing with empty abstractions: (1) I explain one of the great Christian beliefs. (2) We all discuss the reasons for and against believing it. (3) We consider the practical difference it makes if it is literally true. (4) We think of what we ought to do about it. A sequence for a group that a minister does not lead starts with a question, which may come from questions the group listed in advance. They discuss: (1) what the traditional answer to that question is, (2) what the people present believe about it, (3) what difference it makes in anyone's life, and (4) how close they can come to agreeing on the answer.

People who have been wondering whether they are Christians can be moved considerably ahead by such discussions. Some whose religious interest has been dormant may have it reawakened. Misunderstandings can be removed. Those who participate get to know each other at a deeper level.

A class for those who are going to join the church can also serve as an enquirers' group if it is opened up to those who have not yet made up their minds. They all study and discuss together. Some who have not been sure may decide they want to join the church. Those who do not may have their thinking clarified.

6. Personal Attention. The bell that brings people to the church is the doorbell. The best way to let them know that they are important to the church is to go to their homes and tell them so. A house call gives a chance to learn about people and to tell them about the church. A caller can take literature about the church and its faith into a home. A call can bring people into various sorts of church participation.

Evangelism cannot be a mass production. Each person must be

looked at as a separate individual. At its meetings the Evangelism Commission can look at the names in the evangelism file and ask what is happening with each person and what needs to be done. This may bring news of some family event—an illness, promotion, graduation—that will give the minister reason to stop by or write a note. During the period of cultivation, brief personal notes from the minister can assure people that he knows them and is interested in them. There may be a note of welcome to the community, or of pleasure at having seen the person in church. If this is only a technique, it is dishonest. But if the church really does care that much about people, it is vitally important to let them know it.

8

Conversion and Decision

1. What Conversion Is. Conversion is the glorious transformation of a human being by faith in Jesus Christ. It is the continuing joy and marvel of Christianity. It is the aim of evangelism. It changed Paul from a vengeful hater of Christ to a radiant Christian. It changed Augustine from a dissolute teacher of rhetoric who was sick with self-disgust to one of the noblest men this world has known. It has totally changed many people whom we all know.

Broadly understood, conversion is a phenomenon that occurs when a life that has had no unifying center, or a different center, becomes organized around some dominating loyalty. A personality can be integrated at a low level, as around a passion for money or alcohol. Hitler made converts. Arthur Koestler gave this description of his conversion to Communism: "Something clicked in my brain which shook me like a mental explosion. To say that one had seen the light is a poor description of the mental rapture which only the convert knows. The new light seems to pour from all directions across the skull; the whole universe falls into a pattern like the stray pieces of a jigsaw puzzle assembled by magic at one stroke. There is now an answer to every question."[1] A Chinese student explained to an American friend: "I am no longer the former man you knew. Apart from my body, which is the same, my whole mind and thought have changed. I have become a new man in the classless revolution. . . . I shall never live for self, but for the masses."

Conversion is known to all the great religions. The Greeks and Romans strove for it. Seneca said, "I regard myself not so much as a reformed, but as a transfigured man." The conversion of Gautama has been the source of the conversions of countless Buddhists. The Old Testament knows converted individuals, like Jacob, but its strong collective emphasis makes conversion very much a matter for the whole people. The nation is called to be reconverted to God, and to receive the blessings of the transformed life that he will give.

Any consuming interest can give a personality unity and force. To get organized around the right center is the life-and-death issue for everyone. Christians believe that human beings were designed to be centered in God, so that when they try to operate around any other center they pound themselves to pieces, like a flywheel that is off center.

Figures of speech are inevitably used to help us get at something so far beyond our ordinary range of understanding. Conversion is described in the New Testament as dying and being reborn as a different human being (Rom. 6:6–11). Or it is like transmigration: the old soul leaves the body and Jesus Christ comes in and takes control (Gal. 2:20). The word *convert,* from the Latin *convertere* ("to turn"), means that a person who has been facing in some other direction, or in no particular direction, has turned to face toward Jesus Christ. The one who has turned is at the same place as before, but now pointed in a different direction. Conversion is not a leap, it is a turning, and the converted person may at first seem much the same. Evangelism has the double responsibility of getting people to face toward Christ, and getting them to walk toward him. That turning is in the deepest sense a revolution.

Changing the direction in which a life is pointed is like changing the angle of a sail. Ella Wheeler Wilcox described it:

> One ship drives east and another west,
>   While the selfsame breezes blow;
> 'Tis the set of the sail and not the gale
>   That bids them where to go.

> Like the winds of the air are the ways of fate,
>   As we journey along through life;

'Tis the set of the soul that decides the goal,
And not the storm or the strife.[2]

There is a basic slant, deep in the heart of every person, on which everything about that person depends. All that strikes one life will drive it steadily toward happiness, usefulness, and strength. Exactly the same fate could strike another life and drive it just as steadily toward misery, frustration, and weakness. It is not what hits a life from the outside; it is a fundamental slant on the inside that makes the difference.

Judas and John both sat at the feet of Jesus; they shared the same experiences with him. Then one went out to be a traitor, and the other a saint. Two students can go through school together, and all they learn will equip one to be better and more useful, and the other to be worse and more dangerous. The same sort of misfortune that makes one person say, "There is no God," will make another hold more tightly to the hand of God that brought him through. Changing that basic slant is so important that everything in life depends on it.

2. The Results of Conversion. Conversion produces a new person. Every attitude, value, and desire is transformed. "When anyone is united to Christ he is a new creature: his old life is over; a new life has already begun" (2 Cor. 5:17, NEB). To become a Christian is not just to acquire a new philosophy or some improvements. It makes such a difference that John called it passing from death to life (John 5:24). Not only oneself but the whole world seems changed. Dwight L. Moody said that on the day of his conversion all the birds seemed to be singing newer and blither songs. The outer world remains the same. Christians are not spared the sorrows and disasters that are the common lot of human beings. But the world as it is perceived becomes wholly different for one whose daily walk is radiant with Christ's love.

Conversion brings release from the baleful effects of guilt. Those who cringe from what they know about themselves, who are dragged down by the record of past failures, are made to know that God loves them and accepts them. They are given shining new ideals and fresh power to achieve them. Conversion brings a new openness to the guidance and influence of the Holy Spirit, who gives such qualities as love, joy, peace, patience, kindness, goodness, faithfulness, gentleness, and self-control (Gal. 5:22–23).

The result of conversion is often described as a complete reversal of the personality. When you change the sign before a complex equation that is in parentheses, every quantity in the equation remains the same, but every value is reversed. Tolstoy said, "Five years ago I came to believe in Christ's teaching and my life suddenly changed; I ceased to desire what I had previously desired, and began to desire what I formerly did not want. What had previously seemed to me good seemed evil, and what had seemed evil seemed good. It happened to me as it happens to a man who goes out on some business and on the way suddenly decides that the business is unnecessary and returns home. All that was on his right hand is now on his left, and all that was on his left hand is now on his right."[3] This can be misunderstood. It does not mean that a person who before conversion loved beauty and hated cruelty would after it love cruelty and hate beauty. Many qualities remain the same, but the currents of concern are reversed and flow out instead of in. "What do I want?" becomes "What does God want?" "What will this do for me?" becomes "What will this do for others?" Zacchaeus's dominating desire had been to get all he could for himself, even by cheating. After he met Jesus, his dominating desire was to give to the poor and to lean over backwards to be honest.

A familiar incident in the life of Francis of Assisi illustrates this reversal. When he was seeking inner peace, he thought he heard the words, "What you used to abhor shall be your joy and sweetness." Of all disgusting objects, the most horrifying to Francis was a leper. The odor of the suppurating flesh would throw him into a paroxysm of nausea. One day, as he was thinking of the words he had heard, he saw a leper on the road ahead. Francis recoiled and rode past with averted face. Then, strangely, he felt drawn to the sufferer. Sliding from his horse, he placed a gift in the diseased hands. Then he bent down and kissed the loathsome fingers—giving the forsaken creature the human contact and affection his lonely heart needed most. Back on his horse, sweetness and rapture flooded Francis's soul. He knew he had found Christ.

The results of conversion are easy to find. In connection with my work, I wrote to pastors, asking for reports of what was happening to people. These replies are typical:

"I cannot risk identifying people, but deep changes have taken place —despair giving way to hope, trickery to honesty, indifference to sacrifice."

"Two alcoholics have come into the church as new men, devout, humble, sincere witnesses."

"An unhappy divorcée, never having been baptized, and an excessive smoker because of nerves, has found salvation, baptism, joy in church membership, and peace with herself. She has become a faithful member and a teacher in the Sunday School."

"One young husband and wife, who were skeptical and aloof, came into a wonderful experience of salvation and a great eagerness to serve Christ as recreation directors in a new community."

Hugh Price Hughes, a famed mission worker in the London slums, was challenged by an English man of letters, a scoffer at religion, to a public debate on the truth of Christianity. Hughes accepted with the proviso that each bring to the platform as exhibits a score of persons whose lives had been redeemed by each debater's beliefs. The debate was never held. The results of conversion are inescapable evidence of what Christianity can do.

3. What Makes Conversion Happen. When Nicodemus heard that a person can be born again, he asked, "How can this be?" It is God's doing and therefore beyond our understanding. We know it is put within our reach by Christ's death upon the cross. If he had sidestepped the crucifixion and died of old age, we might now have the record of a dozen more sermons like the Sermon on the Mount; we might now know of many more glorious things he did. But these would not do for humanity what the cross has done.

There is no single adequate statement of what the atonement is. The fact that it is explained in a variety of metaphors indicates that none is the whole truth. Each attempts to convey the truth to different sorts of minds. To people who were familiar with temple offerings, Christ's death was explained as a sacrifice for sin. Where Roman law prevailed, the atonement was a penalty to satisfy justice. For the commercially minded, it was payment of the debts of those who had gotten in above their heads. A slave-owning society could understand redemption as the payment that would redeem and free a slave. If our own generation uses psychiatry to explain the atonement, that is one more example of thinking of it in terms that are relevant to the current culture. None of these explanations is literal, of course. God is not a vengeful deity, a Roman magistrate, a banker, a slave owner, or a psychiatrist. But all of these expressions can be useful if they help us to see that the love Christ offers us upon the cross can break down the barriers our sins have erected against God and our fellow men. Christ's death for us can impel us to give ourselves to him in love and trust. An evangelism that hopes to transform human lives must count upon the power of the cross.

The human part of conversion is faith. Faith is not giving your assent, it is giving yourself. You may accept every word of the creeds as true, and still not be a Christian. "The demons believe," the Bible says—but they are still demons (James 2:19). To have faith in Christ means to be so devoted to him that he takes over your whole life. It means that your love of him will so dominate your thoughts that you can literally "have the mind of Christ" (1 Cor. 2:16). It lets the Christian say with Paul, "Christ . . . lives in me; and the life I now live in the flesh I live by faith in the Son of God, who loved me and gave himself for me" (Gal. 2:20). Being taken over by Christ is never complete; there are lapses. But there is no other way for a Christian to explain what he has become, and what he is accomplishing.

Talk of "surrendering to Christ" may sound ignoble, but there is no such thing as an unmastered life. We all are dominated by what we hold to be of greatest worth. If we will not come under the sway of the highest, we will be dominated by what is of lesser worth. God is the one in whose service there is perfect freedom because in that service we are most fully what we were born to be.

There is no way to conversion other than giving oneself in love and faith to Jesus Christ. When the great Jesuit missionary, Francis Xavier, reached the Orient in the sixteenth century, his reverence for the miraculous power of the Sacraments made him labor mightily to baptize many thousands. He was sure that, by the grace of God, this would make them Christians, but as soon as he left, they all returned to paganism. Our evangelistic methods sometimes show a similar faith in mumbled phrases or nodded assent to words that are not understood. It may seem that conversion is supposed to be a by-product of church membership. Or we might try to convert by reasoning, giving the intellectual grounds for accepting Christianity as an ideology. But it is not an ideology. A person might accept it as the explanation of the universe, the basis for mental health, or the one solution to the world's problems, without being a Christian at all.

The giving of oneself to Christ by faith can take place suddenly or slowly. Clovis Chappel said that a horse may be broken over many days by having, first, a rope around its neck, then a halter, then a bit, a blanket, a saddle, a man who walks around leaning on the saddle, and finally a rider. Another horse is subdued in a brief, furious battle with a broncobuster. One horse would never know when it was broken; the other would know just when it happened. Sudden conversions are more common in the Bible because there had not been time for many people to be reared as Christians, as was Timothy. Most people within the Christian community become gradually aware that Christ is their Savior, though they also need some definite time when they recognize what he has come to mean to them. There may be love at first sight, or a boy and girl may gradually begin to know they are in love. They may have no idea *when* it happened, but it is a great time when they first say openly *that* it has happened.

A lightning flash looks sudden, but the electric potential it discharges may have been building up slowly. The Christian martyrs that Paul had seen may have been doing things to his mind and heart that made him ready for his vision. A person who may not have seemed responsive to evangelism may become so because of some experience through which he or she has passed. That is why we can never consider anyone impossible. The Holy Spirit is always working out of sight.

4. Incomplete Conversion. Language is definite, but reality is not. We talk as though we know what we mean by "human being," but the uncertainties about abortion and euthanasia show that we do not. When does a fertilized cell become a human being? At what stage of lost mentality does a body no longer belong to a person? Language makes a clear distinction between "alive" and "dead," but a physician cannot. The sliding scale is a religious bafflement. Theology deals in absolutes, and properly so because there is such a thing as *Church, converted, Christian,* and *saved.* But in real life these always appear as fractions. Depravity has to be total to make dogma come out right, but in experience it never is. Absolutes never match what we know about ourselves. I believe I am a Christian, but only by percentages that can change within the hour. I hope I am generally aimed at heaven, but some days I seem to be quite a few degrees off course.

These frustrating fractions make endless problems for evangelism. Have those you consider converts really been converted? How much evidence of saving faith should you require? To whom can the promise of eternal life be given? Is your congregation a valid fellowship in Christ?

One help in this is the knowledge that the Bible is not as rigid as doctrine is. The Bible has not only the saved and the unsaved, but also the "being saved," which indicates degrees (Acts 2:47; 1 Cor. 1:18). The parable about the servants who received light or heavy beatings seems to indicate that the unsaved are not all at the same level (Luke 12:47–48).

A second help is our knowledge that a main line persists, in spite of wavering and uncertainty. I know only fractional Christians, but many of these across the years have exhibited a beautiful main line of consistency. They follow Christ as an empty skiff that is being pulled on a long line follows a speedboat. The light little hull will not follow straight behind: it darts off toward one side or the other. But in spite of all its skittering, it goes where it is being pulled. Congregations and denominations are blown off course by all sorts of vagrant breezes. But as you look back across the years, there is usually no doubt that they have been getting their bearings by celestial navigation.

A third help with our problem of perpetual imperfections in religion is the knowledge that the perfect is there. Spinoza said that the last Christian died on the cross. At least there has been one. There is an invisible vertical that a plumb line only approximates, and the most precise engineering never quite attains; but the knowledge that there is a perfect vertical makes building possible. There is such a thing as justice. It will never be fully attained in human relationships, but our belief in it keeps us trying. We believe in conversion and salvation and the life in Christ without ever having seen them all the way. In evangelism we keep on working for them because even the fractions of them that we can know are the loveliest, most satisfying, most ennobling attainments this life affords.

Is conversion permanent? If Christ has saved us, we should not have to scuttle fearfully from day to day, wondering whether we are still saved. Calvinists taught "the Perseverance of the Saints," which brought the gibe that Presbyterians do not believe in backsliding, but they practice it. Presbyterians prudently made sure that they could not be proven wrong by declaring that even those who seemed most saintly, if they did not persevere, never had been saints. This is a practical question for evangelism. What has happened when those we thought had been converted fall away? When those who have at one time been church members again join a church, we are never sure whether to consider them converted or reclaimed. There are the regulars who, no doubt with real sincerity, renounce their sins and give their hearts to Christ at every revival. Jesus said that the seed sown where the soil is shallow will quickly spring up but soon wither. The evangelists may be to blame for that. Nels Ferré wrote: "As any chicken farmer knows, you can get a quick green growth, high and lush, by warming a breadpan of soaked oats in the oven at the right temperature. We dread such a growth, for it has no lasting roots."[4] We never know what happens in people's hearts, but we can be sure that the loving care we give to preparing, receiving, and nurturing each new member can greatly reduce the number who are lost.

DECISION

Every waking moment, we are composing our existence by the decisions we make. Life keeps bringing us to turning points where everything ahead will be settled. You may look back some day and wonder why a flighty high school student had a right to decide what your life work was going to be. The uncertain tilt toward a *yes* or *no* may lead to widely different destinies. Harry Emerson Fosdick described a barn in the Chautauqua hills where a difference of one inch at the ridgepole decides whether a raindrop drains off to the Atlantic Ocean or the Gulf of Mexico. Robert Frost gave a memorable picture of decision:

> I shall be telling this with a sigh
> Somewhere ages and ages hence:
> Two roads diverged in a wood, and I—
> I took the one less traveled by,
> And that made all the difference.

A decision about Jesus Christ cannot be avoided. With so many sane people all around us firmly believing that he is the Savior, we have to have an opinion about whether they are right or wrong. Your decision about Christianity is not a matter of spiritual speculation, but a conclusion about history. Bethlehem is not a fabled spot, like Camelot; it has a sports car dealership. Today in Jerusalem, city bus number 43 travels the route of Jesus' triumphal entry, leaving Bethany on the half-hour. Jesus is not a mythical figure like Beowulf; there are few secular early first century references to him, but no one doubts that someone of that name gave history a powerful twist, nineteen and a half centuries ago. A dispute over the site of the temple he frequented affects what I pay for gasoline. If I begin to think of the Jews as characters in religious folklore, I need only walk down the street and look at the synagogue. What happened? Did Jesus actually come to the earth to open up the blessed life that a loving God intends for you? The answer to that can scarcely be, "I neither know nor care."

1. Three Stages of Decision

(1) Unconscious Decision. People may love Jesus without knowing it. Many who adhere to no form of Christianity may know a good deal about Jesus. Secular literature is full of references to what he did and taught. Those who believe in all that Jesus represents may dislike Christianity. Intellectual pride may keep them aloof

from miracles. Some may think of Christianity only in terms of grim-faced Deacons or pretentious hierarchies. All the atrocities committed in Christ's name may make that name repellent. There are some whose loyalties would make moving into a Christian group seem traitorous. In Moslem countries there are graduates of mission schools who are intellectually and emotionally under Christ's control, though they would never dream of calling themselves Christians. "The true light that enlightens every man" may have brought those who have never heard of Jesus to the God whom he reveals. This unacknowledged faith is not enough. The incarnation is not just an embellishment for God's saving plan. The gospel, which Christians are commanded to give to all the world, is the knowledge of the life, death, and resurrection of Jesus of Nazareth, not just an enlightened conception of God. The mind needs to affirm what the heart believes. Jesus wants his followers to "acknowledge me before men." We need to be able to say, "I know whom I have believed." But we can hold to the possibility that people may have a saving faith which circumstances keep them from acknowledging.

(2) Definite Decision. Unexpressed opinions are unstable. Undeclared good intentions are notoriously weak. What becomes explicit becomes real. If Martin Luther had said at the Diet of Worms, "I am inclined to think . . .," he never would have launched a Reformation. It was his saying, "Here I stand . . .," that gave him power. A private esteem for Jesus does not have the force of an acknowledged faith in him as Lord. The purpose of evangelism is to bring people to definite decisions about where they stand. A church loses much of its effect when it counts only on the general benefit of sermons, classes, and good influences without offering occasions for people to make up their minds about what they believe and who they want to be.

The time when people consciously decide what Christ means to them does not have to be anything at all like the "cataclysmic upheaval" which Horace Bushnell rightly insisted is not necessary. But the questions must be asked which require hard thinking and heart searching and definite decisions. "You can't ooze into the kingdom—you choose into it."

(3) An Act of Decision. As you look back and identify the turning points that have determined your path across the years, you will find that they were not just times when you decided something, but they were times when you also did something. You had already decided, but it did not seem actual until you wrote a letter of acceptance, tossed an unfinished pack of cigarettes into the wastebasket, or shook hands over an agreement. Up until the moment of expression, anything was possible; after that, the course was set.

One of the Church's essential functions is to offer people of all ages and temperaments opportunities to express decisions for faith in Jesus Christ. Any act of decision can seem ridiculously inappropriate to the great event. It would be absurd to think that anyone is converted by signing a card, coming down a church aisle, or responding to some questions. But the most prosaic act can become infinitely sacred through what it signifies. Think of Jesus breathing on the disciples and saying, "Receive the Holy Spirit." Any symbol will be inadequate until a church has labored and prayed to make it significant.

2. The Content of an Evangelistic Decision. Evangelism hopes to bring people to a decision about what they believe, how they will live, and what they intend to do about the Church. This can be thought of in terms of what they will be asked when they profess their faith in Christ and join the Church. The wording of these questions is prescribed in some denominations. Others leave congregations some latitude in what they ask of those who come into membership. A church may ask each candidate to make the statement in his or her own words.

Some churches ask questions to which candidates reply. Others offer statements which the candidates may accept. The statements here are not those of any church, but they may illustrate the sort of decisions evangelism hopes will be expressed:

MY FAITH

1. I believe in God, the heavenly Father, who is revealed to us in the holy Scriptures, and most perfectly in Jesus Christ.

2. I believe that Jesus Christ is the Lord of all, and I take him as the Master of my life and the Savior from my sins.

3. I believe that God's love will never fail, in this world or forever.

MY PROMISES

1. I will try, with the Holy Spirit's help, to be a consistent Christian in my thoughts and acts and in all of my relationships.

2. I will constantly try to grow in Christian faith and faithfulness by the use of the Bible, by prayer alone and with others, by the Lord's Supper, and by the other ways of spiritual strengthening.

3. I will help others have what God has given me through Jesus Christ.

MY PURPOSES AS A MEMBER OF THE CHURCH

1. I wish to be a member of the Church which God established to reveal his presence, to teach his truth, to embody the loving fellowship of Christians, and to minister to human needs.

2. I will express my devotion to the worldwide Church of Christ by being a loyal member of this church here, sharing in its worship, friendships, and service, and supporting it by my money and my prayers.

3. If I move away, I intend soon to find a new church home.

It is essential that those who make the most searching statements that the human mind can conceive be given a chance to think and pray about them in advance. Otherwise they will rightly assume that they are not intended to be taken seriously. Helping prospective members understand what they will be saying is an important part of their preparation. Talking about the questions or statements gives the minister an ideal opportunity to deepen his acquaintance with new members and to counsel them on the most important subjects. This may also be important in a new member class. A written copy of what those who join are asked to say is also useful in evangelistic calling.

The statements of faith in Christ are likely to raise the most problems. There may be questions about the reliability of the New Testament record. Do we really know who he was? Does everything the Bible says about him have to be believed?

The Church's belief that Jesus is God makes many wonder whether they can join. When did Jesus find out he was the Messiah? Did he have two centers of consciousness? Did he pray to himself? The Church has no completely satisfying answers to such questions because it does not fully understand God. The best approach may be to turn from the problems and find out what the prospective church members can say about Jesus.

Ask, "Can you say that Jesus is unlike every other human being?" We know there is a difference without being able to put it into words. Charles Lamb said that if the greatest of mortals were to enter a room, people would rise out of respect; but if Jesus came in, they would kneel. We feel that the greatest religious persons, the seers and the prophets, were on man's side reaching up toward God. But we think of Jesus as on God's side reaching down to man. When we read the Gospels we have to echo those who said, "No man ever spoke like this man!"

Ask, "Can you say that, unlike all the other heroes of the past, Jesus is not dead and gone?" He is the only great historic figure for whom a memorial would seem wildly inappropriate. A monument with the inscription "Erected in memory of Jesus of Nazareth who departed this life in A.D. 30" would seem, not a tribute, but a blasphemy. Millions of persons through the years have been sure from their own experience that Jesus is alive. Jesus is the only martyr whose death did not remove him from the world but made his presence always and everywhere available.

Ask, "Can you say that Christ's death upon the cross has a more than human power?" Other heroes have followed their ideals to a painful martyrdom, but it has not redeemed mankind as has the death of Christ. The cross has its more than earthly power to lift and transform life because it was a more than earthly being who was crucified.

Ask, "Can you say that when you use the word *God,* it has the meaning Jesus gave it?" That word can mean anything from a fierce demon to a chilling abstraction. The concept may seem intellectually unapproachable. But Jesus Christ came to the earth to live out the definition of that word. He put the ineffably high and holy in terms that can reach our minds and hearts. That is what we mean when we say that "God was in Christ." Many people who assume that God is good, loving, and wise do not recognize that they are seeing God through Jesus Christ.

So if those who look toward the Church wonder whether they can in good conscience say that they believe Jesus is God, they can be told that they do not have to worry about the too precise wording of the stiff old creeds. If they can say that Jesus Christ is unlike any other person who ever lived on earth, that he is not dead and gone, that his death can bless as no one else's ever could, that they get their understanding of God from him, then they can say in all sincerity that God lived on the earth in Jesus Christ.

3. Postponement. The most common refusal of Christ is not rejection but postponement. Those who cannot say "No" to him can say "Not now" forever. The conception of God's loving pursuit of those who flee from him is deep in our religion. Adam and Eve hid in the garden; the prophets lamented their people's refusal to take what God wanted to give; Jesus sorrowed over the city that spurned his love; and many since have tried to escape from what could have been their greatest blessing. It is the story of the Hound of Heaven: "I fled Him, down the nights and down the days."

Why would anybody do anything so foolish? Pride has been called the original sin; human beings want to be self-directed. They resist letting God control their lives. Sloth may be a reason —the resistance to leaving familiar ruts. Evangelists want people to decide. But to decide, from the Latin *de* ("away") and *caedere* ("cut"), is to cut off. If I decide to take the road to the right, I cut myself off from the road to the left; if I decide to go to a show, I cut myself off from all the other ways I might have spent the evening. People cling to what they would have to cut themselves away from if they were to give their lives to Christ.

All the inner wrong that keeps people from Christ puts up a running fight behind the defense, "Not now—later." Augustine in his *Confessions* tells of the struggle between his "two wills." When the struggle apparently was over, and his intellect was sure he would give all his love to the Christian God, his love entanglements "plucked" at his "fleshly garments" and whispered, "Dost thou cast us off?" So he went into a state of drowsiness and postponed doing what he thought was already settled. He kept saying "anon" and "presently, presently, presently," and "in a little while." This went on for a long time. Wrong attachments can make people delay what they know they should prefer.

Those who are converted often describe what happened by saying that they quit running and let God catch up. C. S. Lewis was an Oxford scholar who proclaimed his irreligion to all. Here is how he tells his story: "You must picture me alone in that room in Magdalen, night after night, feeling, whenever my mind lifted even for a second from my work, the steady, unrelenting approach of Him whom I so earnestly desired not to meet. That which I greatly feared had at last come upon me. In the Trinity Term of 1929 I gave in, and admitted that God was God, and knelt and prayed."[5]

Evangelism must try to introduce some people to Christ, and it must try to persuade other people to quit running away from a Lord whom they already know. Most of those whom our churches try to reach are of this second sort.

That is why the time of decision cannot be hurried. It takes a struggle for someone who has been saying, like Augustine, "presently, presently," to get to the point of being able to say, "now." People sometimes smile at how evangelistic preachers have the invitation hymn sung "one more time," and then "one more time," and then "one more time." But the preacher knows that the old self that has been barricaded behind postponements does not readily give up. Evangelistic callers have to know that evasion by delay is what they are struggling against. So when people begin explaining that now is not the best time, the callers listen politely, but they do not quit.

Making that decision is like breaking through the sound barrier. As the plane approaches the barrier, resistance builds up, and the plane labors and shakes. But when it breaks through the barrier, the resistance and stress subside, and the plane speeds freely on its way.

9

Youth Evangelism

————————————————

Young people offer an inexhaustible evangelistic opportunity for every church. They are a sure source of prospects. The work of evangelism can never be finished, because unbelievers keep being born into our communities. They are not only our greatest opportunity but also our greatest danger. A new horde of invaders gets into our country by the millions every year. They do not speak our language. They have no moral code, no faith in God. Their outlook is completely secular. They establish their beachheads in the maternity hospitals and swarm out across the land. There are no defenses that can keep them from taking over the country. Our only hope of escaping heathen domination is to change the invaders. We have to meet them with the Christian faith and persuade them to accept it.

The evangelism of young people is urgent also because of their special needs. Life's most critical decisions have to be made early. All the rest of a lifetime depends on youthful choices about schooling, vocation, marriage, and what sort of people to become. A person with no clear ideals or purposes is dangerously unprepared to make such choices. Those who believe that the right guidance for life is found in Jesus Christ cannot delay getting this guidance to those whose needs are so pressing.

Youth evangelism is urgent also because it offers the greatest possibilities. Human character is most easily shaped before it begins to harden. John R. Hendrick, in his 1973 Settles Lectures at Austin Theological Seminary, said, "Studies have consistently shown that adolescence is the most religiously active period in the life cycle; it is the time of most conversion experiences. Anyone who is concerned with personal evangelism will do well to view middle and late adolescence as the 'teachable moment' *par excellence.*" He finds that the studies of Jean Piaget and Ronald Goldman show that "the intellectual ability necessary for faith in the full sense becomes possible for most persons in adolescence [with] . . . the advent of formal operational thought." Erik H. Erikson has written that "the adolescent looks most fervently for men and ideas to have *faith* in, which also means men and ideas in whose service it would seem worth while to prove oneself trustworthy."[1]

Evangelism starts in childhood. The evangelism of children has been a troubled subject in American church history. Horace Bushnell praised revivals, but he denounced their minimizing of the home and church as vehicles of God's grace. He insisted that "the Child is to grow up to be a Christian, and never know himself as being otherwise. . . . Only unchristian education brings up the child for future conversion." This was, of course, strenuously opposed. It was said to ignore innate depravity and to replace the work of the Holy Spirit with educational techniques. These views have retained their rivalry. It sometimes seems that the evangelizers have heard Jesus say only that "repentance and forgiveness of sins should be preached" (Luke 24:47), while the Christian educators have heard only the "teach them to obey" part of his commandment (Matt. 28:20 TEV).

Most churches today do not have to decide whether children come into the Kingdom by nurture or conversion, because they see that both training and conscious choice are necessary. Bushnell agreed with the evangelists that children who have always thought of themselves as Christians need some experience that makes it definite. He even referred to this as "a truly supernatural experience."[2] A church which puts children on the assembly line, with the assumption that when they reach the proper age they will do the expected thing and join the Church, is depriving them of an experience of decision which Christians need. No one can take Jesus Christ for granted. There must be the consciousness of having deliberately given one's life to him.

The primary responsibility for bringing children to the Christian faith belongs, of course, to their parents. The child dedication service in churches that do not baptize babies, and the baptism service in churches that do, ordain the parents to the office of evangelist. It is the highest office they can hold, and they must be completely devoted to it. Partly they reveal God by their bearing and attitudes. John Baillie has said: "As far back as I can remember anything, I was somehow aware that my parents lived under the same kind of authority as that which, through them, was communicated to me. I could see that my parents, too, behaved as though they, *even they*, were not their own."[3] The parents' teaching of their children must also be like that enjoined in the Old Testament: "These words which I command you this day shall be upon your heart; and you shall teach them diligently to your children, and shall talk of them when you sit in your house" (Deut. 6:6–7). Parents convey the Christian faith to their children by their examples; they pray *with* them and *for* them; they encourage the reading that will help them to appreciate Christianity. They expose the children to significant experiences —at church, at conferences and summer camps, and by the guests they bring into their homes.

When Robert Raikes organized the first Sunday Schools, he had no idea of enrolling children from church families. He assumed that their religious nurture was their parents' responsibility. His whole purpose was to teach the Christian faith to children who would not hear of it at home. When the Sunday Schools turned from the non-Church children to the children of the Church, many parents in the Church assumed that their children's Christian training was the church's task. Church schools need to recover the zeal for enrolling children from non-Church homes, and parents have to be shown that the church can only be their helper in a task that is mostly their own. One church school wrote the parents, "You are going to do the teaching, and we will check once a week on how well you are progressing." A church's major contribution to evangelizing children from Church homes is the help it gives the parents to be better Christians and better imparters of Christianity.

The church also has its own priceless opportunity with its pupils. It has access to children and young people for a significant amount of time each week during the years when their characters and life purposes are being formed. A successful school will be gathering children from homes where there is no understanding of the Christian faith. For them the school has the whole evangelistic task. With all its pupils, it has an awesome opportunity that it needs to understand in larger terms than the mere imparting of knowledge. Bryan Green puts the matter pointedly: "The old-fashioned teachers may have had poor methods and inferior equipment, but they did very often keep a prayer list; every day they prayed for each member of their Sunday school class by name, and earnestly longed that each child should personally come to love and know Jesus Christ as Saviour, Master and Friend."[4]

When a young Navy flier from our church was killed, his mother told me sorrowfully that Fred had never become a Christian, meaning that he had never joined the Church. She said that no one ever asked him to. I tried to assure her that he could belong to Christ without belonging to the Church, but we at the church did believe that confession of faith and church membership are very important. If none of us—ministers, teachers, youth leaders, or friends—had ever talked about this with Fred, our neglect was unforgivable. A church needs to be sure that the question of becoming a professing Christian is discussed with every young person with whom it has contact. This can be planned by every church activity that deals with youth. It requires a periodic checking through the names of all the young people.

A church has to decide the age at which it will invite all its young people to become church members. Opinions differ. If maturity were the guide, it would be different for every person. Girls are likely to be interested in matters of faith and able to understand them a year or so before boys are. But a church cannot tell about the differences in individuals, so it has to choose the age that will come closest to being best for all. Protestant Churches now seem to be raising this age. In my denomination, for a long while the usual age was twelve; for many congregations it is now fourteen to sixteen. In the Roman Catholic Church the age for the first Communion has long been thought of as six or seven, but an Archbishop has proposed that it should be seventeen. There are conflicting considerations. Little children can be sincerely religious, but they are not able to understand important aspects of the Christian faith or what it requires. Adolescents sometimes view joining the Church as their graduation, so that they need come back only for the annual alumni reunion at Easter. They might have a more mature attitude to membership if it were postponed. On the other hand, church school enrollments often become smaller after the ninth grade, so there seems to be reason for offering the opportunity to become members while more of the pupils can be reached. What is certain is that the age for joining the Church should be the age at which it will have the most meaning for a whole lifetime. (Denominations that consider baptized children to be members of the Church will regard "joining" as meaning entering into the full responsibilities of adult membership.)

There are important reasons for having a class to prepare young people for this momentous step. The class can be a means of evangelism. It can enroll those who know they want to come into full church membership and those who are still undecided. At the designated age, the question of joining the class can be raised through the church school or youth activities, by letters, or by personal contacts. Whatever method is used, the cooperation of teachers, youth leaders, and parents is important. A letter to the teachers can describe the class and ask them to discuss it with each pupil. Guidance for these conversations can be offered. A letter to the parents can tell of the purpose and importance of the class, and urge them to make it a subject for their prayers and for a serious talk with their children. They are told what participation and work will be expected of the pupils, and they are asked to prompt their children to do what is prescribed. A meeting with the parents just before the class starts can answer their questions and show them how very important the class is.

Older young people may come into the Church through an adult New Member Class, but for many reasons younger boys and girls need their own class. One reason is that their classes can last longer, cover more material, and have a wider variety of teaching methods. In some denominations the established practice is to take three years to prepare young people for Church membership. A generation ago, most other Protestant Churches used about five ninety-minute periods, often on the Saturday mornings before Easter, to prepare their boys and girls to join the Church. That time has increased until now there are many churches that have these classes through most of a school year, from September to Pentecost. Often these classes meet during the Sunday church school period, but many have them on afternoons after school. The minister may do the teaching, perhaps with helpers, or he or she may teach the teachers. Most ministers need to learn about good teaching methods for such classes.

There may be assigned reading, tests, papers, field trips, and spontaneous drama. The pupils may be expected to attend the church services, to make reports on the sermons, and to discuss the worship. It is not always easy to find the right printed materials and audiovisual aids. Large churches with professional educators may prepare their own courses; most churches have to depend on outside sources. Some denominations provide excellent courses; what others offer is sadly inadequate. A church that is not pleased with its denomination's materials would do better to adapt what another denomination offers than to limp along with inadequate resources.

The pupils should be told in advance what they will be expected to do. They participate more seriously if they have been made to feel the importance of the class for their relationship to God and for their whole lives. They can be told that enrolling in the class does not oblige them to join the Church. The whole course may be intended to help them decide whether or not to do that. Some time before the class ends, the minister or one of the helpers should have a private conversation with each pupil about his or her religious beliefs and practices. Some of them will talk readily, others will need help in saying what they want to say. A good way for the counsellor to get to the most important subjects is to work with the young person on his or her own statement of faith. This might be read to the congregation at the time of reception as the new member's testimony.

What to do about those who fall short of the class requirements is a hard question. Refusing to let a person accept Christ as Lord is not an appropriate penalty for academic failure, but it may do lasting harm to let the boy or girl believe that religion is not something to be taken seriously. The crisis is less painful if a poor performance is recognized early, so that the pupil can be advised to wait for the next class.

Some Christian educators believe that the regular Church School is preparation for membership, so that no special New Member Class is needed. This is a misunderstanding of what is happening. For young people, joining the church is one of the "rites of passage" by which they leave childhood behind and become adults. They are likely to take it very seriously. They will do more work for the New Member Class than they have ever done for the Church School, or will ever do again. Their regular teachers are astonished to see how they read books, write papers, prepare for tests, attend church, and worry about absences. They feel they are being mentally and spiritually readied for the impending great event of acknowledging their faith and taking their full place in the holy and historic Church. They are likely to be thinking more seriously about their faith and praying more intently than they ever have before. It is a serious mistake for a church to throw away this once-in-a-lifetime opportunity to accomplish so much in so brief a time.

All of a church's normal methods of evangelism apply to young people, but there is often opportunity to use them in specially effective ways. Youth organizations have their own ways to make *contacts* with those outside the church. The attraction of youth choirs, camps, sports, social events, and working for good causes has brought the first step toward faith for many Christians. The school years offer perhaps the best chance in American life for open contacts between church people and those with no apparent religious interest. Students can talk enthusiastically about what is happening at their church, and invite acquaintances to join them.

A church has very effective ways of *cultivating* Christian faith in young people. Worship that is designed for youth can be very real for them. Retreats that take youth to an attractive spot for a weekend can accomplish much in a short time. Summer conferences do the same thing on a larger scale. They appeal to some who would not at first come to a church, and may open up unguessed vistas to them.

The most important influence on a young person is another young person. Many mature Christians recall conversations that they had in high school or college as among the most formative events in their religious development. These take place on dates, trips, or late-night gatherings when no one wanted to go home. The church is the natural setting for them.

Confession and *Church membership* can follow. The many young people who drift in and out of church activities without ever being asked to think about their relationship with Christ are sad evidence of a church's blundering ways. The subject never comes up.

Whenever there is to be evangelism from the pulpit, there must be plans to have the young people present for whom it might be decisive. Lay calls for decisions in homes where there are young people should be directed also to them, perhaps with a young church member on the calling team. Young people and their leaders should be given special help in learning how to talk to young people about decisions, and in finding occasions for doing it. Young people should be invited to join classes that prepare for church membership, whether or not they have decided to become members.

There are two requirements for keeping evangelism in a church youth program: (1) it must be a continual subject for meetings, conversations, and prayers—otherwise it will be crowded out and forgotten; and (2) there must be carefully laid plans for it. It will not come from vague enthusiasm, but only from definite decisions about what is to be done and who is going to do it.

10

Using Lay Callers

Conversations have always been the Church's best evangelistic method. That was true for the New Testament Church; it is true today. A program for lay evangelistic calling simply arranges for such conversations to take place. Many Christians sorrow over their inability to talk with others about Christ. They deeply want to, but the right occasion seems never to arise. A calling program offers those occasions, and under the most natural and helpful circumstances. There is no difficulty getting on the subject— when people receive visitors from the church, they expect to talk about religion. There is a clear reason for the conversation. The setting is ideal, with the surroundings of the home and daily life. Before the callers start, their instruction gives them the good advice that has come from many such experiences. They do not go alone, which makes it easier for everyone. They gain confidence and competence with every call. There could be no better chance to have the happiness and satisfaction of doing what Christ wants all his followers to do.

One of the great benefits of a calling program is the callers' growth in the ability to have their own conversations about the Christian faith, anytime and anywhere. Those who have spent evenings talking about faith to various sorts of people to whom the church has sent them are learning how to get onto that subject with their associates and friends. The experience that evangelistic callers get may be just what can best help church schoolteachers, youth leaders, or parents to know what to say and do.

Home calls have many advantages as a way of bringing people to the great decision to confess their faith and come into the

Church. Such calling is done personally, face to face, at the scene of the family's life, and with a chance to think and talk about any decision they might make. There are other good ways of presenting the appeal for faith. Billy Graham, at present the best-known evangelistic preacher, makes a generous comparison: "There are many methods of evangelism. But the most effective method of evangelism being used in America today, in my opinion, is visitation evangelism. More permanent results come to the churches, more people are actually converted to Christ. . . . I consider mass evangelism as the artillery to soften up the enemy and as a means to break through the line. Visitation evangelism is the occupation force that comes in to possess the land."

There are safeguards around evangelistic calling. It goes only to those who have had some contact with the church and are likely to know what it means to confess faith in Christ and to be a Church member. The callers' training does not give them smooth techniques, but it helps them make their appeals truly Christian and it saves them from mistakes. The intention that is expressed during the call is not the final step into the church. An interview with the minister or what is said during a New Member Class can tell more than the callers could say, and can prevent inadequate decisions. When decisions are not made, the callers can still help people with their religious thinking, and can let them know that the church cares about them.

Evangelistic calling is not associated with any particular theology or style. Every real church—conservative or liberal, formal or unconventional—has to have something to say and some way to get it said. There must be important truths, and the benefits of participating in its life, that it wants those outside to know about. It might try to make these known by skywriting, billboards, or broadcasts, but the best advice is summed up in the saying that if you have an important message to deliver, wrap it up in a person. Evangelistic calling is simply a way of communicating whatever message a church has to those who ought to have it.

There are three quite different sorts of evangelistic calls, and confusing them makes difficulties: (1) *Contact calls* seek only to stir an interest in the church. They are easy to make. Tact and a pleasant manner are about all the qualifications the callers need.

(2) *Cultivation calls* are made on those with whom the church already has some contact. They are intended to draw people into church participation. Those who make them should be able to radiate their liking for people and their enthusiasm for the church. These callers need some preparation, but not a great deal. (3) *Decision calls* are made only on those who may be ready to join the church. These are the "lay evangelistic calls." The callers need to be committed to the Christian faith and loyal members of the church. They should have careful preparation, and their personalities are important.

Though the callers have one of these purposes in mind, they are never sure which sort of call it will turn out to be. A *contact call* may find a stranger eager to talk about joining the church, and a *decision call* may run into complete indifference. But it is important to keep clearly in mind the differences in these calls. Otherwise a church might invite those who know little about Christianity to become members, or it might ignore people between the first contact and the appeal for a decision. A church may think it has had "a fine evangelistic program" and turn its attention elsewhere, when it has actually had no more than a flurry of doorbell ringing and pleasant visits up and down the streets. *Contact* and *Cultivation* calls lose much of their purpose without *Decision calls.*

1. THE ADVANTAGES OF LAY EVANGELISTIC CALLS

1. Validity. Lay calling can be sound evangelism. It is sometimes assumed that lay members are tongue-tied on religious subjects. The truth is that many of them talk about their faith as readily as they talk about any other interesting subject. A member of our church, who had little education, had two subjects he could talk about anytime: how glad he was that he had migrated to America, and what God had done for him. A good many men and women who have never tried to talk about religion outside of the church are often astonished to find out how easy it is. Often the people who are being called on make it easy. Their desire to talk about the most important subjects has been pent up. That is why new callers often come back excited and thrilled. They have tried something that they thought was impossible and found that they could do it. The pastor of an Ohio church reported, "one old elder, always concerned about the spiritual life of others, never had the courage to approach a person directly about Christ. At the first visitation he almost backed out at the last minute, he was that afraid. Finally he went and won four by confession the first night. . . . He can't be stopped now!"

It cannot be taken for granted that the callers will get to essential subjects. A good many calls probably never get beyond remarks like "We have a great choir and the friendliest church in town." That is why advice on how to get to more serious subjects is the most important part of the training. Fortunately, superficial appeals will not result in many superficial church memberships, because they have small pulling power. Unless the callers get to the only real inducements that the church has, the spiritual ones, not much will happen.

It is sometimes objected that lay people with no theological training do not know enough to be evangelists. How much does an evangelist need to know? Not much, according to the Scriptures. Jesus commanded the healed demoniac, "Go home to your friends, and tell them how much the Lord has done for you," though there was scarcely any more that he *could* tell (Mark 5:19). The Samaritan woman used the very little she knew about Jesus to bring her neighbors to him. Anyone who knows Jesus can give another person enough reason to want to love and follow him. The necessary knowledge does not all have to be imparted at the start.

The approach to faith is not intellectual. The president of a theological seminary told me about his highly intelligent brother whom he had tried for years to bring to the Christian faith. He tried to put what he said in a way that would be acceptable to his brother's critical and sophisticated mind, but with no success. Then his brother moved to another city, and a new neighbor, who was far from intellectual, leaned across the fence and asked, "Do you know Jesus Christ as your Lord and Savior?" And in a few weeks he did. Intelligence and learning can be very helpful in evangelism. C. S. Lewis could reach people who would be put off by a too simple faith. But the soulshaking glimpse of Christ that makes people want to follow him has nothing to do with erudition.

Evangelists need enough knowledge to understand what Christianity is *not.* Otherwise, when they witness as callers, or as friends, or as Sunday School teachers, they may be offering untruth. They could make faith shallow, easy, or superstitious. But evangelists do not have to be able to answer all the questions in order to point to Jesus Christ. They can be like the man who had been born blind; his Christology was very shaky, but there was one important thing he could say with no uncertainty: "Though I was blind, now I see" (John 9:25).

In the decade after World War II, "Visitation Evangelism," as a well-defined method, became widely used in American Protestant churches. This was the period when many of the denominations made their greatest gains. When some of these denominations began losing membership during the 1960s, it was sometimes said that they were losing those who had been brought in by incompetent lay callers. This guess was usually made by those whose contact with congregations was not close. The figures show that it was mistaken. Most of the loss of membership has come, not from an increase in suspensions of inactive members, but from a decrease in admissions. The problem is not that calling was used, but that it was dropped. It was a casualty of the collapse of concern for anything evangelistic. Many congregations have continued their calling programs for years because they have found that this is the best way of giving new members an understanding of the meaning of the step that they are taking. One of the surest signs that American churches are taking more interest in evangelism will be an increase in evangelistic calling.

2. Timeliness. Lay evangelism is peculiarly right for the modern mood. The current consciousness includes a rebellion against being handled in the mass. There is now in every field—business, education, healing—a great stress on person-to-person relationships. *Affirmation, trust,* and *openness* have become key words. Lay calling shows people that the church cares enough about them as individuals to come to them in their homes. It shows that these new friends are willing to come out from behind their protective conventionalities and be open about the deepest issues of life. This is the sort of relationship that many people are looking for. The basic human need is increasingly understood in terms of the lack of self-esteem, of identity, of belonging, of acceptance. Christ put his church on earth to save people from this loss of self. A congregation must be a community of trust and caring where people listen to each other, where the unsure know that they are loved. The evangelism that draws people into such a fellowship must exhibit it. For such a church, impersonal evangelism would be like a silent noise.

Modern Christians have properly become uneasy about the conception of the church as a place where Christianity is kept. Our buildings are not supposed to be spiritual refuges to which we can flee from the corruptions of the world. Christ did not intend the fellowship of his disciples to be an enclave of the saved. Evangelism dies when church members turn in upon themselves to enjoy their pieties. The church is not on the job on Sunday, and off the job on Monday. It is most on the job when its members are being Christ's apostles to the world. Christians make their pit stops at the church on Sundays so that they can run the race that is set before them all week long. Great evangelistic events take place in church buildings, but a corps of evangelistic visitors heading for their cars, so they can go out to where people live, demonstrates, both in symbol and in deed, what the Church should be.

3. Lay Superiority. Lay men and women have special advantages as witnesses. They talk the language of the people on whom they call, and they have the same point of view. The minister is a professional persuader. Sabatier said, "It is not easy to hear and apply to oneself the exhortations of preachers who, aloft in the pulpit, seem to be carrying out a mere formality; it is just as difficult to escape from the appeals of a layman who walks at our side."

Ministers are continually astonished to have people with whom they have been working in vain brought into the church immediately by lay callers. There are many like the minister who reported, after his first use of lay callers, "Being in the twenty-first year of my pastorate here, I felt it a real victory to baptize twenty-one adults on Palm Sunday, some of whom I personally have not been able to win in all these years."

The advantage of having the same background is seen in this account: "A young lady went by herself through conviction, outside her prospect list, to talk to a family. This is a farm community. She found the wife helping the husband unload corn, elevating it into the crib. He was up in the crib, but when the load was unloaded, he climbed down. They were busy, and this farm lady Deacon knew it full well. She pressed the claims of Christ as briefly as reverence would permit, doing so in her own words. To her utter amazement and joy, a perfectly natural conversation developed about Christ and His Church, and these people are now dynamic members."

It is often assumed that ministers talk readily about religion, while lay people are inhibited. The exact opposite is more likely. Ministers are afraid of sounding preacherish in private. The smaller the audience, the more likely a minister is to get stage fright. Ministers have more practice talking to crowds; lay men and women have more practice talking to individuals. This does not mean that a minister should leave all the evangelistic calling to the church members. Unless he is doing it too, he cannot be the helper they need. He is a fellow worker. He and the lay workers have a good deal to learn about calling from each other.

4. Numbers. Only the church members can supply the many hours of time that personal evangelism requires. Most of it must be done in the evenings, when people are not at work. For the same reason, most of a minister's meetings and his calls on church members have to be in the evenings. If all the evening time this leaves were used for evangelistic calls, a minister would be hard put to get in as many hours of such calling in a year as a dozen lay workers could contribute in a week. Evangelism cannot be a mass production. If a church is to be evangelistic, only the church members can give the personal attention that each individual must have. A sound Biblical principle has to be applied: Jethro had to tell Moses that he was wearing himself out and the people were being neglected because Moses was not using helpers from the congregation (Exod. 18:13–26). Paul told Timothy, "Teach these great truths to trustworthy men who will, in turn, pass them on to others" (2 Tim. 2:2, LB.) The church is the evangelist, and the full manpower and womanpower of the church is needed for the task.

5. Appropriateness. Lay calling restores to the members a function that Christ intended them to have. He calls every follower to the joy of witnessing. If that is turned over exclusively to the clergy, the laity has been defrauded. Clericalism is an ever-recurring corruption of Christianity. The Reformation, which tried to restore the ministry to every Christian, has yet to arrive in many Protestant congregations.

You may puzzle over a term which we all use. When you call a church "a strong church," what do you mean? What is the quality that marks a church as strong? It is not the size of the membership, the building, the budget, or the mortgage. It is not the stature of the preacher. I believe reflection will show that the feature we instinctively recognize in a "strong church" is the unusual amount of time that its members give to its service. What that reveals, of course, is the members' devotion to the church's mission. Only a church in which the members have a powerful ministry can be what a church ought to be, or can be effective in evangelism. If the ministry of witness is not given to church members, they will be weakened by the lack of exercise, and those they should be reaching will be deprived of the blessings of a faith in Christ.

6. Revival. Evangelistic callers get a firsthand experience of the down-to-life immediacy of the Christian faith. In their calls they participate in the contest between spiritual hunger and indifference, between wanting to know Christ and wanting to avoid him. They can feel as though they have moved into the Bible and become actors in its dramas. This can make spiritual issues a more vivid part of their own lives.

Belief loses force when it is not clear. The faith of many Christians is strong in their hearts but unclear in their minds. We can do our Christian thinking with comfortable and worn-out old expressions that do not require thought. But we cannot use our churchy terms when we talk to non-church people. When callers try to say plainly what they mean in basic English, they must first tell themselves. After each attempt, they will be thinking of how they could have said it better. By this, what they believe will become more clear to them, and a more definite part of daily life.

Changing human lives has to be God's work; trying to participate in it brings a strong sense of partnership with him. The callers' deep longing to bring a blessing to those they call on can make prayer very urgent and specific. When things happen that could not have been expected, there is a direct experience of the miraculous. There are countless testimonies from church members who declare that they have come to a new discovery of the reality and wonder of the Christian life through their evangelistic calling. This can affect the life of an entire congregation.

Evangelistic calling can also bring a fresh contact with spiritual reality to ministers. When a minister talks face-to-face with the uncommitted, trying to tell them about Christ and hearing about their uncertainties and problems, the abstractions of theology come to life. This is the essential truth in the familiar lines of Louis I. Newman:

> I sought to hear the voice of God,
>   And climbed the topmost steeple.
> But God declared: "Go down again,
>   I dwell among the people.[1]

The best sermons are not one-way communication, they are extended dialogues. They start with real conversations, and if the minister can guess what the other person would be saying, the dialogue continues in the minister's mind. It takes real conversations with real people to make preaching valid. P. T. Forsyth said bluntly, "The cure for dullness in the pulpit is not brilliance but reality." Evangelistic calling makes sermons real.

7. Adaptability. A calling program can be used in any sort of church. The organization and frequency will be different in big and little churches. The vocabularies will reflect the church's temperament. But rich and poor, rural and inner-city churches have all used the programs well. It is not just the regular, well-established church that can use its lay men and women for evangelistic calling.

The Mountaineer Mining Mission in West Virginia, with five small churches, got its coal miner parishioners interested in calling. In one year there was a 20 percent increase in membership. The director said, "There was added the great satisfaction of watching the laymen develop. Each and every one of the laymen enjoyed this personal evangelism, and grew spiritually while he took part in it."

An Idaho minister told of the great benefits of the calling; then he added, "I am convinced that if this thing only catches fire in little towns like ours . . . we will have a twentieth-century revival." A Nevada minister spoke of the new spiritual life that lay calling brings "to our churches in the 'out-of-the-way places.'"

A veteran home missionary in the state of Washington wrote: "This construction town has tripled its original six hundred population. . . . Our purpose was to visit every trailer house, construction camp, Quonset hut, and housing project, and welcome them with, 'Only a stranger once.' . . . Membership was thirty-nine, three and a half years ago. Now it is 110. Our congregation is no longer asking: 'What kind of people are these construction workers?'"

8. Completion. Lay calling supplies what is needed for the rest of a church's evangelism program. Evangelistic preaching can begin a move toward faith that calling can later bring to a decision. Or calling may begin what preaching can complete. Those who have been spiritually stirred by devotional groups or classes may be brought the rest of the way into the church by callers. The other parts of the church may in many ways be planting the seed and tending the growth that the callers harvest.

2. HOW A CALLING PROGRAM IS CONDUCTED

1. Get It Started. It is usually the minister who stirs up interest in lay evangelistic calling, but sometimes enthusiastic lay members get it started. The minister, or members who have moved from other churches, may have had experience with such calling, or the inspiration to try it may come from books or conferences. Someone who knows a good deal about this sort of evangelism may be invited in to answer questions and kindle enthusiasm.

A strong committee will be needed to take charge. If a church does not have an Evangelism Committee, it will need one for this purpose. It is important to have an able, respected Chairman.

Some people are reluctant to accept new ideas, and objections to lay evangelistic calling are not unlikely. It may be said that only a minister has the training for evangelism, that lay evangelism is bound to be superficial, or that neighbors will resent callers who raise questions about their religion. Such objections can be answered best from experience. A reassuring description of the experience in another church may be needed. It helps immensely if evangelistic calling is proposed to the churches by their denomination, or by some division of it. If there are training conferences, delegates from reluctant churches may be persuaded.

Sometimes a minister has to get his church started by finding just one person who is willing to go with him on evangelistic calls. They study together the advice that is given for such calls. If the experience is good, the helper takes out a new teammate and the minister trains someone else. By geometric progression, a corps of callers comes into being whose enthusiasm will convince the church.

There is a temptation to make a tentative start as an experiment. A few workers may be asked to make some calls without much training or knowledge of what they are supposed to do. Or the people on whom the calls are made are not carefully selected, so the callers find themselves asking people to become members who scarcely know about the church. The reports of such halfway attempts are very likely to be depressing, which can make it difficult to get real calling going.

2. List the Prospects. A list is made of people who might be approached about decisions. If a church has not been doing calling, there may be a backlog of such persons. The number of calls and the frequency of the calling depend on how well the earlier stages of evangelism are supplying people who are ready to be called on. If the church waits for people to bring themselves, their numbers may be few. If a church is working hard at making contacts and at cultivating these newcomers until they know about the Christian faith and life, then there will be a constant need for calls that ask about decisions.

Callers usually go in pairs. Two are more impressive than one, and they have more to offer. They help each other, and it is less of a strain to talk with two people than with one. Three might seem overwhelming, though some advisors prefer three, partly because this makes it easier to have a man and a woman on each team. A husband and wife can be an excellent calling team if they can guard against the tendency to make a social call, with too much small talk and too little conversation on the serious subjects they came to talk about.

If the homes are not too far apart, callers can complete an average of two-and-a-half calls in an evening. So they will need to carry three assignments, plus two more because some people will not be at home. The number of callers who will be needed can be calculated by allowing five assignments per team on the first evening. The ones they do not get to are reassigned on the next evening. For four evenings they will need twelve assignments ($2\frac{1}{2}$ x 4 + 2), with the two extra left over at the end. If a church has 120 people to be called on, it can use ten teams for four evenings. (There are too many variables for this to be better than a loose estimate.)

3. Set the Dates. When a church is starting a calling program and instructing new workers, it is well to have several afternoon or evening times for calling as close together as possible, with a training period each time. A training course is better if it is not too spread out. First experiences are often the least satisfying, so those who go only once or twice may not learn how good calling can be. Enthusiasm and assurance build from one time to the next. On successive evenings, callers can discuss their experiences and learn from each other. The high spirits of those who did well encourage those who fear they did not accomplish much. Preparatory classes for those who decide to join the Church can be larger and come sooner if the calls are concentrated on a Sunday afternoon and evening and the next two evenings, or on four evenings in one week, or (which is not as good) on an evening a week for four weeks. If the dates are set far enough ahead, callers can promise times that are close together as readily as times that are spread out. When most of the callers are experienced, and need only reminders and fresh inspiration, a single time for calling can be good enough. The best times are different for compact urban areas than for widespread rural ones.

Some times of the year are better than others. Fall gives more time to assimilate new members during the liveliest part of the church year. Fall is the time when there are the most calls to be made on those who have moved into the community. The weeks just before Christmas have much that makes people ready for conversations about Christ and about Christian homes. The period just after New Year's is the least crowded in many churches. The mood of Lent can be helpful for evangelism. Those who join at Pentecost do not have time to get well started in a church before vacations interrupt its normal life.

If dates for a New Member Class or for receiving members are set before the callers go out, that can be given as a reason for their calls. Such dates give prospective members an occasion for making up their minds. The dates for a calling program need to be set well in advance so the church calendar can be cleared, the callers engaged, and preparations adequately made.

4. Arouse Church Interest. The whole congregation needs to feel the importance of the program. Interest can be stirred at church services and meetings of organizations and through publications. Prayer for a calling program, when church members are together and also in their private prayers, is important.

There are reasons for and against letting the people who will be called on know when the callers are coming. It is more considerate to make engagements in advance. It avoids having callers come at an inconvenient time, or when the house is in disarray. Prearrangement also can make a call seem more important, and it saves the callers from wasting their time going to where no one is at home.

But the reasons for not making definite engagements are usually stronger. It would be impossible to set times for any but the first call. Some calls can be made in twenty minutes. Twice that time is more likely for a really good call. Some calls get into so many important matters that an hour is not time enough. Sometimes callers go straight to a home; other times they spend a large part of an evening trying to find it. So a calling schedule cannot be laid out in advance.

If people know that the callers are coming, they will probably guess the reason. Then they will decide in advance what their response will be. Since they have not wanted to join the church, they are most likely to decide that they still do not want to. Thus the callers find minds already made up before there is a chance for any conversation, and minds that are made up are hard to change. People who have for years delayed making a decision about their faith will often request that the callers not come. If they had come unannounced, the call would probably have been mutually enjoyable. They would have had a chance to talk about the reasons for faith in Christ and for becoming members of the Church. They might have helped the dilatory end their procrastination.

5. Engage the Callers. It is better not to ask for volunteers to do the calling. Some who are not qualified will respond, and some of the best qualified will hesitate to offer their services. A personal invitation makes the work seem more important. Some churches with strong calling programs turn them over to an official group—the Deacons or the Stewards—but I think it is better to use those who have been selected for this purpose than to make it an additional duty for those who have been chosen for a different sort of task. A request to serve that comes by mail is easy to decline, and it gives no chance to reassure those who hesitate. A telephone invitation might be good enough, but those who have not served before can best be recruited face to face.

A strong Christian faith and a contagious enthusiasm for the church are important qualities for callers. So are an attractive manner and a friendliness that makes one more interested in listening to people than in working on them. The intelligence that is revealed by good judgement is helpful. The zeal that runs to tactlessness can be a handicap. A natural ability to talk easily can be well used, but a quiet sincerity that can convey deep feeling in few words is just as important. A knowledge of Christian doctrine and the Bible is an asset, but questions that require special knowledge are not often raised. A caller's personal religious experience is more important than what is learned from books. Jesus said, "Whoever believes in me, streams of living water will pour out from his heart" (John 7:38 TEV).

A mature high school or college student and an older person may do well together. A new caller can be reassured and trained by going out with one who will be a good example. There are good reasons for using new church members as callers if they are otherwise qualified. Their experience is fresh. Their faith and their attachment to the church may be strengthened by talking about them. If callers are to go out several times, beginners who can come only once or twice should ordinarily not be used. If they miss most of the instruction and experience, they will not do as well as they should or get a fair impression of what calling is.

6. Get the Materials. Cards are needed for the calling assignments. These are copied from the section of the prospective member file that lists those who seem ready to be asked to make decisions. Some churches have card forms for this, but a blank card will serve well enough. With the name and address are put the names and relationship of others in the home, the source of the contact with the church, present or past participation in this or former churches, dates of past approaches and what the response was, and personal information that may be useful to the callers—work, friends, interests, etc. Nothing should be written on the card that could cause embarrassment if it is accidentally left in a home.

If decision cards are to be used, they should be carefully planned, with the great statements put in as brief, clear, and beautiful a way as possible. It distracts a call if there are too many statements to be discussed or too many spaces to be filled in.

Recheck all addresses. A family may have moved, a number may be copied incorrectly. A few minutes time at the church can save callers hours of irritated wandering.

Envelopes are needed into which the assignment cards for each team each evening will be put. The names of the callers are written on the envelopes, and help in finding difficult addresses can also be written there. Street maps that the callers can consult before they go out are also needed.

It is not necessary for callers to take literature, and it is unwise for them to take very much. Whatever they bring should not be given out until it is needed in the call, or until just before the callers leave. To give it out at the start suggests that delivering it is the purpose for the call. Callers may take a description of the church and its activities, an explanation of the process of joining the church, a brief pamphlet about faith and Christian living, and a leaflet with Bible references. Evangelistic visitors are not colporteurs, and they should not spend much time talking about any material they bring.

Written instructions may be given to the callers, summarizing what they are told in the instruction meetings and giving them a checklist to review before they call. The instructions can also tell them what to do after they have made the calls.

Films, filmstrips, recordings, leaflets, and books for evangelistic callers are available from various sources. These may have inspiration or instruction. Some of this is good, but an instructor must be sure that anything he gives out says what he wants to say.

7. Plan the Instructions. The minister is usually the instructor, though someone for whom this is a specialty may be invited in. There are a number of books that give the information an instructor needs. He has to start early to work out what to say and do. Lay workers may give some of the instructions and pass out the assignments.

8. Work Out the Details. Such things as meals, finance, cars, and clerical help have to be prepared for.

9. Fix the Callers' Packets. Put five or six cards into each assignment envelope if there are enough to allow for this surplus. Three good calls can sometimes be made in an evening, and it is not unusual for no one to be at home at half of the addresses.

Calls are grouped geographically. If the addresses are not too scattered, callers can be matched with those they call on according to age, occupation, family situation, and interests. This is not important enough, however, to sacrifice a great deal of convenience for it. Some people like to call in their own neighborhoods and among their friends; others prefer not to. If decision cards are being used, they are put in the packets.

Calls that are most pressing are assigned first. Those on persons who seem least likely to make decisions are saved for the last evening, unless there is some reason why they specially need attention. There is a better possibility with younger couples than with older ones. Having children in a home increases the receptivity. Addiction to weekend recreation decreases it.

Never give callers a card from the file—always give a copy of it. When a file card is lost, a connection with a family may be lost. If callers were to delay returning a file card, no one else could make the call. Keep a careful record of which cards are in each assignment envelope, and which team has each envelope. This will require alertness in changing the records if the callers exchange teammates, envelopes, or cards.

The teams should be chosen in advance, though trading teammates may be permitted. One member of each team must have a car. The calls should be assigned, not spread out for the callers to pick over. Anyone who especially wants, or does not want, an assigned call may trade it, or trade the whole envelope, but this should not be encouraged. There may be a special team for a special sort of call—as on university students or on people with the same foreign background. When one more caller is needed, the Evangelism Chairman or the minister may be available to complete a team.

10. Instruct the Callers. A typical schedule has the callers come to the church at two o'clock on Sunday afternoon for an hour's training before they call. They return for supper at the church and another half-hour of instruction before their evening calls. This is repeated on succeeding evenings. The timing is close for callers who have to get back to the church after a Sunday morning service, or who come after a day's work for a six o'clock supper, so they must be urged to be prompt. If there is a late start, or if the instruction takes too long, precious calling time is lost. A call should usually not be started after 9:15 P.M. If the callers had to go to their homes for supper after a day's work, or after a Sunday afternoon calling, there would scarcely be enough time for instruction and calling. It saves time to commence the instruction while the visitors are finishing their supper, which need not be heavy. If the preparatory talk and discussion come from 6:30 to 7:00, and if the assignments are finished by 7:15, then some of the calls can commence by 7:30, which is about as early as doorbells should be rung.

In some rural churches, where distances are great, callers stay at the church after the Sunday service for lunch and a long period of preparation. They are given all of their assignments, and they and their partners arrange their own times for calling. They return the next Sunday to discuss their experiences and make their reports.

The basic training period can commence with an explanation of evangelistic calling, of what it can accomplish, and of why it is right. This is to convince and reassure. Those who might think of this as a routine task are shown that God can use them to bring measureless good to those on whom they call.

Next, the callers are given practical information about why they go in teams, the difference between *cultivation* and *decision* calls, and how to turn in their reports.

Then the leader goes through a typical call, step by step, giving advice for each stage. (The content of this comes in the next chapter.) There is danger of being too specific, as though David could fight Goliath in Saul's armor. Each one must call in his or her own way. There has to be room for a great deal of freedom and spontaneity. The callers cannot be given prepared speeches, but they can be told what it is likely will be said to them. There are common mistakes they can be warned against, and they can think in advance of how to move a call toward its great purpose.

Callers can ask the group for advice about problems they have met. Role-playing can be instructive and fun. The leader secretly tells two people what parts to play and in what circumstances; then two callers do their best, starting with the doorbell. The audience discusses what was good or bad. This is usually unrehearsed, but sometimes a call is planned in advance to dramatize mistakes or good calling. Large numbers of people can be put in groups of five, with two calling on two, and the fifth a critic. The parts change with each call.

Those at the training session may be asked to tell briefly what the Christian faith means to them, or why they are grateful to the church, or how they came to believe in Christ. This reminds everyone of the great purpose of what they are about to do. It helps them learn how to talk about important things naturally and well. It may supply quotations for those who can say during a call, "Why just this evening a friend of mine said. . . ." The consent of those who are asked for such testimonies should be had, but others may give spontaneous ones.

The callers can be advised about their continuing relationship with those they visit. Long-lasting friendships have been started by such calls. The callers may be able to introduce those they call on to church activities, to help them get a good start as new members, to give them help with some problem, or to get together with them again for more discussion. None of this is a caller's duty, but a desire to continue a connection can be encouraged. If people are to be called on again, it may or may not be well to send the same callers back. The callers are the best guides in this.

A short and earnest time of prayer closes the instruction period. The names of the teams are then read, and they come to a table to pick up their assignment envelopes. They look over their calls and try to find any uncertain addresses on the map. Leaders are available to give information about the people to be visited, or to answer other questions.

11. Get the Reports. There is great value in having the callers return to the church when they have finished, to discuss their advantures and make their reports. They enjoy telling about interesting experiences while the excitement is still fresh. They ask what they should have done in unforeseen situations. Any who had a disappointing time can be cheered up by the good experiences of others.

Sometimes it is too difficult to reassemble the callers. The last calls may be miles from the church, with more miles to get home. Some may finish a considerable time before others do. There can be some discussion of what happened the next time the callers assemble, but the dramatic interest in experiences that are still fresh, and what is learned from them, are worth a good deal of inconvenience. Many of the callers will have to come back to the church anyway, because the partners' cars were left there. If there is to be more calling within a week, the reports have to be in soon so that unmade calls can be reassigned. As a compromise, all for whom it would not be very inconvenient can be urged to return for a report meeting. The others can make a preliminary report by telephone.

The callers should report in writing, on the cards or on supplementary sheets, everything of importance to the church that they learned from each call. Any need for immediate attention should be underlined. The caller's recommendations for future action are important.

The evangelism leaders go through the reports without delay. The names of any who have decided to join the church are listed for immediate attention. The cards for calls that were not made are put with those that are ready for assignment, noting any which the same visitor wants to try again. Important information and recommendations are copied from the reports onto the permanent cards in the evangelism file, with the names of the callers.

The question of whether or how soon to go back to the same homes is often difficult. The callers should make recommendations about this. As long as calls are welcome and are making progress, they can be repeated. When people make it plain that they are not interested, or that they are receptive only from politeness, something else must be tried. The church may be able to attract their interest in some other way. We believe there are no hopeless cases. A development in someone's life may bring a turning to faith that just before would have seemed impossible. But it does not seem practical to keep sending callers back to where they are not wanted. A church will probably do more good for more people if it goes first to those who seem most receptive.

A church should not have a "Hopeless" section in its file, but it may have to have a section labelled "Not Much Chance."

12. Continue Calling. Special programs of lay evangelistic calling have great value. They give a chance to recruit and train new visitors. They keep a congregation intent upon evangelism. A church that has limited chances for new contacts may not be able to have such a program more than once a year. New churches in growing communities may have them every month. Many churches have calling programs before Thanksgiving, Christmas, and Easter. There is usually a New Member Class soon after a calling program.

Experienced callers do not have to be retrained every time there is a calling program, but they do need to be reinspired. New callers go out apprehensive and knowing how much they need God's help; they are likely to come back thrilled by what has happened. But when they go out repeatedly, that may fade. They may begin to think of this as just a task they can do well. A Catholic priest once wrote: "Never count your converts; you will come to think that you have made them." Preachers find out that when they say on Saturday night, "I'm going to ring the bell tomorrow," that is a day when no bells ring. Evangelistic callers need to be repeatedly reminded of the infinite importance of what they are trying to do, and of the impossibility of doing it without God's help. A quick review of the basic instructions and a renewal of their awe are what experienced callers need.

Churches need some way of making calls between the special programs. Someone who seems ready to make a decision in the spring should not be ignored until the fall. There may be veteran visitors who can be asked to make a call any time. Some churches have a calling organization that meets monthly to make *Contact, Cultivation,* and *Decision* calls. It usually has an interesting name like "The Seventy," or "Saint Andrew's Fellowship," or "The Fishermen's Club."

Callers who have gained experience in evangelistic conversations should be urged to seek out their own opportunities. There are many openings in ordinary social contacts if we are looking for them. Any shocking news or apprehension about what this world is coming to gives us a chance to speak of what we can count on. It is as easy to refer to your enthusiasm for your church as to any other hobby. There is no great benefit in praising a church, but mention of the church leads readily to a reference to something the church does and why it is important. Telling about a book that one has been reading can turn a conversation to the most important subjects.

Dwight L. Moody was so grateful for what God had done for him that he promised he would never let a day go by without trying to help someone else have it too. Sometimes this made difficulties. One night he was in bed when he remembered that his promise had not been kept. He dressed and went to the door and found the rain was pouring down. A solitary figure was going by. Moody got drenched getting to the street, where he asked the man, "May I share the shelter of your umbrella?" As they walked on, Moody smiled at his companion and said, "Have you any shelter in the time of storm?" Then he told the man what his shelter was. There is no limit to what a self-directed evangelist can do.

11

Instructions for
Evangelistic Callers

Evangelistic callers need training because they do better when they know how. The skills they need do not come just from goodness and common sense. They are dealing with the most sensitive areas of human lives. Their success can bring the greatest blessings life can know. But if they blunder, they can do spiritual damage. The only reason they have the courage to try is their knowledge that the only thing worse than doing evangelism poorly is not doing it at all. But they can be warned against the common mistakes that evangelistic callers make. And they can be given the accumulated wisdom that comes from much experience.

Let us think of a call, step by step:

1. Pray. There is something ridiculous about evangelistic calling. An artist could make a hilarious picture by drawing two typical evangelistic callers sitting on someone's sofa, with the picture entitled "The Soul Savers." The only thing that keeps us from laughing ourselves off the scene is our knowledge that apparently impossible things do happen. The promises turn out to be literally true. Jesus told his disciples that in a time of need, "It is not you who speak, but the Holy Spirit" (Mark. 13:11). He said, "I myself will give you power of utterance" (Luke 21:15, NEB). The results of our blundering efforts show that such promises are extended also to us. Jesus said, "You shall receive power when the Holy Spirit has come upon you; and you shall be my witnesses" (Acts 1:8). The Bible's two conditions for receiving that power are to have a use for it, and to ask for it. The power of the Holy Spirit is not given just so we can enjoy our private raptures, but because of something important that we are trying to do. And it is given only to those who know they have to have it. Callers are sent out from the church with prayer. They can pray together before they start their calling. They can be praying silently as they drive to the first house. It also helps to have other people praying for the calls. We do not have to be mystics to feel the difference that prayer makes. There is likely to be a warmth, a confidence, and an earnestness that are lacking when we do not pray.

2. Read the Assignment Card. Get all possible information about the people freshly in mind before ringing the doorbell; then put the card out of sight.

3. Pick the Leader. One caller needs to be designated to make the introductions and start the conversation. It may be the one who has had more experience or who knows the people they are visiting, or they may take turns. A caller who is not leading takes a lively part but does not guide the direction the call takes.

Sometimes a person will start a separate conversation with a caller. There should be a polite response; then the conversations should be merged. Two conversations at the same time make the call fall apart.

4. Get In. As soon as the door is opened, the leader makes the introductions and tells in general who they are: "We are from Grace Church, and we hoped we would find you at home." Sometimes people hesitate to bring strangers immediately into the house, so the caller may have to add, "We would like to come in, if it's convenient." A satisfying call cannot be had at the door. Trying to talk there will do little good, but it may go far enough to leave no reason for a real call.

If people give a reluctant invitation because they seem to prefer not to be bothered, the callers can go in. We all prefer at first to keep on with what we were doing. The mood can soon become a great deal brighter. If someone says, "You're going to find the house a mess," the visitors can laugh and go right in. But if the response is, "We were on the way to the theater, but we would much rather talk to you," or "We were just starting dinner, do come in," the visitors know they have to leave. If there is company, a good call is unlikely. If the company says, "We were about to leave," let them. If the invitation is, "Come in, I wish my wife (husband) were at home," the visitors have to decide whether they want to make a partial call. If they hoped to see the couple, they may be wise to postpone the visit. If they do not come in, they try to set a date to return. Then, when they come back, they will be off to a good start because they were considerate.

5. Get A Good Situation. Try to sit where you can talk easily with everyone. If someone you also wish to see is not in the room, say something like, "We hoped to see Janet too, if she's at home."

An audible or visible television program makes a good call impossible. Even well-mannered people may be so used to its continual playing that they leave the set turned on. If children are watching it, the visitor may say, "We don't want to spoil their program. Can't we go into the next room to talk?" If it is near the end of a period, the visitor may ask, "Don't you want to see the rest of this program? We can talk when it's over." That calls attention to the program, and suggests a time for turning off the set. A visitor may say, "I didn't catch what you were saying; do you mind if the volume is turned down?" Or the visitor may lower his or her voice so people have to turn the set off in order to hear.

6. Establish a Friendly Connection. Evidence of a personal interest is helpful, especially if it is complimentary: "Your son's developing into quite a track star." "Didn't you use to live in Eldon?" "How did you get such a good lawn?" "I think you know my friend."

7. Get Soon To Your Real Purpose. There is a tendency to linger on small talk, sometimes out of nervousness; but important matters should not be delayed. The people you are visiting are curious to know why you have come. It is well to start by mentioning the connection with the church—children in the church school, attendance at church services, helping in

the nursery. This can lead to saying, ". . . and so we thought
we would like to talk to you about the church."

8. Ask Questions. There are several reasons why visitors need
to ask questions: (1) It shows a personal interest. (2) The visitors
have to have information. Until they know about the church
background and religious attitudes, they are groping. (3) Questions get people to talk. Those who did not expect the visit may
not have much to say, so the prepared visitors may do all the
talking. But unless there is a real sharing of thought and feelings,
the visit cannot be a good one. (4) People make more progress
in their thinking when they talk than when they listen. They talk
themselves into what is right better than they can be talked into
it. So progressive questions can help them think their way
through to what they want to do. Big decisions are often difficult
to get to at one leap. The thought might move on through questions like these: "Were you married by a minister?" "Don't you
find, as I do, that we have to have ways of keeping religion
important in our homes?" "Could our church help you with
that?" "Wouldn't it be a great thing for your whole family, and
for you, if you were to confess your faith in Christ and join a
church?"

Of course, in a real conversation, questions would not be that
sudden. Callers need to ask questions at the start; then more
questions come when they are natural, not in strings. It is not like
a cross-examination, but like wanting to get better acquainted
with someone you enjoy, or asking for the opinions of someone
you respect. An obvious question, such as "Don't we need God
in our marriages?", can sound condescending.

9. Talk About God. Some of us have been slow to learn that
you cannot run a church without religion, and you cannot have
Christian evangelism without Christ. We try. We tell people they
ought to join the church for their children's benefit, or to keep
this a Christian nation, or because a community would be a sorry
place without churches. We speak of the fine people one meets,
the popular minister, and the lovely building. None of this seems
to have much pulling power.

I am perpetually torn between two astonishments—I cannot

see why anyone ever comes to a church, and I cannot see how anyone can stay away. You can have better sermons on your bookshelves and better music on your record player. Church fellowship is pleasant, but there are better-managed clubs. The church's education program is amateurish, its movies flicker, its library is pathetic. The world can outbid the church in everything it offers except its one specialty. But if that specialty is authentic, if people can actually get the divine presence and power that God has promised through his Church—why does everyone not come for it? Right here is the make or break point for lay calling. If it can tell of God and his promises, it can be tremendously worthwhile; if it cannot, little will be accomplished.

It is easy for their leaders to underestimate how difficult it is for most callers to talk of what is spiritual. They hear all the good instructions, but in actual conversation they may find it impossible even to say the words *Jesus Christ.* Some church members love above all to talk of Christ, and they do it beautifully. But there are not enough of them to take care of evangelism. How do you sit on someone's tufted divan and talk about what the Holy Spirit does?

There is a strange difficulty. It is hard to talk about Jesus because there is so much to say. We cannot just chat about him. Justin Martyr was beheaded for his Christian faith in 166 A.D. At his trial, the Roman Judge asked him, because of his fame as a philosopher, to explain the mystery of Christ. Justin answered, "I am too little to say something great of him." So he missed an incomparable chance to witness to the Lord because he had so much to say. My former roommate asked me, some years after our graduation, to be in his wedding. When I met the bride, I was just overwhelmed. She seemed to me ideal in every way. After the rehearsal, my friend and I were left alone. I knew this was the time for me to say something complimentary about the bride. If I had been less impressed, I could have been eloquent. But everything I could think of seemed as crudely inadequate as "She sure is swell," so I said nothing, and the evening ended rather awkwardly. Our adoration of Christ may make it difficult to speak of him. But if Christians could not overcome this difficulty, there would have been no Christians after the first century.

We can hope that callers will get to where they do not have to be told how to get a conversation easily and naturally to the Christian faith, but at first most of them will need suggestions:

(a) *Church.* Callers can start by talking about the church. A familiar instruction is: "Make your calls Christ-centered, not church-centered." That is right for the whole call, but not necessarily for the start. A caller's enthusiastic comment on something that takes place at the church—a Lenten class on prayer, a human-relations action group, a special service, a study group for parents—can lead immediately to talking about the reason for it or the good it does. There is no use talking about what a great preacher you have, but if you quote something he said, you can be right on the most important subject.

(b) *Questions.* A good way to get straight into matters of belief is to tell about the questions that are asked of those who join. A caller can say, "I wish some time you could be a member of our church. Do you want to know what they ask those who join?" That will usually get an affirmative reply, so the caller goes on, "The first question is, 'Do you believe in God, the heavenly Father, who is revealed to us in Jesus Christ?' You could say that, couldn't you?" If the answer is yes, the caller goes on to the next question. If the answer is "I don't know. What do you mean by that?", the caller is right on the most important things he has to talk about. Going on through the questions and promises will get to most of the essentials, and the caller in commenting on them has a completely natural way to talk about the Christian faith.

(c) *Jesus.* Simply speaking the word *Jesus* or *Christ* can change the atmosphere from social to spiritual. To say no more than "The children learn about Christ" can make the room seem different. Even non-Christians have a regard for Jesus that makes the mention of his name bring a feeling of seriousness, or even reverence.

(d) *Experience.* Speaking of a personal experience is a convincing way of telling what God can do. When we are trying to get a verdict in Christ's favor, we are not all equipped to be his defense lawyers, giving the arguments for faith; that may be a task for theologians. But we are all able to be his defense witnesses, telling what we know about him. A brief account of some experience in your life that made Christ real is the most effective evidence. You can say, in answer to some obstacle, "You know, I used to feel like that until something happened that completely changed my mind. Let me tell you about it."

A caller who is too reticent to talk about himself can tell about what Christ has done for someone else.

(e) Bible. Callers may count on the Bible to let them say things that they hesitate to say on their own authority. Some of the Bible's statements about sin, redemption, God's promises, and the need to profess Christ are what the evangelist wants to say; but to give them as our own opinions invites argument. Reciting a series of memorized verses or reading from a pocket Testament may not be effective. The people we talk with may not pay much attention to the Bible. But it is more impressive than we are. We can quote something deeply spiritual from the Bible with less embarrassment than we might feel in presenting it as our own thought: "You know, I always remember what the Bible says about that. . ."

(f) Plan. Callers can improve their methods by thinking in advance of how they might get into spiritual subjects, or by thinking afterwards of how they might have done that better. At their meetings they can tell each other what they have said. They can ask, "How would you have put it?"

10. Avoid These Mistakes:

(a) Tension. There are reasons for evangelistic callers to be on edge. They are frightened by the gravity of what they are attempting. They are intensely anxious to succeed. They may be embarrassed at talking about a very personal matter, or ill at ease with strangers. They fear the hazards of an unfamiliar task. Their apprehension may have mounted until, when the conversation starts, it is almost unbearable. But tension is contagious. The more uncomfortable the callers are, the more uncomfortable they make the people they are calling on. To have everybody ill at ease is a heavy handicap.

166 The Church As Evangelist

Telling callers to relax may seem like the stewardess telling the passengers that if something dreadful happens to the plane, they are to "breathe normally." But there are reassurances. An unfriendly reception is almost unheard of. People are impressed when someone else takes that much trouble for them. Very few feel that an interest in their religious welfare is meddling. New callers usually come back vastly relieved and delighted. Those who are shy never get over their anxiety, but they come to look forward to calling as one of their happiest experiences. Prayer relaxes tensions and relieves inhibitions. And William James's principle that outer bearing affects inner feeling applies here; if the callers act as though they are feeling relaxed and having a good time, they can be—and so can the people they are calling on.

Anyone who is tied in knots at the thought of having to do what is unnatural can be relieved to know that a rule for all evangelism is: *Never do anything awkwardly pious because you think you are supposed to.* Preachers should not give altar calls that do not feel right. Workers do not offer to pray with someone unless they really want to. And callers do not have to force themselves to say anything that keeps them from being themselves. But the rest of the rule is: *Keep pushing out your limits.* God exists, and it is natural to talk about him; it is only our not doing it that makes us clumsy. So if there is something good we wish we could do, we do not give up and say, "I guess I'm not the type." We keep coming closer by trying until we can do naturally what would once have seemed impossible.

(b) Asking too soon for a decision. If the callers say soon after they arrive, "Do you want to join our church?", there is a good chance that the answer will be no. Once a negative decision has been expressed, it is a roadblock. People do not like to reverse themselves. Callers should wait until they have had time to make some progress toward a favorable decision before they ask the big question about faith in Christ and Church membership.

(c) Argument. Argument is conflict. The opponents dig in their heels and pull against each other. Each thinks of more reasons why the other one is wrong. A flat contradiction makes agree-

ment too humiliating. We do not get people to come with us by pulling against them, but by walking beside them. We try to find some point where agreement is possible, and then go on from there together. If someone says, "I worship God by the lakes and in the mountains," the best answer is not "But probably not very often!" It might better be: "So did Jesus. That's good Christianity." Then you two nature lovers may later agree that the God you worship out-of-doors has to be learned about somewhere else. When there is an irreconcilable difference, do not belabor it. Change the subject to one on which you can agree.

(d) Talking too much. Callers may be so full of good things to say that the listeners are not convinced, but only benumbed by the battering with words. The callers have important things to convey, of course. They may be entitled to half the time. But it is conversation, not being talked *at,* that is convincing.

(e) Unnecessary subjects. If people want to talk about where Cain got his wife, faith healers, the salvation of the heathen, or Church union, a caller can say, "Christians need to look for more light on those questions. But the first thing we have to decide is what we think of Christ."

(f) Changing the subject. An evangelistic call tries to make progress toward its goal. Wandering off on other subjects wastes time and throws away the progress. Interest is cooled by interruptions. The people who are being called on are not as aware as the visitors are of the purpose of the call, and they may jump to unrelated subjects. Those who have been running away from what they know they ought to do may prefer another topic. The visitors have to show a polite interest in the new subject, but as soon as possible they should get back to what they came to talk about. Unwary visitors may make problems for themselves. Talking about church worship may prompt a question about where a couple spend their summer weekends, which leads ineluctably to a half-hour description of their cabin and water sports. Careless teammates derail each others' conversations.

11. Ask for a Decision. The purpose of a *Decision* call is to offer a definite way of making a profession of faith and joining the church. As we have seen, a life depends on its key decisions, and it is the business of a church to offer opportunities for such decisions to be made. A decision needs to be definite and openly expressed. If a call were to bring only a general statement of belief in Christ, most of its value would be lost. Unless intentions are fixed by something tangible, they tend to drift away. The visitors hope that, before they leave, something will be said and done that marks a turning point. This can be one of those landmarks by which a life forever after finds its course. It is psychologically damaging to talk about the possibility of a great decision without offering an opportunity for a definite decision to be made. That simply confirms the habit of indecision. It is the sin of sermons that stir hearers to great intentions without proposing what is to be done about them. Callers must be able to offer definite proposals. "Our New Member Class is starting a week from Sunday. Can we count upon your being there?" "Our church is receiving members the first Sunday of next month. Can we ask our minister to call to arrange for your reception?" "Would you tell us where we could write for your certificate of transfer?" (See pp. 121–124.)

It helps to make matters definite if the callers ask for permission to write down a record that the decision has been made. This will be even more definite if those who make the decision write down their own record. Many churches use cards for this purpose. Such a card usually has just two or three brief statements: "I accept Jesus Christ as my Lord and Savior," "I intend with his help to lead a Christian life"; and "I desire to unite with the (Name) Church." A request to sign a card might seem inappropriate. It is presented, however, not in terms of signing up, but of accepting a faith. Putting one's name to something—a Mayflower Compact, a Declaration of Independence, a marriage certificate—can be deeply significant. A name is symbolic. A person who is hesitating over whether to put down his or her name to express an attachment to Jesus Christ and to his Church knows that something of great spiritual meaning is in the balance.

There are practical reasons for a written record. It leaves no doubt of the expression of faith in Christ or of what the intentions are. The written statement gives a focus for the conversation.

The caller can read the statement and ask, "Is that not what you want to say?" If the answer is yes, the next question is: "Don't you want to write your name there?" If the answer is hesitant, the card is a visible sign of what the issue is. When the caller has read the statement, he usually hands the card to the other person, and if there is no clear decision, he does not immediately take it back. The person who is holding the card is still considering what to do with it, and this makes the purpose of the continuing conversation very definite. For a person who has been postponing a definite decision, the card ends the vagueness by making *now* the time and *this* the way by which either acceptance or rejection must be faced.

The use of a card is not essential. A decision can be made definite in other ways. When it has been given verbally, the visitor can reach out with a warm handclasp to express great happiness. That act can make the turning point tangibly real. If there is a mutual friend, the visitor can ask, "Do you mind if I tell . . . what you have decided?"

A decision cannot be hurried. It is too important for that. People need to deliberate before they take so great a step. There can be more talk about what the decision means. Additional reasons for making it can be introduced. The talking can go on for as long as it is welcome. But the instant there is the slightest sense of pressure or overurging, the trying has to stop. A decision might be forced by insistence, but it should not be. Most people will rightly resent the attempt.

The callers have to know that what they are up against is not rejection of Christ, but postponement of him (see pp. 127–128.) "Men have excluded God from their lives, not by decision, but by indecision." We have seen how human beings flee from God's pursuit when they say, "Not now," and keep on saying it. They do not admit to themselves what they are doing, and the excuses they give the visitors sound so plausible: "I've always thought I liked the Quakers. I want to get that settled first." "There is talk of a merger in our company; I'd better wait to see where I'll be living." "My father's not been well. We'd better wait till things are not so upset." To accept these excuses too soon can be a mistake. A postponement now will make the next one easier. The habit of indecision grows harder to break with each repetition. The callers have to receive what is said respectfully, but they do not have to give up immediately. They can say: "Isn't every day you wait losing something good you want to have?" "Wouldn't it have been better for you if you had done it a long while ago?" "I think this is something God wants you to do." "If you settle this tonight, you'll be glad tomorrow that you did." "Your friends at the church are all hoping you will do this."

Often people will say, "We are not ready to make up our minds right now, but if you'll leave the cards, we'll let you know." That has to be recognized as a polite way of saying no without being too abrupt. The cards might as well be left; the visitors may say, "Can we see you (or phone you) about this?" But almost never does such a postponement end in a decision.

Callers often think that the minister can bring people who are so close to a decision to make it. They will tell him, "If you talk to them, I know they will say yes." That is unlikely. Ministers are rarely as effective as lay callers. The lay caller is supposed to do the whole thing if he possibly can, without counting on the minister to finish it.

Evangelistic visitors do not work for a congregation, but for Christ's Church. If it appears that there is some other congregation that might serve people better, a decision for it should be sought. If people say that they are thinking of joining some other church, that church should immediately receive the information. Or the visitors can say that what they greatly hope for is the decision; if it is made, they will be glad to give it to whichever church is preferred.

Sometimes it is easier to win a family than to win one person. Their happiness in being together in a church is an inducement. At the start of a call, the visitors should try to bring into the room everyone in the family who might become a member of the church. They should address the first appeal for a decision to whichever adult seems most likely to decide.

Callers rejoice when people decide to confess their faith and join the church, but calls when there has been no decision are usually very worthwhile too. We do not know what is in other people's hearts. We have to believe that whatever they decide to do, or not to do, may be right for them. Callers who have been received into a home and given a chance to speak a good word for Christ and his Church should be happy. They can hope that their call has moved people closer to faith and given them a favorable impression of Christians and the Church. After the call is over, the caller can still pray about it.

12. Tell What Happens Next. The visitors should be able to explain the process that leads to church membership, and to give the dates for the classes and reception. They should know the ways of joining for those who have never belonged to a church, those who come from another church without a certificate, those who come with a certificate, and former members of a church who are not now on any roll.

When people are not going to join the church, the visitors should try to plan ways the church can serve them. They may be able to make dates to introduce them to organizations or classes. They may offer to take them to some meeting, or to get their children into church activities.

13. Leave. When a decision has been made, or declined, the call should soon be ended. Continued social visiting after a call has left its main subject is usually a mistake. The callers do not need to grope for a graceful way to taper off; they simply rise. After that, everything slopes toward a conclusion. Sometimes it seems clear early in the call that not much will be accomplished. The people do not seem interested or have much to say. It is usually unwise to keep struggling. The callers leave as pleasant an impression as they can, give a cordial invitation to church participation, and leave.

Visitors may misread a situation. In a home where a couple had looked glum and answered in monosyllables, as the callers were leaving, the husband suddenly said: "You may think we seem strange. When you came we were having a real quarrel. We have about decided to separate. It might do us good to talk to you about our problem." The wife agreed, and the callers stayed. The couple eventually became members of the church.

Often there is a prayer before the callers leave. It depends on the callers and the situation. Some people can ask for a blessing on a home as easily as they would ask for a blessing at the table. Others would be too ill at ease. When something important has happened, and everyone is feeling deeply moved and happy, it would seem incomplete just to say goodbye and go on out. A caller can say, "This has been a great evening. Let's thank God for it." A conversation in which people have talked earnestly about Jesus Christ and what he means for life can make a prayer seem right. By prearrangement, one visitor can say to the other, "How about your offering a prayer before we go?" No one needs to pray just because the occasion is supposed to call for it. But when it seems right, the prayer can be the high point of the call. It is often surprising to find how grateful people are for it. It may be offered at the door.

14. Make Your Report. Write legibly on the assignment card everything you learned that will be useful in future contacts with the people you have seen. Put it down soon, because recollections quickly fade. Add your recommendations. Try also to make a verbal report to the pastor or chairman. Call special attention to those who are going to join the church. Turn in at once any unused assignment cards.

ANSWERING OBJECTIONS

Most of those who hesitate to join the church will give one of a dozen or so of the most familiar reasons. If the callers have thought about these in advance, they will be prepared for a majority of the negative replies. The instructor can go over these and make suggestions about what to say. What the callers actually do say will depend on their personalities, and on how the conversations develop.

Callers have to assume that people believe the replies they give. Sometimes an excuse will seem so thin that it is hard to take it seriously, but people may have given inadequate reasons to themselves for so long that they believe them. Something that seems frivolous to a church member may look important to someone who has no background in a church.

Often it is best not to say much about these replies. The caller encourages the person to get it said, and may restate it thoughtfully or add a word or two of comment, and then goes on to other things. The real problem may be something else. Or if a strong motive for joining the church can be given, the problem may be no obstacle. Prolonged argument is never useful. The suggestions given here are for those times when the difficulty is a real barrier. In many cases a briefer response is better.

People may be kept from the Church by worldliness or bad habits, or by resisting God—but often the reason is not anything that could so readily be identified with sin. They may just not want to get involved. Most Americans are already overorganized; they shrink from joining something else. Some who think of themselves as followers of Christ may not enjoy group activities. Callers may forget how much they are asking for. The promise to be a faithful member would require a minimum of 156 hours for the church each year, including going and coming, or 1,560 hours for each remaining decade. The expected giving of money and work may look massive. People with a strong religious feeling will not be deterred, but those whose church interest has never been lively can find all sorts of reasons for not taking on church obligations. The callers may be sure that what they are asking for is God's will, but working against them is a great deal of not necessarily very evil human nature. They can believe that those who decline are missing immeasurable good, and still sympathize with their reasons. The marvel that keeps callers going is their knowledge that, with all the obvious reasons against it, people still join the Church. If commonsense advantages were all that need be considered, the Church would have disappeared long ago.

1. Practical Difficulties.

"We do not know how long we'll be here." Ask, "How long have you been here?" If it has been a considerable time, the humor of the situation may take care of this problem. The visitors can point out that a transfer does not change Church membership, which is in the great Church of Jesus Christ, but it changes only the record of local church participation, which should match the facts. The local connection can be changed as easily as the children's

schools or the family's bank account. One's present hometown should also be the church address. Americans are on the move, and if they did not readily transfer, they would spend too much of their lives with no real church home. Most of those who maintain the church, and are maintained by the church, are not long-time residents, they are a procession.

What should be provided for is not the possibility of moving but the possibility of staying. If the stay could last as long as a year, the membership should be transferred. If the time turns out to be less than that, the membership can be moved again with no great trouble to anyone. A church that has been left does not like to keep meaningless names on its roll. Rapid transfers are a sign of taking the church seriously; it is delay that seems neglectful. People who defer transferring are in the impossible situation of being church members without being members of a church. Church membership is like a fern: the longer the roots are in the air, the less chance there is of a successful transplant. Habits of church neglect soon become established.

"We haven't decided yet which church to join." Ask what is needed in order for the decision to be made. Offer to help get the membership transferred to some other church. The visitors can tell why they like their church and describe also the advantages of other congregations. Later send the information to any other church that is being considered.

"I could not bear to leave the dear old church." If it actually has been left, leaving a name on the roll does not change the fact. It is no favor to the old church to clutter up its roll, and it may cost it a denominational per-member assessment. People need to see that they will be closer to the old church if they are members somewhere than if they are in midair. If they are inactive members, they are evidence that the old church failed with them. If someone says, "I love that dear old church so much I want to be buried there," an accurate, though not very tactful, answer could be: "You already are."

Family tradition may interfere: "It would break my parents' hearts if I left their church (or denomination)." When people marry, the center of their loyalty moves from their parents' home to their new one. Most parents would rather have their children active in another church than without a real church home. Our religious decisions cannot be made by the sentiments of another generation.

"There is no use in my joining a church, because I cannot attend." Here the callers have to guess whether attendance really is impossible. If it is, then they can tell the people about the many other reasons for belonging to a church. Their membership lets their faith be known. It enrolls them among the followers of Christ, where they belong. It gives them a home. The church has much besides Sunday morning services. An invalid or a person with Sunday employment should be encouraged to join the Church.

But sometimes the problem is not really the possibility but the priority. There are other things people would rather do. With these the talk should be about the advantages of faithful participation. Those who say that they need their Sundays for rest can be told of the renewal and peace that come from worship. We must avoid the temptation to say, "What you do as a member is a matter for your conscience, the church does not dictate." If people start with a low view of what church membership is, the stream may never rise above its source. People are not helped by being given what is not real Church membership. A man who is prominent in the community told a minister I know, "I have decided I want to be part of an organization that does as much good as the church does, and I intend to make a substantial contribution. I should tell you, though, that I am not a churchgoer." My friend answered, "We will be happy to take your money into the church any time, but we can't take you unless you are going to be a real member."

"I can't join because I can't afford to contribute." Here again, the callers have to guess whether the person cannot or does not want to. A hard financial situation may rightly prevent a normal contribution. The callers must allow for this possibility by pointing out that the church is one organization with no fixed dues. Contributions are not published, and the person who gives the least is as honored as the largest donor. But they must also explain that a church's existence and how much it does depend upon its mem-

bers giving. Those who claim to put Christ first, but who spend their money largely on themselves, are not consistent Christians. The way we apportion what we have shows what we actually believe is most important; our real confession of faith is written in our checkbook stubs. Consecration has to be expressed by giving. Callers should explain the principle of "according to his financial prosperity" (1 Cor. 16:2, PHILLIPS). They cannot encourage the ungenerous to think that they are dedicated followers of Christ.

"I am waiting for my husband (wife) to join." It is natural to think that the other person is more likely to join if they both come together, but experience shows it does not work that way. A person who has an attachment to a church is more likely to draw the spouse into it than is one who is also unconnected. When either is a member, they are more likely to be making church friends and getting into church activities. Moreover, each person has to take care of his or her own spiritual life and Christian responsibilities.

"We were so busy at our last church that we want to take a rest." This reason may be true. It is heard from the sort of people who hate to say no to any worthy request for help, so their church work may have become too burdensome. When they settle in a new community, they enjoy a blessed relief from running to all the church engagements, and they shrink from ending it. The callers may compliment the people for having been such good church members, and also reassure them. A church would be remiss if it did not offer opportunities for service, and it would collapse if its members did not share its work. But each member is trusted to decide which church activities and work to undertake. The church will keep asking, as it should, but there is no reflection on those who know they should not take on more. A Christian's obligation to support the Church is not escaped by keeping one's name off any active roll.

The pleasures of visiting various churches do not supply what Christians need. It is like a delectable diet from which the essential nutrients are missing. Church duties are blessings. We come to know Christ and feel his presence as we do his work. Those who get without giving go stale.

People who do not join should be assured that the church welcomes them to all it does. But as long as they remain unattached, they will feel like tourists. The church cannot make them feel at home until they really are.

2. Self-Doubt.

"I do not know enough." This may be true. Perhaps the callers are asking for a decision when what is needed is a *Cultivation* call. They cannot explain the Christian faith in one call. Lay evangelistic callers should go only to those who already know what Christians must believe and what it means to join the Church. If a little conversation reveals that people need to know more, then the callers try to plan with them how they can learn about Christ and Christian living. If they are not interested, there is no way, at the time, to go ahead.

But there may be an exaggerated idea of how much Church members ought to know. A person can rightly accept Christ as Lord and still be ignorant of much Christian truth. People can be told that it is only the basic faith that is required of those who join the church. Then they spend the rest of their lives inside the Church learning more of what they need to know.

The best way to work this out is to go over the questions that are asked of those who join. The callers will know, at least in general, what they are. If there is enough understanding of what the words mean, paraphrased in ordinary terms, then the people need not feel unready.

"I have too many doubts." There needs to be some talk about what these doubts are. Sometimes people think they cannot join the Church because they do not believe that Christ descended into hell, or because they cannot understand the Trinity. They can be told that they do not have to wait outside the Church until they can make up their minds about each doctrine. That is a lifetime occupation for Church members.

The callers may try to give help with some doubts, though there will not be time for much of this, nor is it necessary. It is more important to get to the positive side and think of what the person does believe. The grandeur of the affirmations may make the doubts seem less disquieting.

If there are doubts about the faith that is asked of those who join the Church, then there can be talk about what the statements mean. The most frequent problem is with the belief that Jesus is the Son of God (see pp. 125–127). It may help to put that faith in other terms: Is Jesus unlike any other human being? Is he present, and not just dead and gone? Did his death give blessings that no one else's ever could? Does your conception of what God is come from him?

The callers may be able to show that the doubts are not an obstacle. But if the problem remains, this is one of the few sorts of calls that the minister may be needed to supplement. The callers may offer to have him stop by.

"I am not good enough to call myself a Christian." The question here is: "Do you want to be good enough?" The businessman who knows his practices are unethical, and who has no intention of changing them, should not be encouraged to give Christ an only partial obedience. The person who will not try to give up what he knows is wrong should not be told, "The Church is for sinners." The Church *is* for sinners, but only for sinners who want to be good. The person can be told: "You are honest with yourself, and you know you ought to give up what you are doing; that is the first great step. You cannot be happy when you are leading a divided life. It will be a great day when you decide to do what God wants you to do."

The problem may be something that the Church is supposed to consider sinful, but the person thinks is all right. If the callers see it as clearly and flagrantly wrong, they may try to explain why the Church takes it so seriously. But if it is a matter on which consciences may well differ, then it is one of the "unnecessary subjects" that callers should avoid (see p. 167). The caller can say: "You may hear that criticized in church. The church is a teacher, and teachers have to take positions. But if you believe you can do that with no disloyalty to Christ, and that it does not hurt you or anybody else, then it will not keep you from being a member of the Church. The Church permits anything that Christ permits."

It may be that a person wants to change but feels unable to. The problem might be alcohol, drugs, hatred, or an ugly temper. Bad habits may seem unshakeable. Honest people may feel that they cannot promise to do what is right when they may not be able to keep the promise. Such people need to know that the Church is the only organization in the world where feeling unqualified is the first requirement for membership. A person who felt that he or she was good enough to join the Church would not be eligible. We have to trust in Christ for help. We join the Church in order to get the power to live as we should.

3. Criticisms of the Church.

"You don't have to join a church to be a Christian" (see pp. 11 15–16, and 69–71), or *"Church members are no better Christians than nonmembers are."* There are no statistics on the comparative virtue of members and nonmembers, so it will be better to pass up debate on the truth of that statement and get straight to the real question it raises, which is: "Could the church help you to be a better person?" A caller can begin with his own testimony: "I am one of those church members who has a lot wrong with him, but I know I'm a million times better than I could ever be without the church." He may tell what the church does that helps him to be better, and why he wants his children to have its guidance and ideals. He may speak of how, in a world which threatens to crush our souls by material pressures, the church gives us spiritual experiences and reminders of religious truth. We need its calls to duty and service and its regular prompting to what God wants us to be.

Christ calls sinners into his Church, and they bring with them all their unpleasant human qualities; but as long as they are getting better, the Church is a success. A caller could say, "If Jesus will let you and me be in his church, we cannot expect too much of the members. Some of the most wonderful people you will ever know are what they are because of what they have gotten from the Church." The two practical questions to keep in view are: "Are you as good as you would like to be?" and "Could you be better with the church's help?"

"The church is too reactionary," or *"The church is too radical."* Some will declare they have no interest in joining an institution that is the bulwark of established privilege, the defender of the status quo, and the chief obstacle to social progress. At least an equal number will say they lost all respect for the Church when it ceased to be a religious institution and became a propaganda center for supporting criminals, Communists, and traitors. Perhaps a church is kept straight by being assaulted from all sides.

The callers may do well to give some brief information to those whose criticisms are based on hearsay, but the time will be better spent in telling what the Church is and does. It tries to help people understand their private and group problems in the light of the Christian faith. Every political and social question is at its deepest level a religious question whose answer depends on one's belief about God and man. Cities are factories where human beings are formed; schools and neighborhoods shape character. The Church has to care very much whether these are tooled and equipped to make the sort of persons God intends. Wars are fought for what is proclaimed to be holy, but war resisters declare that they speak for God. Racial restrictions institutionalize a doctrine of man. Churches fail their members if they do not expose public questions to examination from the Christian point of view. Churches do not dictate what their members think, but they have to help them think from the presuppositions of the Christian faith. The criticisms usually come when people do not hear in church what they already believe, but going to church to hear one's own opinions is not a profitable use of time. Hearing what you do not believe has two uses: it can show you that you were wrong, or it can make you think of better reasons for believing you were right. A Church could not be a Church if its ministers were not allowed to say things, or its officials to do things, which some of the members will regard as mistaken.

Most of this sort of criticism is directed at denominational, national, and world agencies that have little to do with the ordinary member's church life. It would be foolish to miss all the joys of a church home because of discontent with remote officials. Members can arrange to give their time and money only to the sort of church work they believe does good.

"My parents made me go to church, and I got too much of it." There may be reason to call attention to the logical absurdities of this. Many people have convinced themselves that a childhood rebellion keeps them from wanting or needing a church again. You may ask, "Isn't it time to undo the damage of being turned against something good?" or "Could you find out so young that no church anywhere could ever be of any use to you?" This excuse may cover up the real reason. Or the memory of adolescent conflicts that should now be outgrown may make a person try to get even with his parents by saying, "They even spoiled church for me." The best response may be to listen thoughtfully to the account of early bad experiences and then go on to other things. Those experiences will not be a barrier to anyone who can be brought to think seriously about his or her relationship with Christ and the need for what a church could give.

"I am already a Christian; I have no desire to be a denominationalist." People often point out that Christ never intended to have all the separate Churches, and if you join any of them you are contributing to the sin of schism. They can be told that the local church and the denomination are simply doors into the one timeless and worldwide Church of Jesus Christ. The reasons for separate Christian groups are not all bad. Geographical separation and language differences had much to do with it. Different convictions about what a Church should be sometimes make separate organizations necessary. The United States is populated by immigrants who brought with them all the diverse languages, nationalities, and belief groups of Christendom. Many of these groups have now united, and many of those that have not are essentially one Church with different names and administrations. They freely pass ministers, members, and literature among themselves. Roman Catholics, Orthodox Catholics, and Protestants are coming closer to each other all the time. The visitors can say: "We are not making our calls for our demonination, but for the great Church. If you join any Church, you are coming closer to them all. One does not become a better member of the human family by slighting his own home, and we become better members of Christ's Church when we have our own congregation."

"We found your church unfriendly." The callers can say: "No wonder that gave you a bad impression. I don't believe it was typical. Visitors often speak of how warm and friendly they find our church. It depends partly on whom you happen to run into, or the people near you may not have been members. Can I meet you at the church next Sunday? I think I can help you find out how cordial it really is."

"I don't like the minister." The callers can talk, first, about how much weight this should have and, second, about the minister. They can say that it would be a mistake to join a church because of the minister, who might soon be gone, and it would be a mistake to stay out because of him. The *ecce homo*, "Behold the Man," that draws people to a church does not refer to the preacher. The great benefits of church life are there for the members, whoever the minister may be. All human beings have virtues and failings. Church members love a minister for his good qualities and try to make up for what he lacks.

The callers can also say that when people really know their minister, they come to appreciate him. They can talk about good things the minister has done and of traits for which he is admired.

"After what happened in my last church, I decided I would never join a church again." It is well to find out, if possible, what that bad experience was. Describing it to a sympathetic listener may make it seem less grave. Perhaps a caller can show that it was highly exceptional, or can point out some mitigation.

Those who say they have been disillusioned can be shown that a church is a gymnasium where people are trained through ordeals to behave like Christians. The cantankerousness that makes human beings mistreat and offend each other is brought with them when they join a church. Bad things happen, but in a church they happen under the instruction of Christ's teaching and the guidance of his love. Not just by theory, but by practice within its walls, the church teaches us both to cure our own meanness and to deal with the faults of others.

One of the virtues that we must learn by practice in the church is forgiveness. The person can be told: "Your grievance is still rankling and interfering with your spiritual life. God will help you to forgive it, and that will bring a glorious sense of freedom. Your forgiving and becoming free again can be expressed by your getting back into a church."

12

Evangelistic Sermons

In all ages, preaching has been gloriously used to bring lives to Christ. There have been famed preachers to great crowds—Chrysostom, Savonarola, Wesley, Moody—but the most effective of all evangelistic preachers have been pastors in their churches. Public meetings are important, but our concern here is with a minister's use of his own pulpit for evangelism.

All the right methods of evangelism supplement each other. Preaching can finish what lay calling was not able to complete, and lay calling may bring to decision those who have been moved toward it by preaching. Preaching services can be powerful in youth evangelism. They can complete the good work that was commenced by Christian education.

Preaching offers some unmatched advantages. It can tell more than a conversation can, and tell it in a better planned, more stirring way. There is no other way for a minister in person to convey as much to so many people in so short a time. The setting for preaching enhances its effect. The assembled congregation is a witness to Christ. A belief that might seem fanciful in solitude becomes credible in a company of believers. In the midst of a praying, praising, singing congregation, cold hearts may be kindled by the feel of faith. We are both private and social beings, and there are some realities that can be apprehended only in fellowship. Christian love and the presence that Jesus promised when his followers are together can be known in church. The sermon is only one part of the evangelizing that can take place in a worship service. Those who are reached in a church will not have to make the readjustment to ordinary church life that sometimes is a problem for those who have been converted in the excitement of an exotic situation.

Some ministers do not attempt evangelistic preaching because they think they do not have the special abilities it requires. Or they might be affronted by the suggestion that they are the evangelistic type. But any competent preacher who longs to help people find what Christ can do for them can be an evangelist. The great evangelistic preachers have been as intellectual as Helmut Thielicke, or as calmly matter-of-fact as Bryan Green, or as consummate models of good taste as James Stewart, or as unpretentious as many an uncelebrated but warmhearted pastor.

Almost every subject that is proper for a sermon can be used for evangelism. Doctrinal preaching may reach those who are looking for answers to the urgent questions about themselves, and about God, and about the purpose of their lives. Sermons on personal morality may point those who are dissatisfied with what they are to the new life in Christ. Preaching on social problems can show how Christ and his teachings are the way out of the appalling social evils that keep mankind lurching through tyranny and injustice toward the disasters that loom ahead. Evangelistic preaching can deal with the healing of troubled souls that are distraught by such personal problems as fear, discouragement, family upsets, hatred, and boredom. Sermons on prayer, on the Bible, and on the other ways to know God may appeal to those who have an aching emptiness that only God can fill.

THE QUALITIES OF EVANGELISTIC SERMONS

Evangelistic sermons can use a wide variety of styles—logical, dramatic, expository, The preacher's manner may be that of an orator, a teacher, or a friend. Certain qualities, which all good preaching needs, are specially important for evangelism:

1. Relevance. A Scottish professor used to tell his classes: "Every sermon should begin in Jerusalem and end in Aberdeen, or begin in Aberdeen and end in Jerusalem." Many a Biblical sermon never gets to the congregation's daily needs at all. God's saving acts can be presented as a drama that is played out on a distant stage without touching real life at any point. P. T. Forsyth said, "The cure for dullness in the pulpit is not brilliance but reality." A sermon is real when it deals with the real people in the pews, with real situations they confront, and with the real needs they have. A preacher has to deal with abstractions—love, sin, grace, salvation—but the bare abstractions must be clothed in human flesh: sin is the hatred that a worker feels for a domineering boss; hope is what a person wonders about the night before his fiftieth birthday.

The best evangelistic preaching comes out of conversations. This saves the preacher from offering what nobody wants, and answering questions no one asks. The great preachers—Charles Spurgeon, F. W. Robertson, Phillips Brooks—were also tireless personal evangelists.

2. Personal Warmth. An evangelistic preacher asks the most personal of all questions: "What are you going to do with Jesus Christ?" It helps if there is the sense of a personal relationship, and not just a communication between a pulpit figure and a faceless unit in a crowd. Popular mass evangelists understand this well. They like to be known by their first names or, better, by their nicknames: "I want you to know that I've been praying for you. Won't you come down here tonight and take me by the hand? Right now you're saying, 'Chuck, I can't do that.' But I want to say to you, friend. . . ." Most settled ministers should not try to be that personal, but they do need to recognize the importance of being real persons, and not just transmitters of messages.

There are hazards in this. It lets the self-advertiser talk about his favorite subject. What he tells about himself is likely to reveal a truly noble soul. But if he can resist the temptation of the hero's role, he need not be shy about the pronoun "I." "I believe" puts the thought right in the room. "There is reason to believe" leaves it nowhere. The preacher's eyewitness evidence is more convincing than something he has read.

"You" turns the congregation into actors in the sermon drama that would otherwise have a faceless cast. The desiccated pronoun "one" and empty nouns like "people" are poor substitutes for living persons.

3. Clarity. Evangelistic preaching must be crystal clear. The hearers' minds are fully occupied with the greatest of all subjects. They have no attention to spare for puzzling out obscure wordings or complex lines of thought. The preacher has to go through the hard labor of translating the way he thinks and talks into what sounds simple. Jimmy Durante described the same process in preparing a television show: "We woik a munt fer eighteen hours a day to make it look unrehoised."

Christians may not understand that their familiar words—*covenant, redemption, grace*—can be meaningless to others. Sometimes it is not the terms but the conceptions that are incomprehensible —*union with Christ, the hand of God, come to Jesus.*

A mistaken idea of the dignity that is required for sacred themes may make sermons difficult. The artless, even breezy directness of clear preaching is more reverent than a propriety that is a barrier to God.

4. Interest. Evangelistic preaching is not directed to trained sermon fans who follow religious discourse avidly. It is for those who are not motivated to do the hard work of listening without immediate rewards. It requires more than the usual number of striking illustrations and arresting stories. These can also make the meaning clear to beginners who might be puzzled. Humor has important uses. It can expose human folly, make painful truth acceptable, unite the members of the congregation with each other and with the preacher as they laugh together, and relax the strain of listening. Listening to a serious discourse is hard work, and minds will periodically take a break. If they take their own breaks, they may miss something essential. But if the preacher puts in from time to time something that gives a breather, the audience will still be with him when they return together to the serious theme.

5. Emotion. Evangelism can be cheapened by sentimentality or discredited by abuse of the emotions. It has been associated with dangling terrified sinners over hell, or with ecstatic references to Christ's love and beauty that evoke a maudlin mysticism. But that is not the sin of most parish preachers. They tend to hide the emotions that they really feel and to deal with the most

moving subjects at arm's length. Congregations can remain emotionally starved. Preachers need to make people care intensely,
to rejoice over what is joyful, and to sorrow over what is sad. The
famous art critic Bernard Berenson said that the purpose of art
is to make us feel with an intensity of 4 some loveliness that
before had been felt only with an intensity of 2. That is the
purpose of evangelistic preaching. Sermons need to melt the ice
that encrusts cold hearts. They need to heat the resistant iron till
it can be shaped. Emotion is life's motive power. Preaching that
does not intensify emotions would be as barren as preaching that
does nothing for the hearers' minds. Evangelism cannot truly tell
of the wonder of Christ's love, or the joy he offers, or the awful
folly of resisting him, without emotion. It takes a moving sermon
to propel hearers toward what they ought to do.

6. Urgency. Much of the success of evangelistic preaching
depends on its persuading those who have long said, "Not yet,"
to say, "I will do it now." There are dubious ways of stirring up
a sense of urgency. During the 1967 Six Day War in the Middle
East, I heard an evangelist tell his audience that if the Jews went
through the Mandelbaum Gate into Old Jerusalem, the condition
for the coming of the last days would be fulfilled. An impressive
number came forward to be saved. When the Israeli forces did
go into Old Jerusalem that week, I wondered how surprised the
preacher was when the world kept right on going. Those who
come to Christ out of a contrived panic may later find that their
motives were not good enough. But the preacher does not have
to work up an urgency. It is always real. "Listen! This is the hour
to receive God's favor, today is the day to be saved!" (2 Cor. 6:2,
TEV). The preacher must make it clear that every minute's delay
is a disaster. The old invitation hymn that asks, "Why not now?",
is raising the right question.

THE APPEAL

Evangelistic preaching has a specific purpose. The preacher
wants people to take Christ as their Lord. He needs to make that
plain, and to give reasons why they should. Everything in the

sermon is designed to build up to that great result. There has to be a progression toward it. It might be: (1) Show the hearers what their need is. (2) Show that God is ready to satisfy that need. (3) Persuade them to enter into the new existence that God is offering. Whatever the line of thought may be, it is designed to lead up to the new life.

Most preachers feel inadequate for evangelism. They do not see how what they say could possibly transform a human life. But the amazing experience is that even a poor sermon can have an incredible result. Cardinal Suenens of Belgium told of one of his priests whose sermon resulted in a conversion. The priest afterwards looked up the convert and asked him, "Could you tell me what it was in my sermon that convinced you?" The man replied, "O Father, I will never forget that place in your sermon when you said, 'I have finished the first part of my sermon and will now start the next part.' That struck me very strongly, and I said to myself, 'Dear boy, you have to finish the first part of your life and start a new part.' "[1] The preacher—like the teacher, youth leader, parent, or evangelistic caller—has to believe that God has been working on people all their lives. They may be so near the edge that our inept efforts to bring them into the new life may be all it takes.

There are as many sorts of evangelistic invitations as there are preachers and sermon subjects. A preacher learns how to give an invitation from those who do it well. Many of the published sermons by contemporary preachers end with strong calls for decision. Every preacher can find ways that fit his temperament and style.

The effect of the most moving appeal for faith is likely to drift away unless it is anchored by some act. To bring people to desire to give their lives to Christ without offering them any way by which that desire can be expressed will only fix more firmly their habit of doing nothing. To close with some platitude about making up their minds can be damaging. The way a decision is expressed is symbolic. It has no great value in itself, but it marks a turning point. Its validity depends on what happens next.

It takes time for people to make up their minds about something of such gravity. They may have to struggle through their long-established habit of postponement. They may be slow to do anything in public. Some preachers follow their invitation with a time of silence during which people may reflect on it. The invitation may be repeated in a variety of ways to give more time for decisions to be made. People may be helped to reach the big decision by progressive steps. For example, those who want Christ's help may be asked to raise their hands. Then those who raised their hands may be asked to stay after the service to learn more about what Christ has for them. Then those who stay may be invited to join a class that will help them to decide whether to become acknowledged followers of Christ.

RESPONSES

The minister may follow his sermon with a prayer of commitment, or a statement of faith, given in short sentences that people can repeat after him. They are asked to say nothing they do not seriously mean. If the prayer or statement is on cards that are in the pews, it can be thought over before those who wish to do so read it in unison. Those who say what is on the card may then sign it and keep it, or leave it at the door.

There may be decision cards in the pews that people are asked to sign after they have thought and prayed about them. The cards may also have a space for recommitment for church members. These may be collected, or given to an usher at the door, or taken home to be signed and returned.

Raising hands while all are praying may indicate a desire to be prayed for, to have a Christian home, or to take Christ as Lord.

The minister may make one of these requests:

"Won't you right now set a time today when you will think and pray about what you want to do? Then tell Christ and someone else what you have decided."

"Before you leave the church, tell me or someone here of your decision."

"When you have made your decision, won't you tell me about it? I will be by the phone all afternoon waiting for your call."

"I wish you would drop me a note this week to tell me what you have been thinking."

Those who decide to profess their faith or join the Church may be asked to come forward during the singing of a hymn. The minister may come down to give them his hand. Church officers may also come to receive them. Having the officers coming to the front helps those who might feel it was improper to walk down the aisle alone.

There may be a meeting after the service for those who are still undecided, or who have expressed a decision of some sort. The minister can speak of what it is to follow Christ, and he can also answer questions or explain how one becomes a member of the Church. Church members may speak of what their faith and the Church mean to them. Lay counsellors may talk privately with each one who has stayed. Enrollment in a New Member Class may be arranged. Literature may be given out. The names and addresses of all who stayed should be recorded.

GETTING HEARERS

Evangelism in church services is silenced by the absence of anyone to be evangelized. In my first pastorate, I incautiously announced that the first Sunday of each month for the next year would be Evangelism Sunday. I had to go on with it, but it became comic, each time I gave the invitation, to look around and see no one but the old reliables. The problem was that neither I nor anyone else had given any thought to how to bring people to whom such an invitation could be addressed.

The minister can bring the evangelistic message, but only the members can bring hearers for it. The members have the contacts outside the church and they can praise the preaching. They need to know that there will be evangelism Sundays on which the sermon will make a specially direct appeal for faith, and a way of responding to it will be offered. On those Sundays the worship will be designed to reach those who are not used to church services. There may be unusual features which will give the members reason to invite their friends, perhaps a noted singer or a popular public figure who will give a Christian testimony. An evangelism Sunday might be set for any time, or it might be on every Sunday of some month, or on the first Sunday of each month throughout a year. Special Sunday evening services can be designated for evangelism. Church members can be frequently reminded to be thinking of those they want to bring on the next evangelism Sunday—friends, relatives, Church School classes, fellow employees. Those who are listed in the evangelism file can get invitations. *Visitors Sunday* will sound more appealing to nonmembers than will *Evangelism Sunday.* (For more on bringing hearers, see pp. 95–96 and 106.)

A week of special evening services can be powerful evangelism. The build-up from one sermon to the next can be more effective than a single sermon. It is easier to get nonmembers to special evening meetings than to regular Sunday services. They can be strikingly advertised. Church members can be stirred to use their contacts to bring those who have no church. Telephoned invitations can be planned. The revival of church members can also be a purpose; services that present the faith can strengthen it. Having the minister of the church do the preaching gives him a connection with those who are reached. But a guest preacher can provide a fresh experience, and can be advertised in more exciting terms than can the pastor—especially by the pastor. There can be unusually attractive features—a song leader, an orchestra, dramatic skits, brief talks by gifted lay speakers.

Weddings and funerals give access to those who do not know the Christian faith. Wedding homilies can speak of what Christ means to human love and homes. At funerals the minister can tell of God's comfort, of the life in Christ, and the triumph over death. Many who are not Christian come to funerals and listen closely. The thought of death makes them interested in what a preacher has to say.

13

Commencing Church Membership

Paul set down the two essentials for becoming a Christian when he said, "As ye have therefore received Christ Jesus the Lord, so walk ye in him" (Col. 2:6, KJV). It all must start with receiving Christ Jesus as Lord. No amount of teaching or training can make a Christian out of someone who has not done that. "You can't teach an egg to fly before it has hatched."

But the second part also is necessary—the convert must walk in Christ. Someone who has turned and faced toward him is now converted, reoriented, pointed in a different direction. But unless the person now walks in that direction, there has been no transformation, no matter how ecstatic the conversion may have seemed. In the excitement of a revival, the preacher declared, "I don't care how high you jump; what matters is how you walk when you come down." Evangelism must not only bring people to look to Christ as Lord; it must also start them on their Christian walk.

In Jesus' commandment to evangelize, "baptizing" believers is followed by "teaching them to observe all that I have commanded" (Matt. 28:19–20). Those who turned to Christ on the day of Pentecost next "devoted themselves to the apostles' teaching" (Acts 2:42). Two key words that the New Testament uses many times in speaking of converts are "to walk," *(peripateo)* and "way" *(hodos)*—meaning "path" or "highway." The "way" on which Christ calls us to "walk" is marked by an unprecedented sort of thinking and acting. Apollos had ardently accepted Christ, but he was for a while strangely off the Christian path until Priscilla and Aquila "took him and expounded to him the way" (Acts 18:26).

That is the second part of our evangelistic task. In many ways it is the hardest and most important part. As soon as people have decided to follow Christ, and before they have become church members, the church commences trying to give them a sound start by showing them how to "walk" in the Christian "way."

The Church's neglect of this is the great scandal of evangelism. President Herschel Hobbs told the Southern Baptist Convention, "We have dipped them and dropped them." Evidence that other Churches are doing the same is seen in the shocking figures on suspensions from membership. We abandon our new members to make their own way into the new life toward which they have turned, and as might be expected, an appalling proportion of them never make it. This does not have to happen. Most of those who join a church expect to remain as active members. Those who drop away have been disappointed. Things did not turn out as they had hoped. As a lapsed member said, "I wish they had cared about me as much as they cared about my soul."

Part of our neglect comes from a mistaken theology. A person who has decided to take Christ as Lord is not by lightning from heaven suddenly given the knowledge and habits that a Christian needs. Only the Holy Spirit can make a person a Christian, but the Spirit works through the Church, both in the calling and the establishing.

The bad theology lets churches give their new members a poor start. Such churches feel that any requirement beyond a confession of faith is an interference with the Holy Spirit. They make it so easy to join the church that new members are not aware that much of anything has happened. So all that really happens is that an outsider is called an insider. Jesus did not hesitate to make demands of those who were moved to look to him as Master. His demands were astonishingly difficult.

1. INSTRUCTION

The basic knowledge a person needs in order to make a right profession of faith is not all that a Christian has to know. There is more that must be learned before one can even start to lead a Christian life—knowledge about God, about Christ's promises and demands, about the Church. Two thousand years of accumulated wisdom about Christian living is available for new Christians.

1. The New Member Class. A church can transmit the most information in the shortest time through a class. It cannot teach all that Christians need to know—a lifetime of learning in the church is inadequate for that. But it can give a basic orientation and a start toward continued learning.

A class is a safety device. It protects a church from adding to its membership those who should not be there. And it saves people who would not join if they knew what they were getting into from making that mistake. Required classes keep off the church roll people who are not enough in earnest to bother to attend. Classes make decisions valid. A half-hour call or a sermon can bring someone to a valid decision to accept Christ, but it cannot tell enough about what that means. A class can take such a decision far deeper. It is sad when a class deters someone from joining the church. But joining improperly might end the chance of ever learning what a Christian really is.

Some churches require all who join to complete a class. Others require it only of those who have not been members of a church before, but urge it on all others. Some require those who come by transfer to take only the last class, on the life of their new congregation. Classes are valuable for those who have been active in other churches. Entering a new church home is an important, and sometimes precarious, transition. A class provides for review, renewal, and reorienting. It starts newcomers in the church with an attachment to a social group and to the teacher. If classes are required, the teacher has to try especially hard to make them good. People resent being forced to spend time on what is of poor quality.

Six one-hour sessions can provide a fairly adequate course, though twice that number can be well used. There may be just two long Sunday afternoon conferences. There are churches that start their adult New Member Classes in the fall and end them after Christmas. Some classes meet during the Church School hour as a special adult course. Often the minister and his wife have the class in their home on Sunday evenings, or only the final meeting may be there. A weeknight can be a good time.

The number who join governs how often a class is offered. When only four or five join during a year, some might have a long wait until the next class. But a small class can be excellent. I remember one with just two members that was more like a series of interviews than a class, but we got to important matters at a depth that would have been impossible with a larger group. People may be allowed to join on their promise to attend the next class. However, those who have already joined the church are the poorest attenders. Those who look forward to membership are more eager to learn than are church members who regard the class as a troublesome leftover duty. And any who should not have joined will find it out too late if the class comes after they have already joined. Classes often follow Lay Calling programs. Churches with many joining are likely to have classes in the fall, winter, and early spring.

The minister is usually the teacher. There may be no one else available who has had schooling in the class subjects, or the minister may value the connection with new church members he gets in the class. If the class meets while the minister is preaching, a retired minister, or a lay person, or a series of lay persons may teach. If there are several ministers, the one who does most of the preaching may arrange to teach once or twice during each series of classes.

Ministers have to learn to be good teachers. Their tendency is to review old sermons or to lecture. With all its critics, lecturing is the most used method for instructing adults. It is necessary for some subjects. Church history could not be taught by class discussion; prayer could not be taught without it. Being a good lecturer is a special art. A good deal that is neither straight lecture nor random discussion is needed. The use of a blackboard, projectors, recordings, written assignments, oral reports, dramatizations, and dividing into small groups can be considered. Christian Education offices supply booklets on how to teach. The class members should be expected to do some studying at home. Some denominations furnish excellent study books, with a guide for teachers. If yours does not, you may look for what is available from other denominations or from independent publishers.

Classes deal with belief, the Bible, public and private worship, service, stewardship, Church history, the denomination, Christian homes, private and social morality, and the life of a congregation. Separate booklets on these subjects can combine to make an excellent textbook for the course.

Class members often become warm friends. One large church, which tries to have all of its members in some *Koinoneia* (fellowship) *Group*, continues each new member class as another "K Group," which meets regularly for friendship, prayer, and study.

Sometimes church members who are interested in the subjects of the new member class are allowed to attend. These members should never be so many or so talkative that they take the class away from those for whom it is intended. The age at which young people come to the adult class instead of to the youth class must be determined.

2. Literature. All that new members are taught does not have to get to them in classes. They can learn a great deal from their own reading (see 109–110). Much appealing literature which new Christians and new church members need is available as books, pamphlets, or leaflets. To receive one free piece of literature is a delightful surprise; to receive ten is a blow. So literature for new members should be given to them in broken lots and with commendation that will make each piece seem excitingly important. A church has to search through many sources to find the literature it needs. Denominational publishers could do more good if they did not put limiting titles on their publications. *Presbyterian Prayer* or *Baptists and the Bible* could just as well be called *Christian Prayer* or *You and Your Bible.*

It is essential that those who are going to assent to a transforming faith and to bind their whole lives by awesome promises be given a chance to consider in advance what they will be saying. This is often put in a printed form that may be called the APPLICATION FOR MEMBERSHIP or the INVITATION TO MEMBERSHIP. With this there may also be spaces for the needed personal information—address, age (if under 25), occupation, marital status, names of others in the home, whether or not the person is baptized, and where to write for a certificate of transfer. There may also be a list of services that the church needs, with spaces to check any that the prospective member is willing to perform. The form may be perforated so that the half with the information can be kept by the church and the part with faith and vows, which has been signed by the candidate, can be countersigned by the minister or clerk and returned. It will then be a certificate of membership and a reminder of what has been professed and promised.

2. THE RECEPTION

The manner of their reception into membership should impress the new members with its sublime importance. This is one of the very great times in a Christian's life, and it should seem like it.

There are reasons why it may be slighted. It is a frequent happening for ministers and church officers. Many denominations do not require very much and provide only the bare bones of a service for reception. The assumption is that local churches will find their own ways of enriching this, but they often do no more than the minimum that is prescribed.

Churches that receive new members in a meeting of the official board can make it either perfunctory or full of meaning. Except under unusual circumstances, such a meeting should never be held after a Sunday service. Officers' husbands or wives, waiting outside, will be impatient to get home. An indecent feeling of being hurried cannot be completely hidden. It is better not to receive new members at a meeting which also has some other purpose. The great event has to be crowded in with routine concerns. The new members must be sent on while the officers remain to continue their meeting.

The atmosphere of a meeting to receive members should reveal happiness and solemnity. New members may be ill at ease, so officers should be designated in advance to meet them at the door, sit with them, and introduce them to others. When the candidates are presented to be voted on, it is not enough just to read their names. Enough information should be given with each name to show that the person is important. The action to receive should not be a bare motion, but rather something like: "With gratitude to God, I move . . ." or "With great happiness, I second . . ." Officers may give short talks of welcome or advice. New members may be asked about families, interests, or former church experiences. With their permission in advance, they may be asked to tell something of their faith or what they look for in the church. The prayers at this meeting have a special significance. When the meeting has adjourned, it is well to linger so that the officers and new members may visit with each other. Refreshments can provide a time for forming friendships.

In denominations in which the minister receives new members, he must find ways to make it a memorable time. Receiving or introducing new members in a worship service should be a deeply moving occasion. There should be the Te Deum sense that the Angels, Apostles, Martyrs, and the holy Church throughout all the world are gathered round. When there are baptisms, the sacred meanings of the sacrament add to the solemnity.

The names should be read slowly enough so that those who come forward can be identified. If the minister goes into the aisle, those who have come to the front can turn around and face him and the congregation. This gives the feeling of a family circle. It is impressive to have the new members profess their faith, and the church members promise their love and care, while they are face to face. A church can find many beautiful ways of making this service impressive. Lay officers may put the questions to the congregation, or express the church's welcome, or give "the right hand of fellowship" (Gal. 2:9). One verse of a hymn of Christian love may be sung. The new members may be given flowers to wear to identify them for personal greetings after the service. Except in large churches, new members may stand at the door so that those who leave can welcome them and introduce themselves. There may be a refreshment time at which the new members are guests of honor.

When a class of young people is received, whether or not it is called "Confirmation," there can be special ways of making it impressive. Each one may kneel for the laying on of the minister's hand and a prayer of blessing.

3. COMING INTO THE CHURCH FELLOWSHIP

The chief reason people fall away from a church is not lack of faith but lack of friends. When people do not make friends in a congregation, they are pretty sure to lose interest. They will feel that the church is not giving them what they need, and they will be right. A church is not supposed to be a public institution, but a family of faith. Those who come only to attend services, as they would go to a theater, lose too much. Human nature works against new members. With all the ritual promises of love, they will still feel as though they have to force themselves into someone else's club. Church members enjoy each other so much that they may not notice strangers. Unless the church works hard to get around these human tendencies, many who join may never feel at home.

Some new members do not have this difficulty. They are outgoing, make friends easily, and will be deep in the life of the church within a month. But the church has to meet the needs of the majority who do not have this gift. Some turn to the church because they long for friendships and find them hard to make. There are the shy who seem to rebuff advances, though they want them and are hurt when they are not offered. There are the people with deep feelings and fine minds who carry too much weight to be nimble socially. The opening weeks are the critical time for getting into the church fellowship. If friends are not made then, so much resentment and dislike of the church may be built up that it cannot be overcome.

1. Getting to Know the Minister. The first friend that new members need is the minister. A warmly personal feeling for him will do much to give them a warmly personal feeling for the church. New members need to feel that the person in the pulpit is not a stranger who is addressing the public, but someone they have talked to who is talking to them.

Soon after the intention to join the church is known, there should be an interview at which the prospective member and the pastor can get to know and like each other. Like the class, this meeting is also a protection against inadequate decisions. There may be questions that callers or sermons have not answered. The minister can say more than has been said about the Christian faith, and life, and Church. He can explain the process for joining the church. He may also give something that a new member will want to read.

2. Sponsors. The ritual of welcome promises the congregation's love and care, but what everybody is supposed to do will not be done unless someone agrees to do it. Sponsors are persons or couples who are assigned by the evangelism leaders to be friends of persons or couples who join the church. If church homes are grouped by zones, the zone leaders may be the sponsors of new members in their zones. Assignments last for a year; the first three months are the most important. Sponsors call on the new members, meet them at the church, introduce them to church members, try to get them and their children into church activities and duties, and report any lack of interest to the evangelism leaders. New members do not feel socially accepted until they have been invited into other members' homes (social science counts "interdining" as a sign of the breakdown of castes); so sponsors invite their new friends to their homes, or arrange for others to invite them. They look for mutual interests in which they can get together away from the church.

Sponsors need a sheet that describes their duties. They may have good intentions but do little, so they should be asked to report what they have done. Dated postcards are useful for this. If they do not report, they should be telephoned. They can choose whether to say they are sponsors or to make their approaches simply as friendly church members.

3. Groups. Church services provide for handshakes, but real acquaintance is formed only in smaller groups. New members should be given glowing descriptions of what is available for them at the church. All church groups in which new members might participate should have an officer to whom the names of new members can be sent. The officer needs a well-designed procedure for recruiting them—by phone calls or offers to stop by for them. They should be nonpaying guests the first time they attend a meeting at which a meal is served. When they come once, they should be given special attention to see that they return. Representatives of important church activities may come to the meeting where members are received to tell about the activities and to invite personally any they meet there who might be interested. Checking on whether recent new members have gotten into church activities is an important part of the meetings of the Evangelism Commission.

4. Pictures. Pictures of new members, which are put on a bulletin board or in a church publication, help other members to know them. Such pictures can be taken by a photo hobbyist at the time of joining. It is hard to identify everyone in big groups; individual or family pictures are more practical.

4. SERVING

1. Work. New members have been told that the Church exists to do what Christ wants done so that those who serve the Church are serving him and humanity. They have been asked to promise to serve Christ through his Church. It is therefore necessary that they be given opportunities for this service, and that they be given a good start in it.

New members are often given a list of services that the church needs, with a request to check those they offer. By itself this is a feeble device. For one thing, unless someone goes through the list with a new member, almost nothing will be checked. They feel it is presumptuous to offer to do something that others might do better. They are wary. They do not want to get saddled with a task that may be done just as well without them. The rest of the failure is the church's. Such lists are often put in a cabinet and forgotten. So the few who offered to sing in the choir or fold bulletins feel rebuffed.

There is no impersonal way to bring church members into service. A minister who appeals from the pulpit for volunteers to teach Sunday School will get few of them, not because the members are slothful, but because he is. Members, new or old, will not believe it is they who are needed unless it is they who are asked. New members have to be asked in person about what they might do for the church. A service list can be useful for such a conversation. Then the new members' names, with the tasks they might perform, must be kept in sight until each one has been asked to serve.

"Use 'em or lose 'em" is an old and faithful saying. People never feel they are fully a part of a church until a part of their lives has been built into it. Most of the work that keeps a church going is donated by its members. Those who have no part in this feel like outsiders. When they have declined all opportunities to serve, they are uncomfortable and therefore critical. Those who have never been asked feel left out.

The names of new members, with a request that they be used soon, can be given to those who recruit groups of workers for such tasks as getting out mailings, making calls, ushering, serving meals, and nursery care. Church work can include service in non-church organizations, as when members are enlisted to read to blind students or to work in summer camps.

2. Money. Most new members do not have to be persuaded that they should make a financial contribution, but they have important questions. One of these is *"How much?"* It does not do for a church to say only, "You must settle that with your God." God expects the church to be a school of Christian living. It is supposed to help Christians know how much to give.

A church can offer tithing as a guide, or proportionate giving, or comparison with other expenses, or the church's average contribution. New members will be interested to know what most members give, which means most members in their sort of situation. Good guidance can be given by a tactful caller who tells how he or she decided how much to give, and how this has been worked out across the years.

After "How much?" the question will be *"How?"* How should giving be divided among local church support, missions, special offerings, and non-church charities? New members need to know about church finance—how the major pledge is divided, what the budgets include and who draws them up, whether pledges can be changed, and whether statements of unpaid balances are considered bills.

The *"Why?"* of giving is important. New members need to be

taught the Christian view of money. The great meanings of stewardship, consecration, and sacrificial living should be explained. Christianity has been called the most materialistic of all religions because Jesus made it so clear that such spiritual qualities as love, mercy, and dedication are not real unless they are tangibly expressed. He said, "Where your treasure is, there will your heart be also." One of the most important parts of evangelism is to bring converts to a Christian understanding of the use of money. This cannot be carelessly done. The Church's guidance about money has to be given to new members in three ways:

(a) In writing. The spiritual insights and practical information need to be given in a form that can be studied, pondered, and kept. A church has to prepare its own statement. It may also use materials from denominational stewardship departments.

(b) In groups. The New Member Class can give extended time to stewardship. It can be emphasized at the time of reception into membership.

(c) In person. Whether or not a church uses an every-member canvass at pledge time, it needs calls at homes to receive the first pledges of new members. They will have questions. A call shows how important giving is. A caller can say some things about the *"How much?"* and *"How?"* and *"Why?"* that cannot be said in any other way. Some churches have wise and tactful members who make financial calling on new members their special service to the church. There has to be some special way of getting the new members' pledges; they should not have to wait till the next canvass to become regular contributors. If a pledge card comes to them by mail and they have to make an uninformed guess, they will probably pick the lowest figure that could be right, and this may establish the level of their giving for the rest of their church lives. The choice of the amount may be determined either by everyday pragmatism or by Christian idealism. Whichever it is may have much to do with fixing their whole slant on life. In that existential moment when the pen is poised above the pledge card, a life-transforming decision may be in the balance.

5. RELIGIOUS PRACTICES

The adherents of any religion are shaped into the sort of persons their faith requires by religious practices. The most authentic Moslems and the most thoroughgoing Buddhists are probably those who best keep the prescribed observances. Most Christians across the years have believed that there are practices that make Christians strong. Church and prayer group attendance, private and family worship, Bible reading, and Communion—these have been counted on to keep Christ's followers living close to him.

A Christian evangelist has a harder task than does a mullah. A Moslem convert can be told exactly when to pray, which direction to face, how to kneel, what to say. The fasts and feasts and the ninety-nine names for praising Allah are strictly set. But we lay before new Christians a wide variety of religious practices with the hope that they will adopt the ones that are best for them. Some modern Protestants, unlike their ancestors, are making the daring experiment of recommending little and requiring nothing. If this produces an earnest seeking for the best ways, it can be a source of strength. But if it turns out to be only the freedom to have no practices at all, that form of Protestantism will disappear. There must be definite ways by which spirits are nurtured and characters formed. It takes disciplines to make disciples.

We do not lack precedents. Through the centuries, Christians have discovered a great deal about the habits that do the most for them. We can recommend to our new members some well-tested practices, and we can give help in getting started on them, though we do not lay them down as rules. Giving this help is an important part of the classes and literature for new members.

1. Private Prayer. Prayer is the only fine art in which every child of God can be an artist, but it still requires skill. When the disciples begged Jesus, "Teach us to pray," his instructions were explicit (see p. 46). New and old Christians make that request, and Christ's Church must answer it. Many new Christians are baffled by prayer. They are not sure what to pray about or what sort of answers to expect. They must be helped to find out what prayer can do by trying it—not just by occasional petitions, but by regular prayer habits.

2. Group Prayer. A discovery of how great prayer can be may come better in a group than by oneself. When Christians are close to each other, it helps them to feel close to God. When both private and public prayer have gone cold for us, the warmth may best come back through that glow which kindles from one heart to another when two or three are gathered together in Christ's name. Trying to arrange for new members to have the experience of group prayer is an important part of giving them a sound start in the Christian life and in the church.

The most important prayer group is the family. Traditional forms of family worship may seem hard to fit into the modern scene. Fortunately, there are newer forms that can fit beautifully. Describing these to the new members is an important part of their instruction.

3. Public Worship. Those who are not used to public worship may not like it. They have not had time to form an emotional attachment to its parts. They do not understand what it is getting at. They need an explanation of the drama so they will know what their role in it is. They need to know what it is supposed to do for them. They have to see that they cannot collapse into a pew and expect a great experience of worship. Worship is refreshing work. They need a homiletics lesson for listeners that will tell them how the preacher sees his task and what part the hearers play in the sermon process. An occasional meeting at which church people learn about hymns and practice singing them will help new members learn how to sing in church and how to appreciate the poetry and music of the hymns.

The reasons for regular attendance at public worship must be impressed on the new members. They may assume that this is one of those church activities that some go in for and some do not. They need to know that a church "service" is a service that we give to God. A God of love must be loved, and his people assemble to express together their love for him. Common worship also ministers to our deepest needs. Church people have to understand why Archbishop Temple said, "This world can be saved from political chaos and collapse by one thing only, and that is worship."

4. Bible Reading. We need the Bible, both for what it says to us and for what it does to us. The Bible is God's word, a wisdom from outside the human scene. It is also a territory in which we meet God; as we watch what he is doing, hear his voice, and see him looking at us, something is done to us. A hearsay knowledge of what is in the Bible will not bring about what happens to us when we are reading it ourselves. New members who do not know much about what the Bible says and what the Bible does must be helped to get what they have missed.

Many who do not know the Bible have a prejudice against it. They have heard gossip about its absurd, offensive parts. The Bible on the shelf has far more problems than does the Bible in our hands. It is its own defender. Anyone who knows the Sermon on the Mount or the fourteenth chapter of John will not be too much put off by questions about Jonah or uncertainties in the ancient manuscripts. New members must be led to want to read the Bible. The temporary is always more pressing than the time-less. Bible reading is never the line of least resistance. It is a "discipline," which means that we have to start on principle in order to discover the delight.

New readers need a plan. If they try to read the Bible from cover to cover, they may end bogged down in Exodus. They might start out with a list of the great chapters, or they might be offered a reading plan, commencing with the clearest and most immediately helpful parts, and circling on out. A good edition and a one-volume commentary can be recommended.

5. Sabbath Observance. When Jesus said, "The Sabbath was made for man," he did not mean, "so you can do as you please with it." He meant, "so how you use this precious gift is of infinite importance." God gave us the Sabbath for whatever is our great-est need. What lets you be yourself at your very best, most com-pletely a child of God, is right for the Sabbath. It is a day for worship and for spiritual growth. It is a refuge from what pursues us all the other days. It gives us a time to know our families better and enjoy our friends.

Whatever rules you make to preserve your Sabbath can be ridiculed as arbitrary—but if you have no rules, you have no Sabbath. Without some distinctions, Sundays disappear in shapeless disarray.

When homework is ruled out, children get to read what they enjoy the most. A father whose principles will not let him touch his weekday work gets to hear about his children's plans or to join the family orchestra. The caricature of the traditional Christian Sabbath as starched and boring does not match the recollections of most people who grew up with it. The Sundays are likely to supply their happiest memories. The Christian Sunday is not what new Christians have been used to. Helping them to find the finest ways to use their Sundays is an important part of helping them get started in the Christian life.

6. Other Practices. Everything that increases our appreciation of goodness, truth, and beauty helps make us into the sort of persons that Christians ought to be. Music, art, great books, friendship, and the enjoyment of the out-of-doors can do it. These are the things that get pushed from our lives unless we take deliberate care to make room for them.

6. THE HEALTH CHECK

It is exceedingly important to know how well new members are getting started. In the weeks after joining, their relation to the church is taking shape. They are deciding what they will do in the church. They are still open to new activities, new friends, and new habits.

The sooner a poor start is discovered, the more chance there is that it can be remedied. Those who are drifting away into the world are within reach at first. But the farther they drift off, the harder it will be to draw them back.

The names of those who have joined during the past eighteen months must be regularly reviewed to see how they are doing. A simple way of doing this is to put the names down the left-hand margin of a sheet of paper, with vertical columns for checking the church's performance; for example: pastor's call, sponsor assigned, invited to club, literature delivered, pledge call. Other columns check what the new member is doing: participation in the New Member Class, church attendance, Church School class, club, financial pledge, duty undertaken. The pastor may have much of this information, or it may be filled in at an Evangelism Commission meeting. Some friendly reason for phoning a new member may provide the chance to get the information this record needs.

When the information shows a problem, emergency action is required. A request to usher at a church service or to wait on tables at a club dinner may start the person toward the church. A friend or neighbor may be asked to show attention and to stir church interest. The Evangelism Commission may discuss what to do.

Young teenagers who have joined the Church need special attention because of their tendency to feel that they have graduated from children's activities, though in fact they have not commenced adult participation. Special activities—a youth choir, retreats, a vacation program, youth ushers—may show them that the church is not just for old people and children.

Some pastors write personal letters to members on the first anniversary of their joining. An annual dinner for all who have joined during the past two years gets each one to two dinners. Those who joined together may sit at the same tables. They may be asked to discuss such questions as: "Are you getting the help you need?" "Is it easy to make friends in the church?" "How can the church be improved?" This can strengthen the church connection at a critical time, and the church can learn what it needs to know.

14

The Message of Evangelism

1. IS THE MESSAGE POSSIBLE?

In evangelism we talk about God and spiritual realities. This is so different from our ordinary preoccupation with things we see and touch that we are bound to wonder, "Is this possible?"

1. Can Human Beings Know or Talk About a God? The ancient philosophers readily showed that finite minds could have no possible conception of an infinite God, and even if they could have some dim glimmerings, there would be no possible forms in which such knowledge could be conveyed. Thinkers in every generation have found their own subtle ways of demonstrating that the idea of God is beyond the reach of human mentality—"God is dead." And all the while, many of the best minds in every generation have recognized the logic of this God-denying reasoning, and have gone right on praying. They did this because they put the rational proof that religion is impossible right beside old Zeno's proof that Achilles cannot catch the tortoise, or Kant's proof that space must both be unlimited and end somewhere. These all demonstrate that logic does not have the last word. It cannot handle ultimate realities. Logic is a useful tool for adding up grocery bills, but when higher mathematics has to use the such concepts as curved space, or parallel lines that meet in infinity, or the square root of minus one, logic gets left behind. So religion simply bypasses the logical proof that God is inconceivable because it has other ways of knowing that God can be both perceived and talked about.

2. Can Reason Bring People to Faith? Some Christians in every age have counted on reason to do the work of evangelism. They have believed that it is possible to prove the truth of Christianity. Only those whom sin has made perversely obdurate, they thought, could resist the arguments for the Christian faith. For example, the cause can be proved from the effect: you cannot doubt that there is a creation, so there must be a Creator. Design proves that there is a rational Designer. Human morality and love point to a moral and loving Source. Dr. Paley was sure that the marvellously clever invention of the human eye reveals a divinely clever Inventor. Descartes thought that by airtight reasoning he had proved the existence of God with the finality of mathematics. But his proof converted no sinners, and gleeful skeptics soon showed it to be full of flaws. Those who do not want to believe can always find a logical loophole to slip through.

We can be glad of that. If the evangelist had arguments that could force people to recognize that Christianity is true, the Christian faith would be no more. God is not going to tie us tight in proofs and drag us to him. He wants us to come to Christ because we choose to, not because we have to. Love cannot be coerced. Reason is only the next-to-the-highest faculty. It is another faculty entirely to which evangelism appeals. It could be called the prompting of the Holy Spirit or intuition. It is a special sort of recognition, like falling in love. Something deep within us says, "That's it!" As Henry Sloane Coffin said, "You do not go into religion head first. You must go in heart first, and the head will go later."

But the head does have to go too. Though reason is only the next-to-the-highest faculty, and can neither forbid nor compel belief, at that next level it is of great importance.

(a) Reason can clear away the obstacles to faith. It can show that it is possible to be both intelligent and religious. There must always be a leap of faith, but reason can at least let you get to the jumping-off place.

(b) Reason can give you some momentum for the jump. A study of the "evidences" of Christianity used to be important in church-sponsored higher education. There are strong indications that make Christian belief look likely, even though they cannot prove it.

(c) Reason can save faith from absurdity. Falling in love is not a logical process, but those who use their heads can be saved from ridiculous infatuations. Faith has to be super-rational, but it cannot be irrational. There is an old saying that faith may ask us to believe that the whale swallowed Jonah, which is unusual, but not that Jonah swallowed the whale, which is absurd. Faith cannot ask us to believe that the sun is shining when we see the storm clouds overhead. Christians can believe that Christ will return to the earth; they cannot reasonably believe that he will descend to every place on the globe at the same time—which is what some skywatchers seem to have expected.

(d) The evangelist can use logic to show what follows from beliefs that people already have. Once faith supplies a starting place, reason can build on it a life-sustaining structure of beliefs that necessarily follow from it. The *pou sto* can be the conviction that Jesus is more than human, that morals have an external validity, that the superiority of love to hate is built into the order of the universe, that we have had an actual experience of the reality of God, that the Bible has a more than earthly wisdom. Evangelism tries to lead a person to accept such a belief, or to recognize that such a belief has already been accepted. Then reason can be used to lead to other beliefs that necessarily follow from this one. Reason can also show the actions that a belief logically requires. A person who believes in a God of love can be shown that the worship of such a God requires fellowship. The inconsistency of an unacknowledged gratitude to Christ or of believing in the Church without belonging to it can be pointed out. Many people miss the full blessings of their faith because they have never thought out its implications. Evangelism can lead people out of their hazy indecisiveness.

(e) Evangelism has to help new Christians use reason to put together a coherent faith. An unrelated jumble of religious views and sentiments cannot hold a life together. We need the support of a logically vertibrate structure of beliefs. The Bible is the journal of God's revelations, so its teachings are not logically arranged. But God gave us the power of reason so that we can relate the Bible's truths to each other in a consistent system that can satisfy our minds and guide our conduct. In other words, it takes reason to make our personal faith mentally respectable.

3. Is the Message of Evangelism Impossibly Naive? The message of evangelism is that God is love, and he made us to live in love with him and with each other. But our sin has alienated us from God and from other human beings. We have spoiled the Creator's plan and filled the earth with misery. But God in his mercy came onto our scene in human form to reveal, in the only way we could understand, the wonder of his love. The redemptive death of Christ upon the cross can restore us to the relationship with God for which we were created. Christ's resurrection assures us of the blessing of his personal presence in our lives. All this we can have if we will believe in it and take it. We can come into a glorious new life that will be our first experience of the life with God that we shall have forever. We can find in the Church that loving fellowship with God's children that we were intended to enjoy.

This is a sublime story, but it can seem too artless. It ascribes human feelings and limitations to the Almighty. It assumes that God can be frustrated, hurt, forced to try again, and that he feels pity and needs love. Could any but a childish mind believe that this is "true"?

We need to apply here the principle of "like this, only more so," which is essential to all Christian thought. Of course, all our conceptions of God are humanly limited and inadequate, but we come closest to the truth when we use the highest conceptions we know. A pond will help us show a child what the ocean is like better than will a sandbox. We can describe heaven better if we say it is like the greatest happiness we have known rather than if we say it is like some lesser happiness, though both will be far short of the reality. When we describe God in personal terms, it does not shrink him down to human size; rather, it expands our conception of him by using the highest qualities we know, which are personal. One might way, "I can't believe in a personal God, but I do believe in a spiritual force," which avoids thinking of God as like a father, and ends up thinking of him as like a storage battery. It gives us some understanding of God to think of him as a power, like electricity; but it gives us far more understanding to think of him as a love, like that of Jesus Christ. Not even Jesus could embody all that God is, but he revealed all that can be expressed in human terms. He takes us as close as we can get to the full understanding, and he points straight at it, though the complete truth is infinitely farther on in that direction.

We do not need to clutter up the message of evangelism with all sorts of qualifications and reservations in order to keep from sounding more primitive than we really are. We can tell the story straight, knowing that in this world there will never be a better way of letting people know what God actually, truly, literally is offering them through Jesus Christ.

4. Is the Message of Evangelism Historically True? The message of evangelism that we long for people to accept is not just a philosophy, a therapy, an ideology, or a set of moral principles —it is a record of events (see p. 122). Saving faith is based on what God did at real places in the Middle East, at actual dates in the first century. But the account of God's redemptive acts is joined in the Bible with other accounts that are difficult to take as literal history. They seem to require belief that heaven is above a flat earth or that devils cause insanity. Does evangelism have to insist that the gospel is history?

One answer to this question is to say that it does not matter. Divine truth can be put in story form, as Jesus demonstrated with his parables. The discovery that there really was a Good Samaritan would not change at all the import of that story. The saving truths about God, man, sin, and salvation can be put in story form. The gospel has the power of God for salvation, and accepting what it teaches can transform human lives, whether it be history or parable. God may have taught the truth about himself through literal events, or he may have planted this grand conception in the minds of first-century narrators and inspired them to convey it through exalted literature. Someone who discovers "I am Adam" does not have to care too much about who else Adam is.

For many reasons, it would be impossible for me to believe that the gospel is a myth, even a divine and saving myth. But I am so sure of the saving power of the gospel that, though I doubted whether Jesus ever really lived, I would still long to tell others what this miraculous story reveals about the awfulness of sin, the boundless love of God, and the life that we can all enjoy.

Most Christians throughout history have believed that everything in the Bible, and most certainly in the four Gospels, happened exactly as it is recorded. In proclaiming the message of evangelism, these Christians have declared what the Bible says with as much certainty as though they had been there when it happened. They saw no need to distinguish between historical and spiritual truth.

There are others for whom it cannot be that simple. They believe that Jesus walked up the same Mount of Olives that cars drive up today. They believe that he was crucified under the Pontius Pilate whose name is found on ancient lists of Roman procurators. But when they read, in Mark 16:19, that Jesus "was taken up into heaven, and sat down at the right hand of God," that does not seem to them to be an actual seating arrangement at a real time and place in history. As a metaphor it says something of great importance about Jesus and the nature of God, but they know that heaven is not physically above the planet earth, and God literally sitting in a chair has no possible place in their religious concepts.

It is no wonder that literalists go to such lengths to interpret every event in the Bible as a historical happening. If you let just one of them be a metaphor, you are in trouble. If you let the plain statements of the facts of Jesus' ascension be a figure of speech, then any such statement can be. Then his birth, virgin birth, crucifixion, and resurrection may also be inspired representations of truth in picture form. Once the cloth is torn, the whole fabric can unravel. When the possibility of deviating from the straight historical line is opened up, the way through the Bible becomes a difficult and dangerous slalom course between fact and metaphor, between real events and myths. This certainly makes Bible interpretation harder, but perhaps God never meant it to be easy.

We do not have to make up our minds about the historicity of every item in the Bible's account of Christ's earthly mission and his heavenly glory before we can present him as the Lord and Savior. Evangelists with different hermeneutical standpoints can give the same message, though their views of the source of the message may be quite different. The words *sat down at the right hand of God* are essential to my Christology, and if sometime I am persuaded that this happened in time and space, it will not make that verse any more or less important.

2. THE MESSENGER'S REASSURANCES

We have been thinking of some problems for those who give the message of evangelism. Now let us think of their reassurances.

1. The Message Is True. The great encouragement for those who ask people to believe the gospel is that it is true. There is such a God as Jesus Christ described. People can believe that "God was in Christ reconciling the world to himself," because he was. It may be assumed that it is natural to believe in common-sense, material things, while to believe in God, prayer, and a life to come is strange and exotic. But if God and prayer to him are actual and life does continue after death, then not to believe in them is unnatural. It could easily seem unnatural to believe that there are people walking with their feet opposite ours on the other side of the planet, but our great encouragement in trying to persuade anyone of this is that those upside-down people are actually there. There are difficulties in persuading people that there is a God who loves them and wants them to love him; but more important than all the difficulties is the fact that it is true. Reality is on our side.

2. The Christian Life Is Normal. If Christ is real, then the life that is in harmony with him is natural; it is in accordance with the way things are. Any other sort of life is going against the grain. There is sometimes the feeling that evangelism tries to get people to do something unusual, like walking on their hands. It actually tries to set people on their feet and it gets them to walking as they were designed to walk. It is not like trying to teach an elephant to fly; it is rather like trying to teach an eagle to fly. Evangelism does not try to make people into something strange; it tries to show them who they really are. Thomas Aquinas said that "grace does not destroy nature but fulfills it" (*gratia non tollit* *naturam sed perficit*). Evangelism makes normal persons out of abnormal ones.

3. The Message Offers Powerful Inducements. There is a famous answer that the early Saxon missionary, Brindon, gave King Brude of England. Brindon had proclaimed the gospel and urged the king to take Christ as his Lord. Brude was impressed, but he hesitated. He asked, "What shall I expect to find if I accept your gospel and become Christ's man?" Brindon made the magnificent reply: "If you become Christ's man, you will stumble on from wonder unto wonder, and every wonder will be true." As we talk to people about faith in Christ, we must be able to say, "This is what Christ will do for you if you take him as your Lord. . . ."

But can evangelism offer inducements? A new graduate of Union Theological Seminary in New York City sent a copy of one of his first sermons back to his former teacher, Professor Julius Beber. The title of the sermon was "Religion Pays Handsome Dividends." Dr. Beber circled the title and returned the sermon with the notation, "Do you know who said that first? See Job 1:9." That verse says: "Then Satan answered the Lord, 'Does Job fear God for nought?' " Can evangelism offer handsome dividends?

Here is a story that evangelists have told in countless variations —each one, very likely, true. A man is a business failure. His children are hungry. His wife is out trying to pawn her wedding ring. He is so desperate that he begins to pray. He says: "God, I've been cheating you. I've used your gifts as if they were my own. From now on I'm giving you my life. I want you to be my business partner. Amen." He counts out his change—ninety cents. He puts nine cents in a fruit jar and says, "This belongs to God." Just then the phone rings. Someone is offering him a job. From then on everything is different. The story concludes: "Tonight that man is president of a million-dollar chain of supermarkets. He let God take control." The truth is that many Christians can point to their conversions as the turning points in their prosperity. The Christian virtues of industry, honesty, reliability, and good manners can have a cash value. If an evangelist believes that becoming a Christian is likely to make a person a more respected citizen and a better parent, as well as healthier, happier, more loved, and more secure—why not say so? Samuel Pepys had no inhibitions about this. A Sunday entry in his diary says, "A good sermon of Mr. Gifford at church upon, 'Seek ye first the kingdom of God.' A very excellent and persuasive, a good and moral sermon. He showed like a wise man that righteousness is a surer way of being rich than sin."

The problem is that it is almost impossible to disentangle religion from rewards. We tell people that if they will give their hearts to Christ they will find a joy and a peace and a strength that they never knew before. We assure them that the Church can bless their homes and help them to face life. God's laws are the rules by which we are designed to operate; if we break them, we break ourselves. The Bible from beginning to end promises benefits for godliness; think of the Proverbs, the Prophets, the Beatitudes.

But honest people are contemptuous of conversions that are purchased. Rice Christians, who praise God from full stomachs instead of from full hearts, are not admired. Jesus never made the Christian life look easy. He told a prospective follower that he could not even count on the comforts that are given to birds and animals. He asked the young ruler to give up his wealth. He said, "If any man would come after me, let him deny himself and take up his cross and follow me" (Matt. 16:24). He rebuked those who followed him for the bread he gave them. But then he immediately added that they should be looking for more satisfying food: "Do not labor for the food which perishes, but for the food which endures to eternal life" (John 6:27).

There is our clue; there are some rewards that evangelism cannot offer, and some that it can. It cannot offer health, prosperity, or deliverance from pain and sorrow. But it can offer the limitless joy of knowing God in Christ. Without him, everything goes wrong; with him, everything is right. It used to be customary to ask candidates for the ministry, "Would you be willing to be damned to hell forever for God's sake?" Paul said that everything which he once had valued most he now saw as trash in comparison with "the surpassing worth of knowing Christ Jesus my Lord (Phil. 3:8). That explains why the martyrs sang songs of joy while the flames mounted, and why they scribbled rapturous expressions of thanksgiving on their dungeon walls.

The benefits of the life with God are not at all remote. They are as immediate as loving human relationships, as a satisfying purpose for each day, as deliverance from crippling self-pity and corrosive hate, as uplifting worship, as love, joy, peace, guidance, contentment with today, and boundless hope for what lies ahead. Those who look for these benefits are, in a sense, rice Christians —but what rice!

3. WHAT PEOPLE WANT FROM RELIGION

If a church offers people what they seek, they will turn to it. If it does not, they will pass it by. Three things they seek are:

1. An Explanation of Human Existence. From the day we first become aware of ourselves, we are baffled by the question "Who am I?" Until we know who we are, we have no reason for doing anything, no motive for the choices we must make. We cannot remain sunk in apathy, but until we know why we are here, we have to toil with no purpose for our striving, and make decisions without knowing whether they are right. The mystery you confront in your mirror deepens when you look into your neighbor's eyes. How are you related to each other? Do you owe your neighbor anything—good treatment or respect? The world seems a crazy mixture of ugliness and beauty, of suffering and happiness. Our lives seem as evanescent as a mist. It is no wonder that human beings are desperate to know whether anything makes sense.

The answers to our questions have to be religious because the world cannot explain itself. The source of human values must be outside humanity. Those who are groping in the dark look at the Churches and wonder whether they have any light.

Dean M. Kelley, an executive of the National Council of Churches, in his book on why denominations grow or decline, says that "the indispensable function of religion" is to explain "the meaning of life in ultimate terms." Man is "a meaning oriented being." When he has no understanding of who he is or why he is here, he is sick with the deadly disease of *anomie*—of meaninglessness. Dr. Kelley gives statistics to show that the American denominations that characteristically have a clear and definite explanation of the meaning of life are growing; those that do not are dying. He says that the explanation people seek must be validated by some organized fellowship: "Neither anthropology nor history records a disembodied religion without any continuing group of people collectively experiencing and transmitting it." Kelley finds that the denominations that are successful in evangelism offer certainties; those that are failing offer speculations.[1]

In this there is important guidance for us. When stumbling people grasp for a support, their hands need to close on something solid. The longing for a definite meaning for their lives is so great that even intelligent people will accept a primitive theology that is firm rather than an enlightened one that is vague. The message cannot be: "One way of looking at it is. . . ." It must be: "We know!"

2. An Experience of God. The hunger for God is a part of human nature. Many unbelievers would be amused by that idea. They have the hunger, but they do not connect it with the thought of God. We all know people who seem to feel no need for religion. Their longing for God may be diverted into some other channel, or dulled by neglect, or killed by sin. They may experience God through beauty, love, or service without knowing that it is God whom they have found. They still need to know God as God, but at least they are not missing him entirely. People may be consumed by their longing for God without knowing what it is. There may be a deep loneliness which no amount of being with people can dispel. There may be a baffling consciousness of something wrong, an aching vacancy.

Christians know that God exists, and that human beings are designed to be in communion with him. When they are not, they have missed the purpose of their being, like a violin that is never played or a seed that is never planted. Prayer is often thought of as an acquired skill, a baffling exercise that may be natural for mystics but problematical for the rest of us. But if there is a God who loves us and wants us to love him, then praying is as natural as breathing. It is the failure to pray that is strange, like living in a house with someone and pretending to be alone. No doubt it looks strange to a fish to see a man walking on the ocean floor and breathing through a hose that runs up to another realm that is out of sight, but it is not strange for the diver. That is what he was designed to do. Martin Luther said: "As a shoemaker makes a shoe, and a tailor makes a coat, so ought a Christian to pray. Prayer is the daily business of a Christian." Every human being has the urge to pray, whether it is recognized or not. If a church offers to help people to know God, to satisfy the longing for him, to make their prayer more real, they will come to it.

Many who know about God have missed a personal experience of him. If God is thought of as *It,* there are few atheists. Almost everyone recognizes that there must be some Ground of Being, some First Mover or Organizing Principle. There are many who go beyond this and think of God as *He-She*—as personal. The source of such personal qualities as love and goodness cannot be subpersonal. But the knowledge of God will be incomplete until God is known as *You,* as One with whom we are in communication. People who believe in a personal God may not have known his presence, and deeply wish they could.

All believers know that their experience of God is not all that it might be. There is always the baffling sense of something wonderful and something incomplete. A church that can help people have a greater experience of God will have what multitudes are seeking.

3. A Guide for Living. People want a religion that will tell them how to live. They want to know what sort of conduct God expects of them, and what will make their lives turn out the best. They dread the ruinous mistakes that they can make. Amid all the moral confusion and the Babel of contradictory voices, they are longing for one voice that they can trust. As they struggle with their own weakness and evil, they want something firm to hold to. They know that God is supposed to be the source of morality, so they look toward the Church and wonder whether it can tell them what is right.

Dean Kelley's study shows that it is the "high demand" Churches that are growing. We might assume that Churches which lay strict requirements on their members would attract only the rare zealots, while the majority would flock to the Churches that are easy to belong to. But the facts are the exact reverse of that. Leniency and permissiveness do not make a Church appealing, they make it unimportant. If the invitation is "Come join us; you will not have to change what you are doing," the response will not be "Then why not?", but "Then why bother?"

I learned about this when a very intelligent young couple left our church to join one of the less traditional groups. The husband said: "Your church told me, 'We hope you won't drink too much.' My new church says, 'If you drink, you're out.' I used to hear that Christians should be generous; my church now requires me to tithe. No one before paid any attention to how often I attended; when I joined my present church, they told me, 'If you're not present twice on Sunday and on Wednesday evening, we'll want to know why.' I like a church that tells me what is right." I do not like his church's rigidity, but I am troubled about my church's fluidity.

A generation or two ago, the argument was over legalism. Should churches have rules about smoking, drinking, Sabbath observance, or sexual morality? For many churches that argument is over. The question now is whether churches should have any definite standards at all. The current tendency is to put morality in such abstract terms that anything is possible.

The Sermon on the Mount is not a rule book, it is a picture book. Jesus described a worshipper who rushes from the temple to patch up a quarrel. Another, who has been struck, turns the other cheek; another is so sorry for a sin that he cuts off his hand. Those who trust God do not give future needs a passing thought. By pictures painted in such startling colors, Jesus made the Christian virtues unmistakable. He did not leave ideals as abstractions. He was definite when he told what an angry brother ought to do and how a sinful woman ought to act. The Church can give, not Pharisaic regulations, but clear ideals and specific advice on how they apply to daily life. It can give its guidance, not by strict rules, but by high expectations.

Dostoevski said, "If there is no God, then everything is allowed." But if there is such a God as Jesus Christ revealed, then some things are not allowed because they are contrary to God and to his intention for his children's lives. Those who take the same Jesus for their guide will have the same devotion to truth, honesty, purity, kindness, service, and love for God and man. And this way of living will be sharply different from the way of the world, just as it was in Jesus' time.

Christian conduct does not have to be improvised. Millions of followers through twenty centuries have learned a great deal about how Christ's teachings apply to families, morals, daily work, government. Much is now known about the behavior that makes life rich and full, and the behavior that empties living. People expect the Church to accumulate this wisdom and to pass it on to them. The evangelistic message of a church that does this can promise seekers the guidance they desire.

4. THE MESSAGE IS JESUS CHRIST

Paul described his evangelistic message—"I did not come proclaiming to you the testimony of God in lofty words or wisdom. For I decided to know nothing among you except Jesus Christ and him crucified" (1 Cor. 2:1-2). As the first disciples went flaming out with the good news, their whole message was "Jesus Christ is Lord!" Evangelism has other themes, but its greatest appeal is the attractiveness of Jesus to people of all sorts. People criticize the Church, scorn the pretentions of church members, and condescend to the naivete of the devout, but you will not find many who criticize, scorn, or condescend to Jesus. At the height of the campus unrest in 1970, I invited myself to a meeting of some very radical students in St. Louis. When I said that the Church was being helpful in the Vietnam crisis, I was surprised to get no argument. They had no opinions about the Church because they never thought of it. But when I asked, "What do you think of Jesus?", the mood changed. There was a regard for him that was close to reverence. One of the students told me of a friend whom he considered extremely radical. In the apartment that this friend shared with a woman student, there were just two pictures—of Che Guevara and of Jesus. The appeal of Jesus is the most wide-open approach to religion for people of all sorts—for hard-hats and intellectuals, for housewives and entertainment personalities. Tributes to him come from the most unexpected sources:

Dr. James Black of Scotland, reporting on the British troops he worked with in France, said, "Amid all the criticism of the Church, I never met anyone who criticized its Lord."

H.G. Wells said, "I am not a believer. But I must confess, as an historian, this penniless preacher from Galilee is irresistibly the center of history."...."The Galilean is too great for our small hearts."

Dostoevski wrote to his brother, "I am a child of this age, a child of unbelief and skepticism. And yet . . . I believe that there is nothing lovelier, deeper, more sympathetic, more rational, more human, and more perfect than the Saviour."

Many of Jesus' first disciples did not come to him because he was the Son of God, but simply because he was the most attractive person they had ever met. They wanted to be near him. It was only later that they found they could not think of him in human terms at all. He took them to such depths that they finally had to say, "You are the Christ, the Son of the living God." Evangelism can trust that progression. If it brings people to think about Jesus, to read about him, to be with those who love him, the time will come when many will take him as their Lord.

Jesus gives what people seek from a religion. From him that baffling three-letter word G-o-d gets a content. When Philip, at a time of desperate foreboding, expressed the longing of all who grope for God, Jesus told him, "He who has seen me has seen the Father" (Jn. 14:9). He puts God within reach of human hearts. The thought of the Supreme Being can be awful and incomprehensible. Human hearts so need a God that is definite, not abstract, that for lack of anything more specific, they will worship a hideous idol or an even more hideous dictator. But Jesus makes God knowable and real. When Christians end their prayers ". . .through Jesus Christ," they mean that they have had before them as they prayed, not an abstract Deity, but the One whom they have come to know and love in Jesus Christ.

In Jesus we find out who we are. Just as Galileo revolutionized astronomy by putting the sun in the center of the solar system, so Jesus revolutionized anthropology by putting a little child in the center of the value system. When he called a child and "put him in the midst of them" (Matt. 18:2), and said that no one was greater in God's sight, he gave infinite value to the humblest human being—to you, and to every potential victim of a super-bomb.

Jesus shows us why we are here: "As thou didst send me into the world, so I have sent them into the world" (John 17:18). His life of love and service is the model of what our lives are for.

Evangelism can offer Jesus as the guide for living. Through devotion to him, we begin to think as he does. "Let this mind be in you, which was also in Christ Jesus" (Phil. 2:5, KJV). It is Jesus' special slant on life that makes us know what job to take, whom to marry, how large a check to write. He guides us less as a lawgiver than as a comrade. We get the feel for what he wants. We know when we have let him down. When a church says, "Let us tell you about Jesus," it is offering the practical guidance that people seek from a religion.

5. APPEALS

A church, like its stained glass, may look lovely from the inside, but dreary from outside. Christians are supposed to be poor in spirit, and more sweet than strong. They disparage the real satisfactions and get their pleasure from singing hymns and listening to sermons. For excitement they have rummage sales and slide shows on foreign missions.

The groups that people join offer something they want—sports, entertainment, health, prestige. If the Church is to be the evangelist, it must offer inducements that will make people look in its direction.

We need to notice how subtly right appeals can slide into wrong ones. The difference between a covenant and a deal is not always made plain: "If you take God for your Partner, how can you fail?" (You can't, but you may go broke.) We can speak of the hope of a future life, but we cannot use the fear of hell to get people to profess a faith they do not have. We can say that joining the Church helps people lead better lives, but not that it certifies respectability.

It is not wrong to offer appeals that fall short of the full truth. Jesus usually comes into a life through a narrow opening. If people are induced to look to him for a partially adequate reason, there is a chance that they may really find him; and those who find him always find more than they were looking for. We often have to try one appeal after another until we find the one that is right for that person at that time. Here are samples of the many possible appeals that can be offered:

1. Security. Widespread upheavals have many wondering what the world is coming to. Political scandals and bad business news can seem to be portents of impending doom. Many are fearful of losing their jobs, or their health, or the persons they love most. There is always reason for cold fear to be clutching human hearts. Evangelism can let people know that there is a security that overrules the threats from which they cringe. It can assure them that nothing "will be able to separate us from the love of God in Christ Jesus our Lord" (Rom. 8:39).

2. Truth. People are desperate for certainty, and in despair of finding it. For daily living we have to have something solid that we can trust. The experts give wildly conflicting answers to our questions. Our only hope is to get some word from outside the world-conditioned babel. Russell Davenport said in an editorial in *Fortune* magazine: "Unless we hear a voice, men of this generation will sink down a spiral of depression. There is only one way out of this spiral. The way out is the sound of a voice; not our voice, but a voice coming from something not ourselves in the existence of which we cannot disbelieve." The evangelist bears witness to this voice.

3. Death. Americans are inclined to dismiss the thought of death as morbid, and many Christians shrink from commercializing goodness by tying it to future rewards and punishments. But this tendency to slip by without looking at death may be the sign of an unhealthy mind. The approaching limit to all our earthly loves, hopes, and interests is a fact with which we have to reckon. Perhaps what we resent most is the insult of death—the implication that we are worth nothing but the crowning indignity of extinction. Thomas Browne said, "I am not so much afraid of death as ashamed thereof." For those who believe in him, Christ has "abolished death and brought life and immortality to light through the gospel" (2 Tim. 1:10).

4. Satisfaction. Many people have an exasperating sense of hollowness. Hearts can hunger for what the repetitious rat race does not supply. Nature abhors a vacuum. When the man in the parable left his heart empty, seven evil spirits moved in (Matt. 12:43–45). Workoholics and political fanatics try in vain to find a satisfying substitute for God.

This is not a simpleminded need that disappears at the higher levels of culture and education. Teilhard de Chardin pointed out that "nothing could be more mistaken than to regard religion as a primitive and passing phase of mankind's infancy. The more man-like man becomes, the more necessary it is for him to know how to adore."

There is a prevalent sense of being trapped and dominated by superficial affairs. People resent the stifling of their souls. Evangelism can tell those who feel empty what Jesus meant by "they shall be filled" (Matt. 5:6, kjv). It can show how the Church keeps souls awake and gives us companions for our spiritual quest.

5. Salvation. The miracle of God's mercy that evangelism offers is release from the ruinous effects of sin and guilt. The evangelist has the hard problem of saying this in a way that will make people connect it with needs they recognize. They have to see that "guilt" is their sense of failure and betrayal. "Repentance" means making a fresh start. And "sin" is those diseases of the spirit that blight every life, not just scandalous misconduct.

The cross is the best-known symbol in the western world, but we still have to connect it with what God can do for us. Talk of Christ's blood will be no more than an atavistic formula until people are helped to see its connection with the dreadfulness of sin and the marvel of God's love.

6. Peace. Eighty-seven percent of a group polled on the West Coast listed inner peace as what they most need and desire. Many minds are battlefields of contrary impulses and crossed-up emotions. Dr. Alfred Adler defined a neurosis as "Yes, but. . . ." Ideals clash with cravings. We are irritated by those we love. In Robert Louis Stevenson's story, Dr. Jekyll and Mr. Hyde at least took turns; in most people they contend for control at the same time.

This is the state from which Jesus saves us. Love of him can so dominate us that the jangling discords come into harmony. It is a special kind of peace that Jesus offers. He said, "My peace I give to you; not as the world gives . . ." (John 14:27). The world gives the peace of apathy or resignation. Jesus does not quiet our feelings, he increases them. He gives us rapture, indignation, eagerness, and delight. At Boulder Dam, the guide stands a nickel on edge on the housing of a generator that is spinning out enough energy to run a city. Christian peace is not bovine placidity, it is the calm of mighty forces in complete control. We can be sure that an offer of release from inner turmoil will be heard with longing.

7. Gratitude. When a man with no church background joined our church, I asked him why he did it. He said, "I am so grateful for my wife and family, I have to have some way to say so." We cannot thank biology or good luck for our blessings. Thanks requires a personal connection that we deeply want to make. Until we have expressed our thanks, there is a yawning gap that we long to close. People can be shown that by confessing their faith they express their thanks to God.

8. Excitement. Many people are bored with their jobs. They are grinding along in occupations that have lost all interest for them. Ennui is a common disease, a bane to spirits and to bodies. This is a state from which Christ can rescue us. He makes us see our work as our vocation—a service to God and man to which we are divinely called. He ties us by our heartstrings to the joys and sorrows of those around us. He transforms commonplace events into rich sources of delight. He turns us outward from our jaded selves to fascinated absorption in the human drama.

God has put in human hearts a gallant urge for adventure in high causes. Those who chafe in dull routines will respond to a call to give themselves to noble striving. This is no fantasy. Millions of Christians who otherwise would be sitting before their television sets watching the shadows of other people's imaginary exploits have heard Christ's call and are helping paroled prisoners, working in day nurseries, leading clubs in deprived neighborhoods, laboring to improve human relations, challenging corrupt political machines.

An evangelistic invitation that one often sees printed in church bulletins begins: "To all who are weary and need rest, to all who are sorrowing and need comfort, to all who are faltering and need strength. . . ." Christ does have an answer to such needs, but there should also be an invitation addressed "to all the vigorous who need action, to all the courageous who are looking for adventure, to all the strong who long for exhilarating uses of their strength. . . ." Evangelism can make a forceful appeal to the lively who need a worthy outlet for their vitality.

9. Power to Be Good. There is a world of difference between a personal moral code and the Bible's guidance: the personal code depends upon our moods, but the objective guide remains the same, no matter how we may be feeling. The house built on sand may look exactly like the house built on rock—until the storm comes. There are times of temptation when judgement is uncertain and principles become confused. At such times we need a sure moral foundation. We also need the power to be good that Christ supplies. Evangelism can tell people who long to be better than they are, whose good resolutions have often collapsed under stress, whose confidence in themselves has vanished, that Jesus Christ can hold them true to what they want to be.

10. Family. What the Christian faith and Church can do for families has a powerful appeal. For many people, the family is the most important part of life. Christians regard a home, not as a human arrangement, but as a divine ordering. The Church and the home are the two earthly institutions that are let down from God out of heaven. A home is a sub-Church, a House of God, where he can be known and enjoyed in a special way. The early Communion services were always held in homes around a family table. Whenever the family gathered around that table afterwards, some sense of the Lord's Supper must have remained. The dining tables in our homes are still extensions of the Communion table at the church. There is a sacredness in the connection of parents and children, brothers and sisters, husbands and wives. The practical meaning of this for the joys, strains, duties, and relationships in families is an inexhaustible part of the message of evangelism.

11. A Better World. The hearts of many people outside the Church are torn by human suffering; their consciences are outraged by the injustices and corruptions of society. If they can be shown that the Church gives them ways to help the distressed and to get into the struggle for a better world, they will be impressed. Those who do not know the Church may not see how it can give them much to do about the problems of mankind. They need to be shown what the Church does:

(a) Each person whom the Church brings to a true faith in Christ is one more healer for a sick society. Gilbert K. Chesterton said that as a young man he thought of himself as too radical to be a Christian. Then, at last, he got around to putting his radical ideas down on paper, and he discovered that Christianity had been teaching them for eighteen hundred years—so he joined the Church.

(b) The Church is a training school for Christian citizens. It does not tell its members what to decide about current issues, but it gives them the Christian point of view from which their decisions must be made. It makes them keenly interested in public matters.

(c) The Church helps the needy. Most welfare agencies—orphanages, hospitals, shelters—were once maintained by churches. Then Christian urging made welfare a government responsibility, but churches still have their own ministries. Many congregations have programs to help the poor, the aged, the unfortunate, the victims of drugs and alcohol. Anyone who joins a church should be offered ways to help those who are in trouble.

(d) By the miracle of money, church members can help the distressed anywhere on earth. The fingers of a stenographer tapping on a typewriter can open blind eyes in a far-off hospital if her earnings help put the surgeon there. Mission schools are supplying a large proportion of the government officials in many new nations.

(e) Words are social action. A word not only says something, it does something. The ancient Greeks had the saying, "By words alone are lives of mortals swayed." The Church hurls the force of its words against social evils through sermons, official declarations, and its members' participation in the decision-making processes of their communities.

(f) A church can demonstrate Christian ideals in its own life. It can reveal how quite dissimilar people can be a loving fellowship. In its business dealings, and in the proportion of its income that it gives to needs outside itself, it can reveal Christian idealism.

12. Witnessing. It would be manslaughter not to let someone know of a doctor who could save his life. We could never in conversations tell all who know us about what Christ does for life. But when we are known to be members of a Church, it inclines all who like and respect us to think more about the Christian faith. Our example may influence some who are adrift to turn to Christ. Paul said, "I am under obligation" (Rom. 1:14). All we have received from Christ puts us under obligation to let others know about it.

15

The Spiritual
Qualifications for Evangelism

1. THE NEED

A church's spiritual qualities determine whether it will be *eager* to evangelize, and *able* to evangelize. This does not mean that a church should first try to become spiritually qualified and then reach out to others. Christians do not become more spiritually minded by thinking of themselves (see pp. 54–55). But a congregation that is already striving to share its faith must be unceasingly intent on gaining more of the inner resources that it needs.

A congregation does not have to be a model of radiance and vitality in order to evangelize. It may have a tired minister and a program that is stuck in tedious ruts, but it can still be offering the saving truths through hymns, Bible readings, prayers, and sacraments. It is often astonishing to see people brought into Christianity through churches that are far from impressive. Evangelism is always a miracle. But that does not lessen our obligation to prepare ourselves to do our best.

Spiritual renewal is not emergency treatment for a person or a church—it is a periodic necessity. Everything tends to roll downhill. Vitality plays out, vision fades, ardor cools, prayer becomes routine. Our awareness of God is like an astronomer's view of a star. Unless he keeps re-aiming the telescope, the earth's turning will put the star out of sight. That is why the Bible keeps reminding us that we need a supernatural power to reverse this natural tendency: "They who wait for the Lord shall renew their strength" (Is. 40:31). "Though our outer nature is wasting away, our inner nature is being renewed every day" (2 Cor. 4:16).

Paul advised Timothy, "Rekindle the gift of God" (2 Tim. 1:6).

We need renewal to fit us for the succeeding stages of our lives. The religious conceptions of childhood will not do for adolescence. Our teenage religious experiences will not see us through our twenties. A church that provides mountaintop experiences for young people, and leaves the rest of life an uneventful plain, misunderstands human nature. We regularly need special occasions, not just for restoring what has faded, but for new spiritual discoveries. "Hardened saints" are those who have been left in the same state so long that they have solidified.

2. SOURCES OF NEW SPIRITUAL LIFE

1. Belief. Members whose lives are dominated by a clear and commanding faith make a church able to evangelize. Vagueness of belief is the reason for the troubles from which many of the denominations are now suffering—declining membership, decreased attendance, diminished contributions, lapsed evangelism.

Evangelism is not tied to any particular theology; both liberals and conservatives can be ardently evangelistic. But a person who has no clear beliefs has no assurances to share. Many ministers are uncomfortable about evangelism because of their uncertainties. They dream of a season of study and reflection when they can work out what they believe. And all the while what they most need is not reverie but action—the striving to help someone who is desperate for something firm to hold on to. They need to preach all the belief they have, knowing that each sermon will take them a little farther. Many a reluctant personal witness or hesitant evangelistic preacher has dragged himself down the sawdust trail by the exertion of doing all he can for those whose needs are great.

We are not going to come to an impelling faith by working our way through all our Biblical and theological uncertainties, because pressing close behind them are swarms of new uncertainties that we have not yet seen. What we really need is to recover the theological method that has served Christians well through the centuries—the method of working from the center out, instead of from the outside in. Everyone who is a Christian has a few great beliefs that are absolutely certain and unshakable. Beyond them is an area of speculation about beliefs that are accepted but not yet worked out—perhaps about prayer, or heaven, or the Church. Then way out at the periphery is a shadow land where everything is confusing and obscure. Too many Christians are so trapped out there that they have lost contact with the certainties they never had to doubt. They are like the geologist at the South Pole who went beyond the line of stakes that, in the total blackness of the polar night, was supposed to connect him with his base. Except for a lucky accident, he would never have been found. Religiously, we need to keep in touch with the last stake that we have driven, but too many good minds have wandered out into the darkness and are lost.

If churches are to be effective in evangelism, or in anything, they have to keep in contact with the great truths that are always there. The whole life of a church depends on its certainty that Jesus Christ is Lord and Master. When other interests divert a church from an all-dominating awareness of this truth, it becomes ineffectual in everything it tries (see pp. 223–225).

In the recent past, we have too much let this truth be pushed aside by interests that are derived from it. I can recognize this in my own preaching. Our Lenten classes, which used to have Biblical or devotional topics, have tended to have more of such subjects as "Religious Themes in Broadway Plays" or "Christ and the Ecology." A summer conference that our group of churches provided for their youth had as its one requirement that religion not be mentioned. The leaders were trying an experiment in interpersonal relations that they felt would be disturbed by blessings at the table or Sunday worship services. Church people in the future are likely to look back on our recent church fashions with some amazement. These fashions can account for much that has been happening. Denominations' reorganizations do not work, so they reorganize again. They devise the best fund-raising techniques they have ever had, and raise less money—especially for causes beyond the local church. Christian education has improved its methodology, but it nurtures fewer Christians. The loss of spiritual vividness and intensity is the reason for the present problems in the Church.

Preaching can do much to build in a congregation the strong beliefs that are essential for evangelism (see p. 184). It is sometimes felt that doctrinal preaching will be dull, but the truth is the exact opposite. Dorothy Sayers put it well: "It is the neglect of dogma that makes for dullness. The Christian faith is the most exciting drama that has ever staggered the imagination of man—and dogma *is* the drama."[1] Classes on belief are important. The reading of books on the Christian faith can be promoted by the church library, a book table, or reading-and-discussion clubs. The use in worship services of brief contemporary affirmations of faith can be helpful, especially if they are examined, and not just read with ritualistic inattention.

The force of our faith depends not only on what we believe, but on how we believe it. Surveys of the beliefs of church members invariably show that over 90 percent believe in a loving God, prayer, a future life, and the Bible as revelation. Then what more does it take to throw them into evangelism with fervent abandon? But mere acceptance of beliefs is not enough. The Huguenots of southern France, as they were hauled in farm carts to their execution, were warned that if they spoke or sang to the crowds that packed their route, their tongues would be torn out. But many of them, seeing this as their last chance to witness to their faith, sang Psalms all the way, and their tongues *were* torn out. I am sure I would have found conscientious reasons to dispense with the Psalm singing. I believe most of what those Huguenots believed, but I believe it in a different way. It is not only what church members believe that makes them eager for evangelism, it is the way they believe it.

2. Prayer. A church that is going to accomplish much in evangelism has to rely on prayer. A church becomes a praying church by praying. There must be many occasions for real prayer. The prayer must be a conscious turning to God, and not just a substitute for a gavel in calling a meeting to order. It is important to increase the number of church members who can lead in prayer. In one of my pastorates, I found the feeling that it was disrespectful, of God or of the minister, for anyone else to pray if a minister was present. That deprived the church members of something that they should do, so I consulted the lay leaders. We came to an understanding that a minister never prays between Sundays. Even on Sundays the minister need not do all the praying.

3. The Bible. Spiritual vigor is nourished by the Bible. Inducing the members to use their Bibles with a fresh delight is an important source of new life for a congregation. A church needs to help its members understand what the Bible has for them. They need incentives and helps (see p. 207). A sermon on a whole book of the Bible can stir great interest in it. A sermon series can get people to do the related Bible reading for each week. There will be more reading of passages that are recommended for private use in Advent or Lent if they are also used in church services and classes.

4. Action. Spiritual power requires spiritual exercise. Pew warmers have poor prayers. Eating without exercise results in sluggishness, and a church that provides wonderful worship without giving ways to serve will have torpid members. The penalty will be what Harry Emerson Fosdick called "a glut of unutilized grace."

God in his mercy lets us share his work. "God created everything, but he manufactures nothing." He calls us to finish what he wants to do for his children. "We are God's fellow workers" (1 Cor. 3:9, NEB). When we are laboring to do what Christ wants done, he can seem very close to us. If you want to understand a sailor, you have to go to sea; if you want to understand Jesus Christ, you have to get into his line of work.

A problem with some churches is that they do so little that they have no way to use their members. So they defraud the world of what the church should be doing, while the members go flabby for lack of any function. There is no shortage of important things for a church to do. If it is in touch with human life, it can never get caught up. A church's ministry need not be confined to its own tasks. It should be willing to recruit workers for wherever there is need. Some churches put in the bulletin, where the staff is listed, some form of the statement, "This church has four hundred ministers assisted by a clergyman."

The act of giving is an exercise that makes souls strong. We are made spiritually more alive by the stirring experience of dedication, by the thrill of doing something unselfish out of obedience to Christ. Spiritual dullness is the result of uninspired giving. When a giver hesitates, more than money is in the balance. The decision to do an unprecedented sort of giving may mark the advance into a new spiritual state.

A fresh program that can jar church members out of the old financial ruts in which they have been stuck can be a source of new life for a congregation. The program may be the adoption of a stirring mission project, a rediscovery of tithing, or the presenting of a creative new work for the congregation to begin. It can make those who think their church is stodgy recognize how exciting it can be.

A new concern for social righteousness can bring renewal to a congregation. It can give some members a heartstretching discovery of an area of Christianity that they have missed, and it can put a fresh interest into church life. A congregation that uses its members for direct ministry to human needs gives them a personal experience of what it is to follow Christ.

Working at evangelism unites church members in a high spiritual endeavor. It makes them recognize their need of clear belief and prayer. It strikingly illustrates the old rule, "What you do not share, you lose; what you give away, you keep forever."

The most vital churches are likely to be known for some particular work in which they are outstanding—as in Christian education, or counselling, or ministry to a foreign-language group. A specialty makes outsiders aware of a church and gives the members the sense that their church is unusual.

3. A CHURCH'S PERSONALITY

Churches have as distinct personalities as do individuals. They may be staid, unconventional, contentious, cheerful, placid, fervent. This is important for evangelism in two ways: (1) An appealing personality can attract outsiders. (2) A church's personality can reveal Christianity.

An attractive church personality is a blend of qualities. One of

these is spirituality. That might not sound appealing; "spirituality" may suggest the heavenly remoteness of those who already
seem to be wearing their ascension robes. But Christian spirituality is more robust than that. Its source is hero worship. Our
heroes tend to move in and take us over. That is what Paul meant
when he said, "Christ lives in me" (Gal. 2:20, NEB). A "spiritual"
church will have some of the attraction that Christ has.

The feeling of a church's members for each other affects the
impression it makes. Sometimes they seem to be acquaintances
who meet formally and warily. In other churches you sense the
delight of dear friends who love to be together. Of course,
friendly people make a friendly congregation, but a church cannot be just a fellowship for extroverts. A church needs to make
much of occasions at which even the shy can develop friendships.
With all the jokes about the "dining car to heaven," close-knit
and happy churches are likely to serve many meals. Companion-
ship comes from breaking bread together (com, "with," plus panis,
"bread"). Elton Trueblood called the church supper "the oldest
Christian ritual." Punch-and-coffee fellowship after a church service is an appropriate sequel to worshipping together.

Any church with more than a few members needs smaller
groups where close friendships can be formed. Some of these are
functional—the choir people, the Church School cronies, the
kitchen crew. Groups meet the members' need for learning, recreation, prayer, or fellowship. A church is deficient if it does not
have some group that is right for every member or prospective
member.

Coming together in groups does not by itself make for intimacy. A little girl is reported to have explained why she did not
like her new Sunday School: "They put me in a room full of
children all by myself." A strange gap in many congregations is
the lack of any opportunity for the members to be known for who
they really are. Even in small gatherings, they may talk only about
the business or the topic for that day, but not about what is most
on their minds and hearts. They may sing, "We share our mutual
woes, our mutual burdens bear," without ever doing it. Prayer
groups where the members pray about each other's problems
give a chance for this sort of sharing. Retreats, or any coming

together when members can talk about themselves, help to make an organization of Christians a real church. Tertullian, a convert from paganism, reported in his *Apology* that the Romans said of the Christians, "Look how they love one another." The love of a church's members for each other is one of its most important spiritual qualifications for evangelism.

Notes

CHAPTER 1: THE URGENCY OF EVANGELISM

1. Walter Rauschenbusch, *Christianizing the Social Order* (New York: Macmillan Co., 1912), pp. 458, 459, 462, 464, and *A Theology for the Social Gospel* (New York: Abingdon Press, Apex Books, 1945), p. 194.
2. Pitrim Aleksandrovich Sorokin, *Man and Society in Calamity* (New York: E. P. Dutton and Company, 1943).
3. Gordon W. Allport, *The Nature of Prejudice* (New York: Doubleday, Anchor Books, 1958), p. 422.
4. Sherwood E. Wirt, *The Social Conscience of an Evangelical* (New York: Harper & Row, 1968), p. 3.
5. Richard F. Lovelace, "The Shape of the Coming Renewal," *Christian Century* 88, no. 40 (Oct. 6, 1971): 1165.

CHAPTER 2: THE OBJECTIONS TO EVANGELISM

1. Leonard England, "Report," *Information Service* 30, no. 39 (Nov. 24, 1951, published by the Federal Council of Churches): 2–3.
2. Keith Miller, *The Taste of New Wine* (Waco, Texas: Word Books, 1965), p. 89.
3. Avery Dulles as quoted in Donald A. McGavran, *Eye of the Storm* (Waco, Texas: Word Books, 1972), pp. 89–90.
4. Ronan Hoffman as quoted in McGavran, *Eye of the Storm,* p. 84.

CHAPTER 3: THE CHURCH IS THE EVANGELIST

1. Edward Gibbon, *History of the Decline and Fall of the Roman Empire,* Vol. II, p. 7.

CHAPTER 4: THE DEFINITION OF EVANGELISM

1. William Temple, *Readings from St. John's Gospel* (London: Macmillan and Co., 1940), p. 386.
2. Philip Schaff, *History of the Christian Church,* Vol. II (New York: Charles Scribner's Sons, 1903), pp. 256–257.
3. William James, *Psychology* (New York: Henry Holt & Co., 1915), pp. 147–149.
4. Dietrich Bonhoeffer, *The Cost of Discipleship* (New York: Macmillan Co., 1949), p. 68.
5. Martin Luther as quoted in *The Luthern Liturgy* (Philadelphia: Muhlenberg Press, 1947), p. ii.
6. J. Milton Yinger, *The Scientific Study of Religion* (New York: Macmillan Co., 1970), p. 10.

CHAPTER 5: THE SUPPORTING STRUCTURES

1. Karl Barth, *Dogmatics in Outline* (New York: Harper Tourch Books, 1959).
2. John A. O'Brien, *Winning Converts* (New York: P. J. Kenedy & Sons, 1948), pp. 239–240.

CHAPTER 6: MAKING CONTACTS

1. Truman B. Douglass, *Mission to America* (New York: The Friendship Press, 1951), p. 69.
2. Karl Barth, *The Humanity of God* (Richmond, Va.: John Knox Press, 1960), p. 53.
3. Donald A. McGavran, *Understanding Church Growth* (Grand Rapids, Mich.: William B. Eerdmans, 1970), pp. 198–215, 249–250.
4. H. Richard Niebuhr as quoted in *Evangelism in the United States* (London: Lutterworth Press, 1958), p. 10.
5. Clyde S. Hale, *The Webster Presbyterian* 32, no. 25 (Sept. 22, 1976), p. 1.
6. Andrew W. Blackwood, *Evangelism in the Home Church* (New York: Abingdon-Cokesbury Press, 1942), pp. 42–43.

CHAPTER 7: CULTIVATING CHRISTIAN FAITH AND KNOWLEDGE

1. James S. Steward, *Heralds of God* (New York: Charles Scribner's Sons, 1946), p. 47.

CHAPTER 8: CONVERSION AND DECISION

1. Arthur Koestler, *The God That Failed,* ed. Richard Crossman (New York: Harper & Brothers, 1949), p. 23.
2. Ella Wheeler Wilcox, "The Ships" in *Quotable Poems,* Vol. 1 (Chicago: Willett, Clark & Co., 1931), pp. 148–149.
3. Leo Tolstoi, *A Confession, The Gospel in Brief and What I Believe,* trans. Aylmer Maude (London: Oxford University Press, 1951), p. 307.
4. Nels F. S. Ferré, *Return to Christianity* (New York: Harper & Brothers, 1943), p. 10.
5. C. S. Lewis, *Surprised by Joy* (New York: Harcourt, Brace and Co., 1955), p. 228.

CHAPTER 9: YOUTH EVANGELISM

1. Erik H. Erikson, *Identity, Youth and Crisis* (New York: W.W. Norton, 1968), pp.128–29.
2. Horace Bushnell, *Christian Nurture* (New York: Charles Scribner's Sons, 1923), pp. 4, 21, 35.
3. John Baillie, *Our Knowledge of God* (New York: Charles Scribner's Sons, 1939), p. 5.
4. Bryan Green, *The Practice of Evangelism* (New York: Charles Scribner's Sons, 1951), p. 180.

CHAPTER 10: USING LAY CALLERS

1. Louis I. Newman, "The Voice of God," in *Trumpet in Adversity* (New York: The Renascence Press, 1948), p. 57.
2. R. A. Torrey, *Why God Used D. L. Moody* (Wilmore, Ky.: Asbury Theological Seminary, 1973), p. 46.

CHAPTER 12: EVANGELISTIC SERMONS

1. Arthur Michael Ramsey and Leon-Joseph Suenens, *The Future of the Christian Church* (London: SCM Press, 1971), p. 56.

CHAPTER 14: THE MESSAGE OF EVANGELISM

1. Dean M. Kelley, *Why Conservative Churches Are Growing* (New York: Harper & Row, 1972), pp. 20–37, 39, 40, 44.

CHAPTER 15: THE SPIRITUAL QUALIFICATIONS FOR EVANGELISM

1. Dorothy L. Sayers, *Letters to a Post Christian World* (Grand Rapids, Mich.: William B. Eerdmans, 1969), p. 13.

For Further Reading

These books on evangelism come from a wide variety of points of view. Some can be skimmed at top speed, others require careful reading. Some are in bookstores, others can be found only in libraries. They all have important insights.

THE BIBLICAL AND SPIRITUAL BASIS

Baillie, John. *Baptism and Conversion.* New York: Charles Scribner's Sons, 1964. 121 pp. Scholarly, lucid, brief, Biblical.

Barclay, William. *Turning to God.* London: The Epworth Press, 1963. 103 pp. A Biblical study of conversion and what it requires of the church and the convert.

Blauw, Johannes. *The Missionary Nature of the Church.* London: Lutterworth Press, 1962. 136 pp. Asks, "Does everyone on earth need Jesus Christ?"

Bloesch, Donald. *The Crisis of Piety.* Grand Rapids: Wm. B. Eerdmans, 1968. 159 pp. Investigates the faith and spiritual life that empower evangelism.

Coleman, Robert E. *The Master Plan of Evangelism.* Old Tappan: Fleming H. Revell, 1963. 126 pp. How we can use Jesus' evangelistic methods.

Ford, Leighton. *The Christian Persuader.* New York: Harper & Row, 1966. 149 pp. Why faith is specially needed now.

Stott, John R. *Our Guilty Silence.* London: Hodder & Stoughton, 1967. 118 pp. A British view of the world's great need of evangelism and the Church's neglect of it.

Stowe, David M. *Ecumenicity and Evangelism.* Grand Rapids: Wm. B. Eerdmans, 1970. 78 pp. Recent criticisms of world evangelism. New strategies for it.

THEOLOGY

Barth, Karl. *Church Dogmatics.* (Reconciliation, 2nd half). Edinburgh: T. & T. Clark, 1950. On vocation, the Holy Spirit, the Christian Community, the Christian hope.

de Jong, Pieter. *Evangelism and Contemporary Theology.* Nashville: Tidings, 1962. 112 pp. On Reinhold Niebuhr, Tillich, Bonhoeffer, Brunner, Barth, Bultmann.

Documents of Vatican II. New York: Herder & Herder, 1966. 792 pp. Specially the sections on "Laity" and "Missions."

Hoekendijk, J. C. *The Church Inside Out.* Philadelphia: Westminster Press, 1966. 212 pp. Evangelizing by reaching out, not by drawing in.

Kantonen, T. A. *Theology of Evangelism.* Philadelphia: Muhlenberg Press, 1954. 98 pp. Scholarly, not lively. Puts evangelism at the center of all church activities.

Kraemer, Henrik. *The Communication of the Christian Faith.* Philadelphia: Westminster Press, 1956. 120 pp. Dry, thoughtful.

———. *A Theology of the Laity.* Philadelphia: Westminster Press, 1958. 191 pp. Widely read and highly regarded.

Stott, John R. *Fundamentalism and Evangelism.* Grand Rapids: Wm. B. Eerdmans, 1959. 88 pp. British. Fundamentalism's relation to evangelism.

THE QUALITIES OF THE EVANGELIZING CONGREGATION

Brown, Fred. *Secular Evangelism.* London: SCM Press, 1970. 117 pp. A British insistence that most people today find religion real and churches unreal.

Drummond, Lewis A. *Evangelism: The Counter-Revolution.* London: Marshall, Morgan & Scott, 1972. 192 pp. Pastoral leadership, preaching, problems, resources, theology.

Hyde, Douglas. *Dedication and Leadership.* Notre Dame, Ind.: University of Notre Dame Press, 1968. 157 pp. A Communist now converted to Christianity thinks that Christians can learn from the strategies of Communist evangelism.

Kelley, Dean M. *Why Conservative Churches Are Growing.* New York: Harper & Row, 1972. 179 pp. A National Council of Churches executive explains why liberal churches lack evangelistic force.

McGavran, Donald. *Understanding Church Growth.* Grand Rapids: Wm. B. Eerdmans, 1970. 369 pp. A global look at what makes churches grow or shrink.

Niles, Daniel T. *That They May Have Life.* New York: Harper & Brothers, 1951. 120 pp. Evangelism by "heroic service and humble kindness."

PERSONAL WITNESS

Archibald, A. C. *New Testament Evangelism.* Philadelphia: Judson Press, 1946. 149 pp. Reasons for lay evangelism and a program for it.

Chafin, Kenneth L. *The Reluctant Witness.* Nashville: Broadman Press, 1974. 143 pp. Wise, pastoral, realistic. How lay people can share their faith.

————. *Help, I'm a Layman.* Waco: Word Books, 1966. 131 pp. All church members are called to be ministers and evangelists. How they can respond.

Ford, Leighton. *Good News Is for Sharing.* Elgin, Ill.: David C. Cook, 1977. 203 pp. Entertaining. Original. Last half specially practical on conversational witness to Christ.

Gibbs, Mark and Ralph Morton. *God's Frozen People.* Philadelphia: Westminister Press, 1964. 192 pp. Work by "ordinary Christians" in British and European settings.

Kennedy, D. James. *Evangelism Explosion.* Wheaton, Ill.: Tyndale House Publishers, 1970. 187 pp. A much acclaimed method of training church members for evangelistic calls. It centers on getting to Heaven. Callers are told what to say and how to say it.

Little, Paul E. *How to Give Away Your Faith.* Downers Grove: Intervarsity Press, 1962. 131 pp. How to share faith by conversation. What to say. How to start.

Mallough, Don. *Grassroots Evangelism.* Grand Rapids: Baker Book House, 1971. 143 pp. Old time style but useful hints on talking about Christ.

PREACHING

Coleman, Robert E. *Dry Bones Can Live Again.* Old Tappan: Fleming H. Revell, 1969. 127 pp. Why and how to use revival meetings for renewal and evangelism.

Dodd, C. H. *The Apostolic Preaching and Its Development.* New York: Harper & Brothers, 1936. 92 pp. New Testament "preaching," this British scholar says, is always evangelistic.

Soper, Donald. *The Advocacy of the Gospel.* London: Hodder & Stoughton, 1961. 119 pp. A brilliant English preacher gives lively advice and sparkling illustrations.

Stewart, James S. *A Faith to Proclaim.* New York: Charles Scribner's Sons, 1953. 160 pp. The Yale Lectures on Preaching. On using the pulpit to appeal for faith.

OTHER METHODS

Baker, Gordon Pratt and Edward Ferguson, eds. *A Year of Evangelism in the Local Church.* Nashville: Tidings, 1960. 210 pp. Various methods of evangelism are described by twenty-eight authors.

Barclay, William. *Fishers of Men.* Philadelphia: Westminster Press, 1936. 113 pp. The popular English Bible expositor urges evangelism by teaching.

Drummond, Lewis. *Leading Your Church in Evangelism.* Nashville: Broadman Press, 1975. 165 pp. Sound theory and practical guidance for evangelism in the local church.

Gage, Albert H. *Increasing Church School Attendance.* Grand Rapids: Zondervan, 1939. 130 pp. Called "the book that made the Baptists big." Practical guidance on an urgent subject.

Little, Sara. *Youth, World and Church.* Richmond: John Knox Press, 1968. 201 pp. On youth evangelism.

O'Brien, John A., ed. *Winning Converts.* New York: P.J. Kenedy & Sons, 1948. 248 pp. Roman Catholic priests and a laywoman describe various methods of evangelism.

Southard, Samuel. *Pastoral Evangelism.* Nashville: Broadman Press, 1962. 185 pp. On various old reliable methods, child evangelism, the pastor as evangelist.

SOCIAL ACTION

Smith, Timothy L. *Revivalism and Social Reform.* Nashville: Abingdon Press, 1957. 253 pp. Describes the social gospel emphasis in the great revivals.

Wirt, Sherwood. *The Social Conscience of an Evangelical.* New York: Harper & Row, 1968. 177 pp. Admits that evangelicals have been slighting their traditional insistence on social reform and calls for its restoration.

COMPREHENSIVE

The Church of England. *Towards the Conversion of England.* London: The Church and Publications Board, 1945. 156 pp. A much quoted classic. Beautifully drafted by a Church of England Commission.

Green, Bryan. *The Practice of Evangelism.* New York: Charles Scribner's Sons, 1951. 258 pp. Spiritual, intelligent, wide-ranging guidance by a Church of England pastor and evangelist.

Hendrick, John R. *Opening the Door of Faith.* Atlanta: John Knox Press, 1977. 112 pp. Evangelism through the congregation. The last half of this book has interesting comments on child and youth evangelism and on the importance of a congregation's commitment, beliefs, and program.

Hunter, George G., ed. *Rethinking Evangelism.* Nashville: Tidings, 1971. 94 pp. Six able authors write on what evangelism should do, and how to do it in contemporary situations.

Jones, E. Stanley. *A Song of Ascents.* Nashville: Abingdon Press, 1968. 400 pp. An evangelist's autobiography, with many striking insights.

Sangster, W.E. *Let Me Commend.* Nashville: Abingdon Press, 1948. 140 pp. An English minister's stimulating observations on purposes, message, preaching. Arresting illustrations.

Turnbull, Ralph G. *Evangelism Now.* Grand Rapids: Baker Book House, 1972. 109 pp. Principles and methods from ten writers.

Webster, Douglas. *What Is Evangelism?* London: Highway Press, 1959. 192 pp. On church social narrowness, conversion, baptism.

Woodson, Leslie. *Evangelism for Today's Church.* Grand Rapids: Zondervan, 1973. 159 pp. On "Meaning, Motivation, Method, Mobilization." Deals with recent controversy.

HISTORY

Green, Michael. *Evangelism in the Early Church.* Grand Rapids: Wm. B. Eerdmans, 1970. 268 pp. Well researched by a British scholar.

Sweet, William Warren. *Revivalism in America.* New York: Charles Scribner's Sons, 1944. 192 pp. An often quoted record of the revivals in colonial times and the early life of this country.

Index

Adler, Alfred, 228
Allen, Tom, 88
Allport, Gordon, 18
Appeals for faith, 71, 217–19, 225–31
Appeals for faith, wrong, 225–26
Application for membership, 197–98
Aquinas, Thomas, 216
Atheism, 5, 40
Atonement, 117–18
Attendance registration, 97–98
Augustine, 32, 33, 113, 127

Baillie, John, 131
Barth, Karl, 74, 86
Beatty, Clyde, 45
Beber, Julius, 217
Beliefs, 144–45, 233–35
Berenson, Bernard, 188
Berlin World Evangelism Conference, 22
Bible, 25, 38, 69, 120, 165, 207, 212, 214–15, 236
Black, James, 224
Blackwood, Andrew W., 103
Body of Christ, 65
Bonhoeffer, Dietrich, 62
Brindon, 217
Browne, Thomas, 227
Bushnell, Horace, 123, 130

Calls in homes, 137–83
   for contact, cultivation, and decision, 138–39
   and cultivation, 111–12, 139
   and decision
   answering objections, 172–83
   arrangements for, 146–58
   asking for, 167–71
   instructions, 159–83
   mistakes, 165–67
   reasons for, 137–46
   talking about religion, 162–65
Calvin College Conference, 23
Calvin, John, 50, 121
Carey, William, 9
Chairman, evangelism committee, 75–76
Changing neighborhoods, 90
Chappel, Clovis, 119
Chesterton, Gilbert K., 230
Children, 98–99; 130–35
Christian sector, 85–86
Church attendance
   evangelistic services, 191–92
   for cultivation, 106–8
   new members, 206–7
   source of contacts, 95–98
Church to be evangelized? 54–56
Church growth, 11–15, 27
Church membership, need for, 10–16, 44, 63–71
Church, necessary, 220
Church polarization, 20–21, 36
Church school, 98–100, 130–35
Church services, 95–98, 106–8, 184–92
Church, visible, 15, 64, 65
Church, what it is, 15–16, 64–70
Church, what people want from it
   answers to basic questions, 6, 219–20, 226

experience of God, 220–21
guidance for living, 221–23, 225
Church work, 202–3, 236–7
Classes for new members
  adult, 108, 138, 148–49, 195–97
  children, 133–35
Coffin, Henry Sloane, 211
Commencing Church membership
  Bible on, 193–94
  church's neglect of, 194
  getting into the fellowship,
    200–202
  health check, 208–9
  importance of, 71–72
  instruction, 194–98
  reception, 198–99
  religious practices, 205–8
  serving, 202–4
  superficial start, 121
Committee and Commission on
  evangelism, 52, 75–78, 100, 112,
  147, 202
Communicants' Class, 132–35, 199
Communion of Saints, 65
Conferences, 77, 80
Congregation, xi, 33, 46–51, 232–33
Congregation's personality, 237–39
Contacts, 56, 85–105
Conversion, x, 16, 43, 113–121
Cross, 117–18, 126, 227–28
Crusades, 103–4, 138
Cultivation, 18–19, 57–61, 106–112
Cultural difference, 86–91
Cyprian, 71

Davenport, Russell, 226
Death, 6, 226–27
Decision, 8, 61–63, 121–28, 130,
  134, 167–71
Decision, act of, 61–63, 119, 124,
  189–91
Declaration of Evangelical Social
  Concern, 23
Definition of evangelism, 49, 52–72
Democracy, 17–18, 45
Denominational assistance, 52, 78–80
Denominational program, 80
Denominations, 66, 89, 181
Descartes, René, 211
Detached evangelism, 51

Dostoevski, Feodor, 223, 224
Drummond, Henry, 32
Dulles, Avery, 41
Durante, Jimmy, 187

Emotion, 187–88
England, Leonard, 29
Enquirers' group, 110–111
Erikson, Erik H., 130
Ethnic Christians, ix, 7–8
Ethnic exclusiveness, 87–91
Evangelicals, 22–24
Evangelism Sunday, 191–92
Evangelist, required qualities, x,
  49–51, 150–51
"Everything we do is evangelism,"
  27, 49
Example as witness, 32, 35, 46
Excitement, 228–29

Faith, 59, 61, 118, 124, 144–45,
  211–12
Family, 3, 94–95, 98–99, 100–101,
  130–31, 229–30
Family, religiously divided, 94
Fear, 6, 226
Feel of faith, 59, 60
Fellowship, 9, 47–48, 51, 59, 62,
  65–66, 93, 141–42, 184, 200, 206,
  238–39
Ferré, Nels, 121
File of prospective members, 91–92,
  147–48
Finance, 203–4, 231, 237
Forsyth, P. T., 145, 186
Fosdick, Harry Emerson, 122, 236
Fractions, 69–70, 119–21
Francis of Assisi, 116
Friendliness, 96–97, 98, 103, 182,
  238–39
Friendship, 92–93, 200
Frost, Robert, 122
Funerals, 192

Galileo, 225
Gibbon, Edward, 50
Glasgow, Ellen, 2
God, conception of, 126, 210,
  213–14, 221
God, relationship with, 5–6, 220–21

Index

God's work we do, 9–10, 31–32, 145

Good acts not all evangelism, 27, 33, 33–35, 49

Graham, Billy, 138

Great Commissions, 20–21

Green, Bryan, 132, 185

Hendrick, John R., 129

History, 122, 214–16

Hobbs, Herschel, 194

Hoffman, Ronan, 41

Holy Catholic Church, 66

Holy Spirit, xi, 31, 36, 37, 39, 55, 70, 115–16, 119, 159–60, 194, 211

Housman, Lawrence, 33

Hughes, Hugh Price, 117

Huguenots, 235

Impersonal evangelism, 51

Inactive church members, 54

Inclusive church, 91

Inner light, 5–6, 39–42

Instruction of new members, 58–59

James, William, 62, 166

Jesus' commandment to evangelize, 9–10, 20–21

Jesus is God, 5–6, 125–27, 178, 213–14, 224

Jesus is the message, 223–25

Jesus, necessary? 1–8, 37–44

Jesus, speaking of, 163, 164

Justin Martyr, 39, 163

Kant, Immanuel, 210

Kelley, Dean M., 219–20

Kingdom of God, 67–68

Koestler, Arthur, 113

Lamb, Charles, 126

Larson, Bruce, 26

Lausanne, International Congress on World Evangelization, 23

Lay callers, 137–83

Lay task of evangelism, x, 49–51, 69, 75, 139–45

Lewis, C. S., 127–28, 140–41

Life, purpose of, 5, 6, 213, 219–20, 228–29

Loneliness, 29, 220

Literature, 109–10, 197–98, 207, 235

Living, a guide for, 221–23

Love, 5, 46, 92, 206, 239

Lovelace, Richard, 24

Luther, Martin, 63, 123, 221

McGavran, Donald, 87

Manipulation, 30

Marginal methods, 47

Marriage, 3, 8, 100–101

Marriage, religiously divided, 94–95

Materials, 79

Members, inactive, 54

Message, 210–31

Message, summary of, 5, 213

Methods, x, 31–32, 46–47, 77, 79, 159

Miller, Keith, 34

Minister, 73–74, 75, 143, 146–47, 200–201, 233

Miracle, 9–10, 31–32, 59, 145, 159–60, 232

Modern methods, 47, 80

Moody, Dwight L., 115, 158

Morality, 221–23, 225, 229

Motives, 1–26
  church growth, 11–15
  Jesus' commandments, 9–10, 20–21
  keep Christian faith on earth, 9–10
  make church a greater source of good, 10–16
  own experience, 7–8, 26
  save society, 16–20
  theological, 24–26
  wrong, 11

Needs everyone has, 6–7, 219–23, 225–31

Neglect of evangelism, reasons for, ix–x, 27–45, 73–74

Neighborhood religious census, 104–5

New member care; see Commencing

New residents, 101–3

Newman, Louis I., 145

Niebuhr, H. Richard, 88
Nietzsche, Friedrich, 93
Non-Christian background, 85–86
Non-Christians, salvation of, 5,
    37–44, 71, 122–23
Normal self in evangelism, 48–49,
    166

Objections to evangelism, ix–x, 24,
    27–45
O'Brien, John A., 60, 80
Observable difference faith makes,
    2–4
Organizations' part, 49, 76, 77,
    100–101, 108–9, 201–2, 238
Organizing for evangelism, 73–78
Other religions, 37–45
Out-of-date, x, 47
Own evidence, 7–8, 11, 26, 70

Paley, William, 211
Parents, 130–31
Peace, inner, 228
Pepys, Samuel, 218
Polarization, x, 20–26
Postponement, 127–28, 169–70, 188,
    189–90
Powell, Sidney, 93
Prayer
    normalcy of, 220–21
    private, 46, 205
    public worship, 206
    reliance on, 76, 145, 149, 159–60,
        166, 171–72, 235–36
    small group, 206
Preaching, evangelistic
    advantages, 184–85
    appeal for decision, 188–90
    expressing decisions, 190–91
    getting hearers, 191–92
    needed qualities, 185–88
Preaching can make a church
    evangelistic, 235
Preaching, special services, 192
Preaching, strengthened by
    preacher's personal evangelism,
    145
Preaching, for building toward faith,
    106–7
Predestination, 38–50

Preparation for membership; see
    Cultivation
Profession of faith, 59, 61–63,
    123–24
Proselyte, 27–28, 37–44
Prospects; see Contacts
Purpose for living, 5, 6, 219–20, 225,
    228–29

Rahner, Karl, 39
Raikes, Robert, 131
Rauschenbusch, Walter, 16
Reading, 109–10, 197–98, 207, 235
Reason, 210–212
Reception into membership, 198–99
Religious practices, 205–8
Requirements for membership, 60,
    222
Revival (Renewal), 36–37, 48, 54–56,
    144–45, 192, 232–37
Rewards of faith, 217–19, 225–31
Robbins, Raymond, 32, 33

Sabatier, Louis Auguste, 142
Sabbath observance, 207–8
Sacraments, 65, 67, 69
Salvation, 7–8, 71, 120, 227–28
Sartre, Jean Paul, 30
Satisfy spiritual hunger, 227
Sayers, Dorothy, 235
Schaff, Philip, 57
Seagrave, Gordon, 8
Second coming, 19–20
Security, 226
Seneca, 114
Sermons, 184–92
Shaftesbury, Earl of, 24
Sin, 6, 115, 117, 118, 127, 178–79,
    227–28
Social action, x–xi, 3, 16–24, 35–36,
    68, 180, 185, 229, 230–31, 237
Social barriers, 87–91
Social time after services, 97, 107–8,
    238
Sorokim, Petrim, 17
Special evangelistic agencies, 54
Specialists, 53
Spinoza, Baruch, 120
Spiritual qualifications, xi, 48, 54–56,
    232–39

Index

255

Sponsors, 201
Stages in evangelism, 53, 77
Statistics, 11–15
Stevenson, Robert Louis, 26, 228
Stewardship, 203–4, 231, 237
Stewart, James, 107
Stowe, David M., 66
Streuning, E.L., 18
Suenens, Leon-Joseph, 189
Supporting structures
  congregation, 74–78
  denomination, 78–80
  pull away from evangelism, 73–74
  seminary, 80–84
Syncretism, 42

Tagore, Rabindranath, 31
Temple, William, 39–40, 55, 206–7
Teilhard de Chardin, 43, 227
Territorialism, 50
Tertullian, 239
Testing, 60
Thanks, 228
Theological seminary, 80–84
Theology, x, 8, 24–26, 38, 40–44,
  120, 138, 194, 233–34
Tillich, Paul, 43

Time is right, ix, 36–37
Tolstoy, Leo, 116
Trueblood, Elton, 238

Urgency, 1–26, 72–73, 188
Ushers, 96

Walk with Christ, 114, 193–94
Weddings, 192
Wellington, Duke of, 109
Wells, H.G., 224
Wesley, John, 23, 89
Wilcox, Ella Wheeler, 114
Wirt, Sherwood E., 22
Words, 32–34, 145, 187
Work, 202–3, 236–37
World Council of Churches, 48
World evangelism, 8, 35, 37–45
Worship, public, 106–7, 184, 206–7

Xavier, Francis, 39, 118

Yinger, J. Milton, 65
Youth, 47, 129–36, 209

Zeno, 210